Small and Medium Powers in Global History

This volume brings together a leading group of scholars to offer a new perspective on the history of conflicts and trade, focusing on the role of small and medium, or "weak", and often neutral states. Existing historiography has often downplayed the importance of such states in world trade, during armed conflicts, and as important agents in the expanding trade and global connections of the last 250 years. The country studies demonstrate that these states played a much bigger role in world and bilateral trade than has previously been assumed, and that this role was augmented by the emergence of truly global conflicts and total war.

In addition to careful country or comparative studies, this book provides new data on trade and shipping during wars and examines the impact of this trade on the individual states' economies. It spans the period from the late 18th century to the First and Second World Wars and the Cold War of the 20th century, a crucial period of change in the concept and practice of neutrality and trade, as well as periods of transition in the nature and technology of warfare.

This book will be of great interest to scholars of economic history, comparative history, international relations, and political science.

Jari Eloranta is Professor of Economic History at the University of Helsinki, Finland.

Eric Golson is a Senior Teaching Fellow in the School of Economics at the University of Surrey, UK, and also teaches at the School of Oriental and African Studies (SOAS), London, UK.

Peter Hedberg is Associate Professor of Economic History at Uppsala University, Sweden.

Maria Cristina Moreira is an Assistant Professor of Economics at the University of Minho, Portugal.

Perspectives in Economic and Social History
Series Editors: Andrew August and Jari Eloranta

47 **Merchants and Trade Networks in the Atlantic and the Mediterranean, 1550–1800**
Connectors of Commercial Maritime Systems
Edited by Manuel Herrero Sánchez and Klemens Kaps

48 **Property Rights in Land**
Issues in Social, Economic and Global History
Edited by Rosa Congost, Jorge Gelman and Rui Santos

49 **Working-Class Community in the Age of Affluence**
Stefan Ramsden

50 **Culture, Philanthropy and the Poor in Late-Victorian London**
Geoffrey A. C. Ginn

51 **The Economic and Business History of Occupied Japan**
New Perspectives
Edited by Thomas French

52 **An Urban History of The Plague**
Socio-Economic, Political and Medical Impacts in a Scottish Community, 1500–1650
Karen Jillings

53 **Mercantilism, Account Keeping and the Periphery-Core Relationship**
Edited by Cheryl Susan McWatters

54 **Small and Medium Powers in Global History**
Trade, Conflicts, and Neutrality from the 18th to the 20th Centuries
Edited by Jari Eloranta, Eric Golson, Peter Hedberg, and Maria Cristina Moreira

For more information about this series, please visit www.routledge.com/series/PESH

Small and Medium Powers in Global History

Trade, Conflicts, and Neutrality from the 18th to the 20th Centuries

Edited by Jari Eloranta, Eric Golson, Peter Hedberg, and Maria Cristina Moreira

LONDON AND NEW YORK

First published 2019
by Routledge
2 Park Square, Milton Park, Abingdon, Oxon OX14 4RN

and by Routledge
711 Third Avenue, New York, NY 10017

Routledge is an imprint of the Taylor & Francis Group, an informa business

© 2019 selection and editorial matter, Jari Eloranta, Eric Golson, Peter Hedberg, and Maria Cristina Moreira; individual chapters, the contributors

The right of Jari Eloranta, Eric Golson, Peter Hedberg, and Maria Cristina Moreira to be identified as the authors of the editorial material, and of the authors for their individual chapters, has been asserted in accordance with sections 77 and 78 of the Copyright, Designs and Patents Act 1988.

All rights reserved. No part of this book may be reprinted or reproduced or utilized in any form or by any electronic, mechanical, or other means, now known or hereafter invented, including photocopying and recording, or in any information storage or retrieval system, without permission in writing from the publishers.

Trademark notice: Product or corporate names may be trademarks or registered trademarks, and are used only for identification and explanation without intent to infringe.

British Library Cataloguing-in-Publication Data
A catalogue record for this book is available from the British Library

Library of Congress Cataloging-in-Publication Data
A catalog record has been requested for this book

ISBN: 978-1-138-74454-7 (hbk)
ISBN: 978-1-315-18094-6 (ebk)

Typeset in Bembo
by Swales & Willis Ltd, Exeter, Devon, UK

Contents

List of contributors vii
Foreword ix
PATRICK KARL O'BRIEN

1 **Introduction** 1
JARI ELORANTA, PETER HEDBERG, MARIA CRISTINA MOREIRA, AND ERIC GOLSON

PART I
Interplay of trade and conflicts in the long run 27

2 **Trade and the new republic: American trade during the Napoleonic Wars, 1783–1830** 29
JEREMY LAND, JARI ELORANTA, AND MARIA CRISTINA MOREIRA

3 **The United States and the Mediterranean during the French Wars (1793–1815)** 52
SILVIA MARZAGALLI

4 **Commercial relations between Portugal and Russia: neutrality, trade, and finance (1770–1850)** 73
MARIA CRISTINA MOREIRA, RITA MARTINS DE SOUSA, AND WERNER SCHELTJENS

5 **Taxation in Brazil in the Napoleonic Wars: neutrality, economy and the outcomes of a royal court in transit** 95
RODRIGO DA COSTA DOMINGUEZ AND ANGELO ALVES CARRARA

6 **Wartime trade and tariffs in Sweden from the Napoleonic Wars to World War I** 116
PETER HEDBERG AND HENRIC HÄGGQVIST

PART II
Trade and neutrality in conflicts — 139

7 Small states in harm's way: neutrality in war — 141
ERIC GOLSON

8 The Atlantic orientation: Norway and the western blockade of Germany, 1914–1918 — 155
KNUT OLA NAASTAD STRØM

9 What was the impact of World War I on Swedish economic and business performance? A case study of the ball bearings manufacturer SKF — 173
ERIC GOLSON AND JASON LENNARD

10 The macroeconomic effects of neutrality: evidence from the Nordic countries during the wars — 196
JASON LENNARD AND ERIC GOLSON

11 No room for neutrality? The uncommitted European nations and the economic Cold War in the 1950s — 213
NIKLAS JENSEN-ERIKSEN

12 Bicycles in rush hour: concluding neutrality and war — 231
TOSHIAKI TAMAKI AND JARI OJALA

Index — 237

Contributors

Angelo Alves Carrara (Federal University of Juiz de Fora, Brazil), PhD, adjunct professor, specializes in the economic history of Brazil.

Rita Martins de Sousa (ISEG, University of Lisbon, Portugal), PhD, assistant professor, specializes in Portuguese monetary history.

Rodrigo da Costa Dominguez (University of Minho and University of Porto, Portugal), PhD, postdoctoral scholar, specializes in Portuguese trade relations and history.

Jari Eloranta (University of Helsinki, Finland), PhD, professor of economic history, specializes in the history of government role in the economy and Nordic economic history.

Eric Golson (University of Surrey, UK), PhD, lecturer, specializes in the history of neutrality and economics of warfare.

Henric Häggqvist (University of Uppsala, Sweden), PhD, postdoctoral scholar, specializes in the history of tariffs in Sweden and the history of the Swedish welfare state.

Peter Hedberg (University of Uppsala, Sweden), PhD, associate professor, specializes in the history of Swedish trade and the impact of wars.

Niklas Jensen-Eriksen (University of Helsinki, Finland), PhD, professor of business history, specializes in the history of Cold War business enterprises and trade.

Jeremy Land (Georgia State University, USA), PhD candidate, specializes in the history of early American trade.

Jason Lennard (Lund University, Sweden), PhD, researcher, specializes in economic policy, financial crises and national accounting in the long run.

Silvia Marzagalli (Université Côte d'Azur, Centre de la Méditerranée Moderne et Contemporaine, France), PhD, professor of modern history, specializes in the history of French and Mediterranean trade.

Maria Cristina Moreira (University of Minho, Portugal), PhD, assistant professor of economics, specializes in the history of Portuguese trade and impacts of the wars.

Patrick Karl O'Brien (University of London, UK), PhD, professor of economic history, one of the foremost experts in the history of global trade and the British economy in the world.

Jari Ojala (University of Jyväskylä, Finland), PhD, professor of comparative business history, specializes in early modern economy, maritime history and comparative business practices.

Werner Scheltjens (University of Leipzig, Germany), PhD, assistant professor, specializes in the history of early modern trade and the Soundtoll accounts.

Knut Ola Naastad Strøm (University of Gothenburg, Sweden), doctoral student, specializes in the history of the Nordic countries and impacts of conflicts.

Toshiaki Tamaki (Kyoto Sangyo University, Japan), PhD, professor of economics, specializes in the history of the North European trade and economic relations.

Foreword

Patrick Karl O'Brien

Two meta themes and questions of strong significance form the chapters of this book. They are of significant interest to historians, economists, and other social scientists endeavouring to achieve rigorous and informed analyses of the workings of the international economy and international economic relations. The chapters focus on small states and their economies that opted to remain neutral during the numerous and more or less protracted and serious interludes of warfare that have punctuated the long-term development of the international economy. Not only do they deal with the costs and benefits of neutrality in the premodern age of mercantilism, but they also augment our limited knowledge of such economies, including Sweden, Denmark, Norway, Ireland, Switzerland, Spain, Portugal, and the young American republic, whose commercial relations with countries beyond their frontiers, although small, nevertheless contributed in several significant ways to a global economy for an exchange of commodities, the migration of labour, movements of capital and diffusion of knowledge by land across the frontiers of countries and by way of oceans, seas, and waterways of an expanding and integrating world economy.

In some degree, particularly if the commodity or service was especially desirable and/or was widely demanded and in inelastic demand and embodied externalities, exports from small economies could play a disproportionate part in increasing the volume of world trade. Nevertheless, as several of these chapters show, their more significant role was to maintain bilateral and multilateral connections for international commerce and diplomacy during the frequent geopolitical conflicts that occurred during the era of mercantilism and in the 20th century's two world wars and Cold Wars.

During such times of military and naval conflict, which included blockades and attacks on trade, the status of neutrality was expedient for weak states to claim, but difficult to maintain. Despite the endeavours of international lawyers to define neutrality, the law was not enforceable and its status depended upon the interests of powerful belligerents and the greed of privateers and naval commanders seeking prizes from predation upon "neutral" ships and their cargoes.

These chapters ask in what ways and to what degree neutrality in particular pre-and modern wars augmented the long run growth of powers that managed to maintain that enviable and envied status. The historical evidence (which includes a cliometric exercise) suggests that for Sweden and the United States it seems that outcomes that flowed from evading the costs of allocating resources to warfare and continuing to trade with belligerents was positive, and in the Swedish case probably significant. No doubt the same intuitively plausible case could be made for all the small and weak neutral powers studied by authors of chapters in this book.

The editors are to be congratulated on posting and mobilizing a scholarly collection of case studies to address this important and neglected meta question for political economy and international relations. Wars have historically been endemic and, for most countries, unavoidable components of the anarchy of international geopolitical and commercial relations. Perhaps, however, their destructive potential has now been attenuated by the prospects of a nuclear holocaust?

1 Introduction

Jari Eloranta, Peter Hedberg, Maria Cristina Moreira, and Eric Golson

The history of trade and conflicts for the last 300 years is typically a story of great powers and great men (and occasionally women), where the smaller states are usually referred to in footnotes. It is, after all, a common assumption that smaller geographic size, or some other indicator of perceived weakness, connotes limited power and importance in the "big picture". In this volume the authors challenge this view. In fact, we would argue that smaller/weaker states have had crucial roles to play in history, especially during conflicts. As warfare has become more consuming, conflicts bigger and deadlier, and more and more of a country's resources are used up in order to win the war, smaller/weaker states have been able to take advantage of the economic opportunities that conflicts can offer. It is, of course, true that smaller nations can end up on the receiving end of military aggression, but in our view they have also been very adept at maneuvering during conflicts, thereby avoiding invasion and direct participation in the war. Thus, we are calling here for greater attention to be paid to the middle and small powers in world history and suggesting that a preoccupation with the study of great powers can distort our view of the nuanced dimensions of conflicts and trade. After all, networks and alliances have always been crucial in warfare, and they have worked only if everyone contributed.

The aim of this edited volume is thus to provide a novel take on the history of conflicts and trade, with a clear focus on the role of small/medium, or "weak", and often neutral states. This volume spans a crucial period in history, namely, from the 18th century with its great power expansion revolutions to the world wars and the Cold War of the 20th century, i.e., crucial periods of change in the concept and practice of neutrality and trade, as well as periods of transition in the nature and technology of warfare. The key findings from the case studies included in this volume emphasize that these states played a much bigger role in world and bilateral trade than has previously been assumed, and that this role was augmented by the emergence of truly global conflicts and total war. In general, we want to explore what kinds of short- and long-run changes we see in the trade flows between the great powers and weaker states during these centuries, especially whether the pressure of a war effort allowed more latitude for these states to explore their trade options or enhanced their bargaining power or market position. Many of the smaller/weaker states were neutral during parts or all of the major conflicts of the period and served as important conduits for key strategic and other goods. The basic argument in most of the chapters here is that weak states were able to expand their trade and discover new markets during the large and protracted conflicts, which more and more characterized this period, due to the industrialization of war.

In what follows, we first discuss the study of smaller/weaker states, state power, and conflicts. After this, we provide an overview of some of the perspectives on the study of trade, as well as the macro-indicators of trade over time. The big changes in the last 300 years involve the rise and fall of powerful states (and the less powerful), the massive increases in world trade, especially since the globalization and industrialization of the 19th century; increases in the scale and scope of conflicts; and the global increases in living standards. None of these processes has been steady or even, and thus they have created winners and losers. We conclude this introduction with a review of the chapters and raise some points about the future research challenges.

Weak states, state economic/political power, and conflicts

Given our strong assertions about smaller/weaker states, it is useful to discuss what we mean by this term. A state that occupies a "small" geographic area is not necessarily weak (consider Great Britain), while on occasion states of wide geographic extent (such as China in the 19th century) need not be strong. In the present volume we focus our analysis primarily on states that had limited economic and/or military power.[1] Thus, for example, the United States in the 18th century was clearly a weak state, whereas the USA that emerged after World War II was most certainly not. In this section we explore different ways of estimating the power of a state, and also how many conflicts we have seen in this period, roughly from the mid-18th century to the Cold War, and what kinds they were.

Here the definition of weak states is not the same as that of failing states, i.e., states which cannot contain internal violence and repression, such as is used in the recent literature on state formation.[2] Our approach is more akin to that of Michael Handel, who argues that even countries with a large area can be weak, in the sense that they are weak players in the international system. Typically, according to him, a weak state tends to have a small population and area, low GNP, a small and specialized domestic market, high dependence on foreign military protection, and limited potential to influence the international system.[3] In Jari Eloranta's earlier work, weak states are presented as perhaps overly dependent on external trade, with fewer policy constraints on domestic trade apparatus, and differing from one another on the basis of geographic and strategic impulses.[4] Moreover, they can have significant options in the global or regional system depending on the relations between them and the great powers and the characteristics of the hegemonic system. As Robert Gilpin and Paul Kennedy, among others, point out, systems dominated by hegemonic powers can be more peaceful than others, since other powers cannot challenge them, thus leaving room for smaller/medium powers to gain from the economic and political networks.[5]

There is, of course, a large literature on state capacity in history, and it is a particularly lively field in economic history.[6] An equally large literature has been devoted to the evolution of fiscal states and fiscal transformations in history.[7] Many of these topics intersect when it comes to analyzing the long-run formation of states, typically in Europe, usually via fiscal expansion impacted by conflicts.[8] The scholars working on state capacity have overwhelmingly used fiscal data – for example, revenue collection and tax analysis – to gauge a state's ability to establish a monopoly of the violence inside its borders. Usually the analysis of conflicts brings in the ability to use public debt as a tool to finance them and shows how the burden of debts affected state formation.[9] Here our focus is not on the growth and evolution of fiscal capacity, but on military capacity and the level of engagement in trade. We particularly want to compare and contrast the position of smaller/weaker states with that of the great powers. Finally, we want to emphasize that the power position of states changed over time, and we want to see if this also holds for smaller/weaker states.

One way to analyze the power position and ranking of states has been to use the so-called CINC (Composite Index of National Capacity) scores, especially in the conflict and peace science research since the 1970s. This index consists of total population, urban population, iron and steel production, energy consumption, military personnel, and military expenditure, all from 1816 onwards.[10] This index is useful in forming a macro-picture of power relations over time, but it also has some weaknesses. First, it can overestimate the perceptions of power versus actual capacity. Second, some of the components can be critiqued, such as the inclusion of two population variables and the lack of GDP (per capita) as a component, especially since more and more of these data are available for the post-1816 period.[11] Still, the CINC scores are a decent starting point for our analysis here.

Based on the CINC scores, Brazil, Denmark, Norway, Sweden, Portugal, and the Netherlands were fairly consistently weak powers in the period summarized in Table 1.1. France and the UK appear to have been declining great powers, while the USA was an ascending power, especially after World War I. Germany's power status waxed and waned in the period; in the 1920s, for example, it was a weak great power.

Military spending is more naturally taken as a comparative instrument of a state's (military) capacity. However, it too is imperfect, since the COW-database figures have been converted to pounds sterling or dollars using exchange rates. Another option would be to come up with the percentage share of military spending in respect of GDP, often called the military burden. However, the data for all these countries are not available, so we have opted here to use the COW figures. However, we treat them as a percentage share of the world's military spending total (= all COW military expenditures summed annually).[12]

4 *Eloranta et al.*

Table 1.1 Composite Indices of National Capabilities (CINC), 1865–1950, as shares (%) of UK CINC

	1865	1880	1895	1913	1925	1938	1950
BRA	2.73	4.13	5.23	9.73	11.46	12.82	21.31
DEN	1.56	1.38	1.74	1.77	2.08	2.56	3.28
FRA	43.36	49.54	51.74	60.18	62.50	58.97	54.10
GER	25.39	48.62	73.26	126.55	85.42	197.44	—
NED	3.13	4.13	4.65	6.19	7.29	6.41	13.11
NOR	0.78	1.83	1.16	2.65	3.13	3.85	0.00
POR	1.95	2.29	2.33	2.65	4.17	3.85	3.28
SWE	4.30	5.05	5.23	6.19	6.25	6.41	8.20
UK	100.00	100.00	100.00	100.00	100.00	100.00	100.00
USA	52.73	57.34	97.67	194.69	264.58	219.23	465.57

Sources: National Material Capabilities data 5.0, based on methods developed in Singer, Bremer, and Stuckey (1972).

Note
BRA = Brazil, DEN = Denmark, FRA = France, GER = Germany, NED = Netherlands, NOR = Norway, POR = Portugal, SWE = Sweden, UK=United Kingdom, and USA=United States of America.

Note
We use the period from 1865 onward to make these figures comparable with the naval tonnage data noted later in this chapter.

In the late 19th century, the only great powers shown in Table 1.2 were the UK and France – the United States had a high military spending share in 1865 only because of the impact of the Civil War, and in subsequent years this share was much smaller. The medium powers here were Germany and the USA, and both were ascending to the status of great powers by 1913, Germany in particular. In the interwar period those rankings changed, and on the eve of World War II Germany was the only military superpower among this group. After the war, it was the USA. The military spending "strength" of the weak powers here did not change very dramatically during the period, although they show a clear trend toward lower relative spending after World War I.

The great leaps in the extension of historical national accounts in the last 40 years have made it possible to look at the relative positions of these states in the 19th and 20th centuries, and sometimes, as in the cases of the UK and Sweden, for longer.[13] GDP is one way to measure the overall economic capacity, and it is particularly well suited for comparisons of the great powers and their ability to prevail in a conflict. However, for example, GDP per capita is in many ways a better measure than the CINC score, since it describes concisely a state's total economic capacity and its potential for mobilization during a conflict. Moreover, it takes into account the size of the population, which can, when large, be both a positive (numbers available for military service, ability to mobilize, ability to sustain losses) and a negative (being hard to control, with potential for revolution, cost to a sovereign of appeasing a large population). At least it gives us another way to analyze state capacity in a comparative way.

Table 1.2 Military spending of select nations as a share of the world's military spending (%), 1865–1950

	1865	1880	1895	1913	1925	1938	1950
BRA	1.44	1.59	1.34	1.42	1.08	0.27	0.75
DEN	0.38	0.47	0.49	0.28	0.21	0.11	0.12
FRA	16.78	19.95	15.83	11.27	7.13	4.40	3.34
GER	4.19	11.79	13.60	14.94	3.25	35.45	—
NED	1.30	1.68	1.34	0.74	0.85	0.36	0.53
NOR	—	—	—	0.19	0.16	0.06	0.11
POR	1.38	1.59	1.40	0.90	0.39	0.24	0.23
SWE	0.60	0.77	0.90	0.77	0.93	0.35	0.49
UK	14.76	13.04	15.74	11.45	12.74	8.91	5.33
USA	21.45	6.94	6.69	10.62	12.95	5.41	32.64

Source: *National Material Capabilities* data 5.0, based on methods developed in Singer, Bremer, and Stuckey (1972).

Note
BRA = Brazil, DEN = Denmark, FRA = France, GER =Germany, NED = Netherlands, NOR = Norway, POR = Portugal, SWE = Sweden, UK=United Kingdom, and USA=United States of America.

The selected countries are analyzed in Table 1.3 in terms of both their real GDP per capita (as potential for mobilization) and rank in global comparisons. First, however, we must note that the rankings take account of the fact that few countries had any data for the early part of the period, and that they do not say anything about the absolute size of the economy. If we start with the UK and the USA, the former unquestionably experienced a decline in the 20th century, similar to the pattern apparent from previous tables. The United States ascended to the top and held on to this position until the late 20th century. France also declined toward the late 20th century. Germany, in its turn, ascended in the early 20th century, but then dropped to the same rank as it occupied for most of the period. Of the smaller/weaker states, Brazil evinced little progress, and in fact declined in rank. The Nordic countries remained at similar levels, relatively speaking, with some rise in the ranks, notably by Norway.

Another way to assess a state's military capacity more effectively is to analyze its military capacity as a stock. Scholars have in the past used the number of battleships as a measure of state capacity, which favors the great powers.[14] Naval tonnage is a better way to gauge naval capacity, and a new dataset offers us a way also to take into account proportional naval power.[15] Figure 1.1 provides us with the great power patterns, and Figure 1.2 what happened to some of the smaller/weaker states. Unsurprisingly, the UK dominated the waves until World War I. Afterwards, it had close to parity with the USA. The latter country's performance in this comparison is quite surprising – typically scholars do not consider the US a major naval power, at least until World War II. But the interwar naval treaties limited naval buildup to a degree in any case. France was a declining naval power for most of the

Table 1.3 Real GDP per capita (in 2011 USD), 1800–1950

	1800 GDP per capita	1800 World rank	1850 GDP per capita	1850 World rank	1900 GDP per capita	1900 World rank	1950 GDP per capita	1950 World rank	2000 GDP per capita	2000 World rank
BRA	600	16	600	34	606	43	1549	84	8316	72
FIN	827	13	1035	23	1813	24	5208	22	32972	23
FRA	—	—	2028	11	4214	12	6869	15	31771	26
GER	958	11	1386	18	4596	9	5536	20	33975	19
NOR	—	—	1562	15	3813	14	7947	12	54594	4
POR	1330	7	1226	22	1729	25	2771	48	21497	37
SWE	1151	9	1446	16	3438	15	8816	9	36374	13
SWI	—	—	2333*	7*	5124	6	9053	8	42752	7
UK	2205	1	2858	1	5608	5	9441	6	34390	18
USA	1980	3	2825	2	6252	1	15241	1	45887	5

Source: Maddison Project Database, version 2018. See Inklaar, de Jong, Bolt, and van Zanden (2018). The figures are in 2011 USD, based on multiple benchmarks.

Note
BRA = Brazil, FIN = Finland, FRA= France, GER = Germany, NOR= Norway, POR = Portugal, SWE = Sweden, SWI = Switzerland, UK = United Kingdom, and USA = United States of America.
* = for Switzerland, the value is the 1851 figure, the earliest data point.

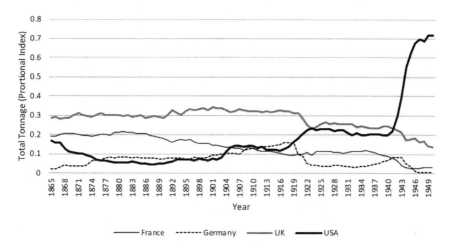

Figure 1.1 Total proportional tonnage of France, Germany, UK, and USA, 1865–1950.
Source: Crisher and Souva (2014).

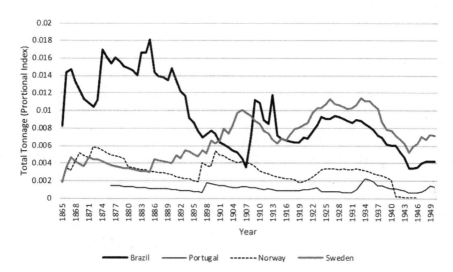

Figure 1.2 Total proportional tonnage of Brazil, Portugal, Norway, and Sweden, 1865–1950.
Source: Crisher and Souva (2014).

period, while Germany was ascending (yet unable to challenge most of the others) until the interwar period. These comparisons may change our perceptions of power in the period, although the trends are somewhat similar to the other indicators used above. Regardless of these patterns, we have to acknowledge that having large battleships, submarines, and later aircraft

8 *Eloranta et al.*

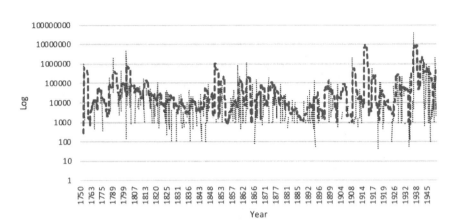

Figure 1.3 Total deaths (military and civilian) from conflicts, 1750–1950.
Source: Conflict Catalog (Violent Conflicts 1400 AD to the Present in Different Regions of the World), retrieved from www.cgeh.nl/data#conflict (cited February 10, 2018).

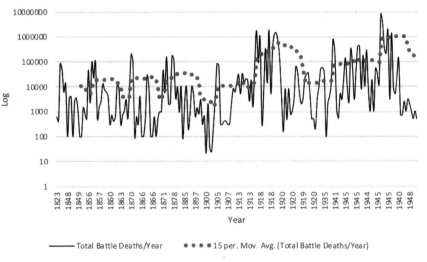

Figure 1.4 Total battle deaths, 1823–1950.
Source: Inter-State War Data, ver. 4.0. See also Sarkees and Wayman (2010). Please note that this database starts in 1816, and the first observations are from 1823 onward.

carriers was vital for global dominance such as UK in the 19th century and US in the 20th. From this perspective, the US was less impressive before World War II. In 1860, the American navy had only five ships of the line, whereas the UK had 76.[16]

In turn, the patterns for the weaker states were extremely varied. For example, Brazil was a substantive naval power in the latter part of the 19th century, with levels on par at times with the US and Germany. Portugal and Norway were fairly similar, with a lowering trend from 1900 onwards, and Sweden increased its naval power in the early 20th century, following Brazil's development in the interwar period. The naval power indices of the weaker powers were around 10–15 percent of the totals of the major powers. It appears that the weaker powers were not a uniform group but more a set of groups, which then followed similar trends, most probably due to external influences (conflicts, markets, etc.).

One of the key external conditions that affected all the states in the global trading system was conflict. While the 19th and 20th centuries saw fewer conflicts overall – in fact, the "long 19th century" from 1815 to 1914 saw few of them – they were deadly centuries. The world wars were, of course, the deadliest conflicts; they developed into global total wars, something that had begun with the wars of the French Revolution and Napoleonic conflicts. These total wars, which were relatively rare, involved all elements of society, and typically also offered new opportunities for neutral and smaller states, due to the resource needs of the belligerents.[17]

As Figure 1.3 shows, the long-run trends in war fatalities, military and civilian, hardly decreased from the 1750s to 1945. There was a slight decline in the early 19th century, then an increase in the mid-century, and more fluctuation and increases due to the world wars. Since the Conflict Catalog figures are still somewhat incomplete, we also decided to confirm the results with the COW data, as shown in Figure 1.4. From 1823, the data show many annual fluctuations and apparently a slightly increasing trend toward the late 19th century and then into the 20th. The biggest jump came with World War I, and then the interwar period. There is certainly no reduction in conflict-related violence.

Importance of the study of trade and neutrality

Since the 17th century, major wars have recurrently been accompanied by declining international commerce.[18] There are several reasons for this. Developments in communications and societal organization have enabled more efficient mobilization for war while increasing the production capacity of states has entailed mass production of war materials, population growth has provided for larger armies, and advances in weaponry have worsened the adverse impact of wars on the economy over time. In addition to tragic losses of lives, numbers of wounded, and ruined material resources, wars and conflicts have persistently distorted markets and disrupted trade. Moreover, and of great importance to this book, after the turn of the 18th century, naval warfare and blockades have been employed and more vigorously enforced than before. The power of a country is typically related to its wealth, i.e., resources buy guns und munitions, foodstuffs, and raw materials, and commodities, which are required to provide for military as well as civilian needs. For this reason, belligerent countries have regularly made efforts to control trade channels, either to benefit from trade in order to increase their wealth, or to deprive the enemy of their resources.[19]

Belligerent countries commonly have accounted for the largest market distortions and trade disruptions. A great number of powers that have waged war against each other have been leading trading nations and each other's major trading partners, and as they have targeted each other the naval warfare and blockade policies of belligerent powers have frequently entailed losses of major markets. Consequently, the decline in the trade of belligerent countries has been strongest.[20] This has opened up opportunities for other nations to fill the void.

Moreover, the impact of wars and conflict on the economy has commonly stretched far and deep beyond belligerent countries.[21] Since the 18th century, trade and integration has increased on a global level. As a result, an increasing number of countries have depended on international trade for their economic growth and development and have thus been increasingly vulnerable to disruptions of international trade and commerce. The larger the trading nations and the more vigorous naval warfare has been, the stricter the blockade that has been enforced. In addition, this has resulted in greater market distortions, and as a result the costs of trade have increased. The costs from market distortions and declining international commerce and trade have sometimes exceeded the direct costs from battle-related casualties and material destruction.[22] For this reason, the resulting decrease in world trade volumes has been assumed to affect both belligerents and non-belligerents – neutral countries – negatively.[23]

However, as is presented in this book, there are ample examples of neutral countries that have benefitted from the changing political and economic conditions brought on by wars and conflicts.[24] Neutral maritime trade and wars have coexisted since at least the 18th century, and since then commercial activities of neutral countries have not been as restricted as the belligerents'. While international trade and commerce has declined, the importance of access to alternative markets and the role of neutral trade conversely has increased.[25] As a result, neutral countries have had opportunities to profit from international wartime demand. Even though such expansions have been temporary – as hostilities eventually have ceased and international commerce have been resumed – they sometimes have entailed long-term positive impact on trade and GDP growth.[26] When the trade between belligerent countries has diminished due to naval warfare and blockades, neutral countries have often managed to maintain old and develop new channels for international commerce. In this respect, expanding wartime trade of neutral countries has mitigated the negative impact of conflicts and wars on the economy in general.

Typically the beginning of the first era of globalization is placed in the early 19th century, which also implies an immense growth in trade and shipping.[28]

As Figure 1.5 shows, the scale and scope of shipping increased (see the Dutch case) for centuries before the start of globalization in the 19th century, though others have challenged the view that it began even as late as this.[29] We also plotted the total number of ships that passed through the Danish Sound, which can be interpreted similarly, as an almost continuous growth trend in North European trade since the early 18th century.[30] Smaller nations were the key players in the trade passing through the Sound, and they certainly joined in this expansion.

Figure 1.6 puts this in the context of 19th- and 20th-century trade, using the latest data from Giovanni Federico and Antonio Tena Junguito. It also gives the impression that the trade expansion in the 19th century may have been a continuation of an earlier pattern, albeit possibly timed later. Whether it was or not, the huge growth in trade in the 19th century is clearly impressive. The dips in the pattern show the effect of World War I and the 1930s' Depressions.

The same database provides an overview of some of the costs of doing trade, namely freight rates. As earlier studies have suggested, freight rates declined in the 19th century, with the exception of a temporary bump in mid-century due to the Crimean War.[31] World War I shows up as a massive peak, and so do the late 1930s. These results were confirmed by another data series and seem to match well. The decline in costs of course benefited all the states, and especially those with large merchant (and military) fleets.

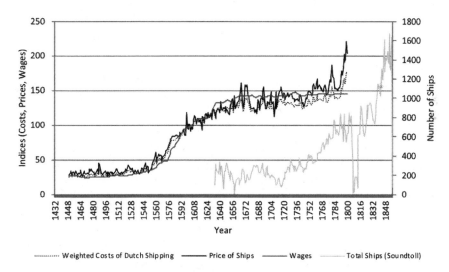

Figure 1.5 Estimates of the economic dimensions of early modern shipping, 1450–1800 vs. ships passing the Danish Sound, 1634–1857.

Source: van Zanden and van Tielhof (2009). On the Sound Toll records, see www.soundtoll.nl. (cited January 5, 2018).[27]

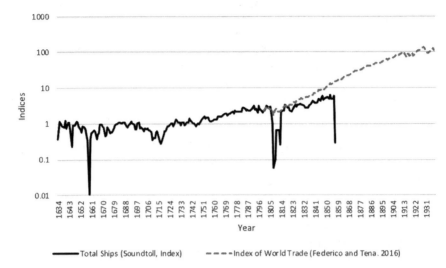

Figure 1.6 Index of world trade, 1800–1938 (1913 = 100) vs. ships passing the Danish Sound, 1634–1857.

Sources: Federico, Giovanni; Tena Junguito, Antonio (2018c), Federico-Tena World Trade Historical Database: World Trade, doi:10.21950/HPW2AK, e-cienciaDatos, V1; on the Sound Toll Records, see www.soundtoll.nl/index.php/en/onderzoek/zoeken-in-de-sonttol-database.

Note
The two indices were equalized at the year 1800.

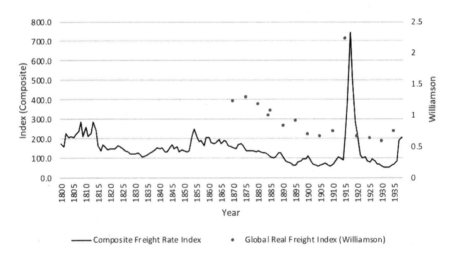

Figure 1.7 Global freight rates, 1800–1938.

Sources: Federico, Giovanni; Tena Junguito, Antonio (2018a). Federico-Tena World Trade Historical Database: Freights Rates, doi:10.21950/LAFKWD, e-cienciaDatos, V; and Mohammed and Williamson (2004).

Note
The Federico–Tena Junguito freights were combined into an arithmetic mean.

What about trade openness, which we have hypothesized as perhaps being a characteristic of a smaller/weaker nation? As seen in Figure 1.8, such openness increased above all in Europe, as a consequence of a network of free trade treaties later in the century. In the world as a whole, the increase was less pronounced, and the Americas remained more protectionist. World War I marked the end to this era of relative trade openness. But how do the smaller/weaker states fit into this picture? Figure 1.9 shows some of the states discussed in this book. Some countries, such as Brazil and Switzerland, were very open economies in this period, Sweden less so but increasingly between the wars. Portugal and the United States were not very open at all, and their dependence on foreign markets was low. Existing and former colonies helped the former to keep its economy fairly completely closed off, while the latter, in contrast with most of Europe, was fairly protectionist in the late 19th century,

Moreover, several of the chapters in this book examine the concept of neutrality, which small states have used as a way of avoiding direct conflict. Neutrality has long been seen as impartiality in war and is codified in international law as part of the Hague and Geneva Conventions.[32] Although we have used this word across the chapters to describe how countries avoid conflict, the individual cases differ widely: consider Finland in the Cold War; Ireland, Spain, Switzerland, Sweden and others in World War II; all the Scandinavian countries in World War I. Neutrals have maintained their independence by offering economic and political concessions to the belligerents to make up for their absolute and relative smallness. Cooperation allows them to survive,

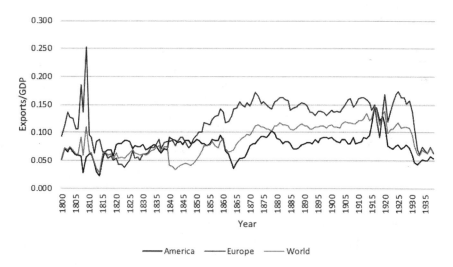

Figure 1.8 World trade openness (= Exports/GDP), 1800–1938.

Source: Federico, Giovanni; Tena Junguito, Antonio (2018b). Federico-Tena World Trade Historical Database: Openness, doi:10.21950/BBZVBN, e-cienciaDatos, V1. See also Federico and Tena-Junguito (2017).

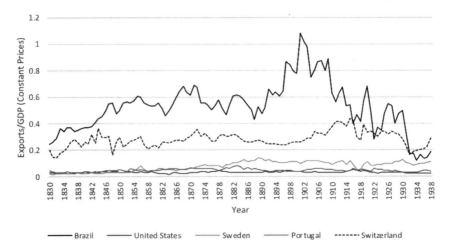

Figure 1.9 Trade openness (= Exports/GDP) for select weak powers, 1800–1938.
Source: Federico, Giovanni; Tena Junguito, Antonio (2018b). Federico-Tena World Trade Historical Database: Openness, doi:10.21950/BBZVBN, e-cienciaDatos, V1. See also Federico and Tena-Junguito (2017).

but still to oppose the regimes against when they were ideologically hostile. However, despite their different starting places, challenges across a wide time period, and unique political and economic threats, the instances of neutrality mentioned in this work show a number of similarities. The credibility of this defense was tested in many areas; in this work we explore the trade and business effects of neutrality, particularly in Scandinavia and the Iberian Peninsula.

The argument presented in the chapters on neutrals in this book is developed on two discrete planes. The first area is explored in order to provide an economic history of small, neutral countries. In each conflict across the neutral case studies, trade is an area where neutrals were consistently threatened. Each of the chapters details elements of the trade and financial relations between the belligerent and neutral countries. Depending on the threats they faced, the neutrals cooperated to ensure their survival. Specific chapters also look at economic and business performance in light of the threats faced. These show how closely the neutral countries and businesses were affected by the war, but also how in the postwar periods they had a strategic advantage over competing firms, because of actions taken during the war.

The second area of inquiry is investigated in order to describe the bilateral relations between nations and the negotiations they engage in. As part of this process, powerful belligerents or groups of belligerents seek to influence neutral behavior – whether between Portugal and Russia in the late modern period, the Western alliance introducing an embargo on Finland during the Cold War to minimize the leakage of trade through Finland to the Soviet bloc, or the German and British embargos on Sweden during World Wars I and II. In the last two cases, informal cooperation with the Anglo-sphere existed; at each turning point in the various wars, Finland and Sweden had to provide evidence of cooperation to placate the belligerent parties.

Although many of the themes are the same, one strength of this volume is that the several chapters on small states and neutrality address a number of different cases to refine the concept of small state neutrality. For example, the trade and commercial relations between Portugal and Russia between 1770 and 1850 demonstrate the misalignment in trade aims due to problematic institutions and conflict. Norwegian neutrality in the Western blockade of Germany in World War I shows how vulnerable Norway became over time because of its unwillingness to negotiate in certain areas. In comparison, the business performance in Sweden during World War I of ball bearings manufacturer SKF displays how business can adapt to changing conditions during war. The macroeconomic effects of neutrality in the Nordic countries during the two world wars comparatively demonstrate a significant export improvement in the early years of World War I, but losses thereafter.

The lessons here show that neutrality was a tool used more and more by weaker states over time, but also that it was not always respected by the other players. The more important the output of the smaller state, and the greater their power to provide access to markets that were otherwise difficult for the belligerents to access, the more their neutrality status was respected. In such situations the weaker states could take advantage of the gaps in the limited wartime markets. These states could also operate between the confines of formal trade agreements, which were in any case abandoned during certain conflicts. In times of war their merchant fleets represented important conduits; and if they maintained enough of a military deterrent, their neutrality status was even more likely to be respected.

Contributions of the volume

The chapters in Part I, which focuses on the long-run interactions between trade and conflicts for smaller/weaker states, shed light on the reciprocal effects between war, or times of conflict, and trade. In Chapter 2, Land, Eloranta, and Moreira analyze the trading practices and trends for the United States from the beginning of its de facto independence, through the Revolutionary and Napoleonic Wars, and all the way to the period of peace in 1830 – during this time, the US was a new and weaker state. This is a longitudinal analysis of U.S. trade flows and behavior over a period that includes several conflicts and provides a fresh perspective on the role of the US as weak political actor. The economic impacts of war on trade are explored here, as well as the role of neutral and/or weaker states during such times, together with the pressure of the war efforts and whether they allowed more latitude for the US and other states to explore their trade options. Were there any changes in the types of goods traded over this complex period and, if so, what was the impact of the changes?

Did economic and business concerns override political and diplomatic obstacles in these trade relations, and how did they open up opportunities for the smaller/weaker states? This chapter explores these points and argues that weak states, albeit briefly, were able to expand their trade and discover new markets even though they faced such large and protracted conflicts.

Silvia Marzagalli's contribution (Chapter 3) provides an evaluation of the role of American shipping and trade in the Mediterranean during the French Wars, and she shows how a country such as the United States could make the most of its situation and the wars in Europe to explore this trading area to its advantage. This chapter also underlines the relevance of guarantees for the United States' trade and the chance to take advantage of neutrality through peace treaties, commercial treaties, and consulates in major ports. According to Marzagalli's findings, American shipping into the Mediterranean increased five to six times from the early 1790s to 1807, part of the trade being with belligerents. The United States' ease in handling belligerents' property relativized the notion of neutrality, giving it more flexibility and making it a system in constant evolution, rather than a fixed legal status. Despite the obstacles faced by the ships' crews, they still seized the chance to expand the country's stay in the Mediterranean and travel further east.

Moreira, de Sousa, and Scheltjens' study of the commercial relations between Portugal and Russia (Chapter 4) analyzes the trade patterns and finance between these two countries. They explore the commercial changes in the relations between these two markets and focus on the Baltic Sea region in the context of the major international changes between 1770 and 1850 entailed by the new global war, and on neutrality and peace, in particular after the American War of Independence and the Napoleonic War. This study also points out that the difficulties of navigation, organization, and finance for Portuguese trade are important variables in explaining the absence of Portuguese merchants from this region's commercial relations.

In Chapter 5, da Costa Dominguez and Carrara bring out a Brazilian historiographic panorama over the last three decades, following economy and taxation as a main conduit and depicting the establishment and consolidation of the two schools of thought regarding Brazil's economic history. In addition, the writers analyze the former Portuguese colony's fiscal capacities before and during the Napoleonic Wars, exploring in particular the case of Rio de Janeiro's supremacy over other major local provinces and Lisbon at the end of the 18th century and beginning of the 19th.

Chapter 6, by Hedberg and Häggqvist, covers how a neutrality stance was adopted, especially by Sweden, following the end of the Napoleonic Wars. Its origins were closely connected to foreign trade, where neutrality was a tool for the country to keep trade links open and to attempt to direct shipping through Swedish ports. This chapter examines Swedish foreign trade, shipping and wartime trade policy strategies during the Napoleonic Wars, the Crimean War, and World War I. Sweden was able to take advantage of its neutral position during these three wars to increase trade and shipping, but it also adjusted its trade policy as a result of the circumstances of war and the encompassing neutrality. The short- and long-run effects of these wars on trade policy are discussed.

In comparison, the chapters in Part II, which focuses on the impact of conflicts on trade and neutrality (and vice versa), open the door to in-depth analyses of conflict-era trade and neutrality. In Chapter 7, on neutrality and conflicts, Eric Golson contributes to the understanding of the origins of neutrality and its legal framework, linking it with a framework from economic history, namely, the analysis of trade, labor, and capital for small states and neutrals in times of conflict. He approaches the subject of neutrality by briefly discussing the concept in legal terms and describes how different scholars have viewed its evolution. This introduction leads to the legal codification of neutrality in legal conventions, providing a framework for the definition of relationships between states. However, this legal framework was often disregarded in practice and neutral states were deeply affected during the Great War and interwar period, which was critical for the concept of neutrality. The realist principles, and the fact that neutrals did not have access to trade and other services, led to a loss of power, the German encirclement being the most famed violation of neutrality.

In fact, the concept of neutrality has evolved over the centuries. Legally codified as impartiality, it took a realist turn with the events of World War II. It is clear nowadays that there cannot be a single rule that covers neutrality and the way in which a country should be able to protect itself. Neutral, small states were able to survive even in a war scenario, avoiding conflict by their own realism and practicality. Throughout the Great War, the Norwegian economy rose and fell with great speed. During this time, not only did the German demand for imports boost domestic production, but Norway also then became a hub for the trans-shipment of overseas goods. Strøm explains in his contribution (Chapter 8) how the British government's failure to implement a coordinated system of blockade may explain how this could happen, in spite of the best efforts of the Entente. The Norwegian government implemented policies that had been made in the prewar era. However, in 1914, the British government controlled the connections between Norway and the West. Therefore, the British government would have had full power to overrule a Norwegian policy in order to avoid direct engagement with the blockade. Once the British government began implementing effective blockade measures, it was only a matter of time before Norway would become fully integrated into the blockade mounted by Germany.

Golson's second contribution (Chapter 9, with Jason Lennard), which centers on the study of Swedish economic and business performance during World War I, focuses on the importance of the Great War in the economic history of Sweden. The chapter proceeds with a microeconomic perspective to show how the war affected the economy at the level of an individual firm and how "the golden age" of the Swedish economy developed. Ball bearings manufacturer SKF saw a healthy boost and eventual longevity through international capital investment, vertical integration, the expansion of subsidiaries, and control of the Conrad ball bearings patent. The authors review the impact of World War I on the entire Swedish economy and Swedish businesses, as well as the flourishing movement and growth of SKF. The Swedish economy placed itself in context with the economic and business development of the time. Sweden's neutrality in this era is often overlooked or understated, but not in this chapter. This new study applies previous theories with updated statistics to the SKF case study. The SKF case during the war is unique because of the growth of competition against the company, but the extent of SKF's growth, in spite of all that was going against it, makes it intriguing to delve into. This study extends into both the Swedish economy and its business to demonstrate how dependent on the progress of Swedish businesses and how closely interlinked it was with the war. World War I was a pivotal time for the recognition of Swedish industry in international markets and set the tone for many years – well into the 1920s and beyond.

In the wake of World War I, the Nordic countries suffered only mildly, and generally recovered quickly. However, in Chapter 10, on the Nordic countries during the two world wars, Lennard and Golson discuss how much more they suffered in the second. They saw almost twice as much loss of output as they had seen during the Great Depression. Still, much of the lost economic activity in the wartime current accounts was mitigated when trade quickly increased afterwards. Meanwhile, countries such as Finland suffered in both wars. Isolation from traditional trading partners appears to have been a contributing factor to its losses. While the focus of this chapter is the short-run implications of the world wars on the Nordic economies, the long-run impacts were also a factor. Lennard and Golson provide a comprehensive methodology for measuring the economic effect of wars based on the cost of crisis in terms of lost output.

During the Cold War, the control of exports, especially protecting them from the influence of the Soviet bloc in the Eastern European countries, was extremely difficult. In Chapter 11, Jensen-Eriksen points out how much some of the officials and companies of the neutral countries wanted to limit the flow of militarily useful goods eastwards. Informal links and agreements made under the radar maintained the appearance of neutrality. This is why, Jensen-Eriksen says, it is important to look at low-level interaction. This study suggests that there was very little some countries could do about the field of export controls to the Eastern bloc. The Soviet Union, for example, could have used items embargoed by the Western alliance to help undermine the embargo itself. This underlines the fact that, the US in the early Cold War was not strong enough to totally eliminate the impulse to reap benefits from being declared neutral. Some of the neutrals believed that the strategic Western embargo was not an "East versus West" issue. It was a threat that forced neutral countries to curtail their exports of strategic goods, which sometimes came from the USA. Therefore, it had a major "West versus West" impact. They were concerned that they would have economic sanctions imposed on them or be shamed by their efforts to stay out of the global confrontation. Throughout this chapter, Jensen-Eriksen explores the advantages and disadvantages of neutrality.

In Chapter 12, the conclusion of this volume Jari Ojala and Toshiaki Tamaki discuss some of the findings and contributions of the book, as well as offering ideas for future research. This volume is just the first step in the process of reassessing the role and importance of smaller/weaker states in world trade, conflicts, and economic outcomes. Our assertion is that their role has been under-studied and underestimated. These nations were key players in the economic and political networks that functioned in the peripheries of the conflicts and of trade, when in many of these conflicts the peripheries were the only places for trading. The great powers had to dedicate their resources to protecting their own trade routes and/or imposing blockades, but they still needed the key commodities. Neutrality was a key tool for the smaller states to explore and exploit these opportunities over time.

As we have said, here we have just scratched the surface of the research opportunities that might be seized, as Patrick O'Brien also points out in his kind Foreword. First of all, we need a larger set of country studies to examine the bilateral and multilateral trade flows over longer periods of time, especially to develop large-scale databases for comparisons. Second, as in this volume, our approach is still too much dominated by European historical cases and descendants of the British Empire – we need a broader coverage of different world regions, and a better balance between colonial mother countries and the colonies themselves. Third, we need comprehensive long-run data on these states, to engage in deeper data analysis, so we can also quantitatively test the ideas explored here. Fourth, we see a dichotomy between the smaller/weaker states and the type of state capacity they had, when it came to conflicts and trade, in various historical contingencies. Finally, we need deeper analyses of the types of conflict they were involved in and the economic consequences of these conflicts, which would link our analyses with the larger literature of state capacity, fiscal states, long-run trade, the economic history of conflicts, and the long-run macroeconomic development of polities.

Notes

1 On the concept of small states, see Joenniemi (1998); Kassimeris (2009); Maass (2009). On the Baltic states in this context, see Lamoreaux and Galbreath (2008).
2 See e.g. Acemoglu (2005); Acemoglu, Ticchi, and Vindigni (2011); Acemoglu, Vindigni, and Ticchi (2010).
3 Handel (1981, 1990).
4 Eloranta, (2002). This is further discussed in Salmon (2002).
5 See e.g. Gilpin (2016); Kennedy (1989); Parchami (2009); Schroeder (1994).
6 For example, see Acemoglu, Garcia-Jimeno, and Robinson (2015); Acemoglu and Robinson (2013); Besley and Persson (2009, 2010); Dincecco (2011); Dincecco and Prado (2012); Gennaioli and Voth (2015); Hendrix (2010); Johnson and Koyama (2014).
7 Such as Bonney (1999); Ferguson (2001); Hoffman (2015); Lindert (2003, 2004); Stasavage (2002, 2011); Yun-Casalilla, O'Brien, and Comín (2012).

8 Many of these arguments are grounded in Tilly (1990).
9 In addition to the literature already cited, see especially the case of Spain in Drelichman and Voth (2014). For a broader analysis of public debt patterns and financial crises, see Kalemli-Özcan, Reinhart, and Rogoff (2016); Reinhart and Rogoff (2014).
10 Singer, Bremer, and Stuckey (1972).
11 Some of this discussion can be seen in the following: Eloranta (2017); Ju (2017); Rauch (2017); Wohlforth (1987). Also, in older conflicts other products and resources could play a more decisive role.
12 On comparative figures for the late 19th and early 20th centuries, see, e.g., Eloranta (2007); Eloranta, Andreev, and Osinsky (2014); Rota (2016); Sabaté (2016).
13 Bolt and Zanden (2014); Broadberry (2016); Broadberry and Gardner (2016); de Pleijt and van Zanden (2016); Meredith (2016).
14 See, e.g., Modelski and Thompson (1988, 1996).
15 Crisher and Souva (2014).
16 Modelski and Thompson (1988).
17 Bell (2007); Land and Eloranta (2016); Moreira and Eloranta (2011); Moreira, Eloranta, Ojala, and Karvonen (2015).
18 Findlay and O'Rourke (2007).
19 There is plenty of literature available on the impact of war and blockades on the economy. On the French Revolutionary and the Napoleonic Wars, see, e.g., Crouzet (1964); Frankel (1982); Heckscher (1964); O'Rourke (2006). On the economic conditions during World Wars I and II, see Broadberry and Harrison (2005); Harrison (1998); Milward (1977).
20 See, e.g., Gowa and Hicks (2015),
21 Chapter 1 in Broadberry and Harrison (2005); Kennedy (1989).
22 Glick and Taylor (2010).
23 Blomberg and Hess (2006).
24 On the experiences of, e.g., the Scandinavian countries during the Napoleonic Wars and World War I, see Häggqvist (2015); Hedberg (2016); Hedberg and Karlsson (2015); Müller (2016); on Spain, see Pinilla and Serrano (2008); on Switzerland, see Müller (2009); on Dutch trade, see de Jong (2005); on belligerent US, Australia, Canada, and South Africa, as well as India, all countries were out of reach of war activities and blockades, see Findlay and O'Rourke (2007) and Hautcoeur (2005).
25 However, it should be noted that the practices of maritime neutral trade have been contested repeatedly in different wars and between countries, and accordingly, immense legal, diplomatic, political, and economic negotiations have been produced in order to reach agreements. The interpretations of neutrality have thus diverged greatly, and the arbitrary nature of the issue is illustrated by the fact that neutral merchant vessels sometimes were accompanied by armed escorts, and as a result, blockade policies of belligerent countries subsequently triggered wars between the neutral and the belligerent country. While neutrals have claimed that "free ships make free goods", the stance of belligerents have differed varied according to the different neutrals (Marzagalli & Müller, 2016), p. 113). If neutral merchants were considered enhancing the military capacity of the enemy side, they often became targeted – such as during World War I, when Germany and the British took aim at the neutral vessels trading with the enemy, see, e.g., Davis and Engerman (2006) and Halpern (2006). But, from the view of the belligerent country, the use of blockade strategies comprised a dilemma: on the one hand, allowing neutral countries to trade unreservedly might benefit the enemy side and extend the duration of the war, but, on the other, too strict an attitude would have

risked that the neutral even joined the enemy as well, and accordingly a loss of a supplier of precious commodities.
26 For instance, neutral Sweden's trade and terms of trade during the Crimean War and the Franco-Prussian War experienced a short- and long-term positive impact, making a significant contribution to Swedish real GDP growth rates; see Hedberg and Karlsson (2015).
27 As examples of other trade databases for the period, see, e.g., TradHist (www.cepii.fr/cepii/en/bdd_modele/presentation.asp?id=32), which provides bilateral trade data for the period 1827-2014, and Ricardo Project (http://ricardo.medialab.sciences-po.fr/#/), which has trade data for the period 1800–1938.
28 Jacks (2006); Jacks, Meissner, and Novy (2010); Jacks, O'Rourke, and Williamson (2011); O'Rourke and Williamson (2001, 2002, 2004).
29 See, e.g., DeVries (2010); Frank and Denemark (2015). In turn, O'Grada and Kelly (2017), for example, argue that a major increase in ship speed occurred in the latter part of the 18th century.
30 Gøbel (2010); Moreira et al. (2015); Ojala and Eloranta (2015); Scheltjens and Veluwenkamp (2012).
31 Harley (1988); North (1958).
32 A small sampling of articles and books relating to the wars and trade of the weaker nations would include: Adams Jr. (1980); Alimento (2011); Aunesluoma (2003); Frey (1997); Little (1985); Marzagalli and Müller (2016); Müller (2016); Welling (1998).

References

Acemoglu, D. (2005). Politics and economics in weak and strong states. *Journal of Monetary Economics*, 52(7), 1199–1226.
Acemoglu, D., & Robinson, J. A. (2013). *Why nations fail: The origins of power, prosperity, and poverty*. New York: Broadway Business.
Acemoglu, D., Garcia-Jimeno, C., & Robinson, J. A. (2015). State capacity and economic development: A network approach. *American Economic Review*, 105(8), 2364–2409.
Acemoglu, D., Ticchi, D., & Vindigni, A. (2011). Emergence and persistence of inefficient states. *Journal of the European Economic Association*, 9(2), 177–208.
Acemoglu, D., Vindigni, A., & Ticchi, D. (2010). Persistence of civil wars. *Journal of the European Economic Association*, 8(2–3), 664–676.
Adams Jr, D. R. (1980). American neutrality and prosperity, 1793–1808: A reconsideration. *Journal of Economic History*, 40(4), 713–737.
Alimento, A. (2011). *War, trade and neutrality: Europe and the Mediterranean in the seventeenth and eighteenth centuries*, vol. 400. Milan: FrancoAngeli.
Aunesluoma, J. (2003). *Britain, Sweden and the Cold War, 1945–54: Understanding neutrality*. New York: Springer.
Bell, D. (2007). *The first total war: Napoleon's Europe and the birth of warfare as we know it*. New York: Houghton Mifflin Harcourt.
Besley, T., & Persson, T. (2009). The origins of state capacity: Property rights, taxation, and politics. *American Economic Review*, 99(4), 1218–1244.
Besley, T., & Persson, T. (2010). State capacity, conflict, and development. *Econometrica*, 78(1), 1–34.
Blomberg, S. B., & Hess, G. D. (2006). How Much does Violence Tax Trade? *Review of Economic Studies and Statistics*, 88(4), 599–612.

Bolt, J., & Zanden, J. L. (2014). The Maddison Project: collaborative research on historical national accounts. *The Economic History Review*, 67(3), 627–651.

Bonney, R. (Ed.) (1999). *The Rise of the Fiscal State in Europe c. 1200–1815*. Oxford: Oxford University Press.

Broadberry, S. (2016). The great divergence in the world economy: long-run trends of real income. In Joerg Baten (ed.), *A history of the global economy: 1500 to the present*. Cambridge, UK: Cambridge University Press.

Broadberry, S., & Gardner, L. (2016). Economic development in Africa and Europe: Reciprocal comparisons. *Revista de Historia Economica-Journal of Iberian and Latin American Economic History*, 34(1), 11–37.

Broadberry, S., & Harrison, M. (2005). The economics of World War I: An overview. In S. Broadberry & M. Harrison (Eds.), *The economics of World War I*. Cambridge, UK: Cambridge University Press.

Conflict Catalog (n.d.). Violent conflicts 1400 AD to the present in different regions of the world. Retrieved February 10, 2018, from www.cgeh.nl/data#conflict

Crisher, B. B., & Souva, M. (2014). Power at sea: A naval power dataset, 1865–2011. *International Interactions*, 40(4), 602–629.

Crouzet, F. (1964). Wars, blockade, and economic-change in Europe, 1792–1815. *Journal of Economic History*, 24(4), 567–588.

Davis, L., & Engerman, S. L. (2006). *Naval blockades in peace and war: An economic history since 1750*. New York: Cambridge University Press.

de Jong, H. (2005). The Dutch economy during World War I. In S. Broadberry & M. Harrison (Eds.), *The economics of World War I*. Cambridge, UK: Cambridge University Pres.

De Pleijt, A. M., & Van Zanden, J. L. (2016). Accounting for the "little divergence": What drove economic growth in pre-industrial Europe, 1300–1800? *European Review of Economic History*, 20(4), 387–409.

De Vries, J. (2010). The limits of globalization in the early modern world. *Economic History Review*, 63(3), 710–733.

Dincecco, M. (2011). *Political transformations and public finances: Europe, 1650–1913*. Cambridge, UK: Cambridge University Press.

Dincecco, M., & Prado, M. (2012). Warfare, fiscal capacity, and performance. *Journal of Economic Growth*, 17(3), 171–203.

Drelichman, M., & Voth, H.-J. (2014). *Lending to the borrower from hell: Debt, taxes, and default in the age of Philip II*. Princeton, NJ: Princeton University Press.

Eloranta, J. (2002). European states in the international arms trade, 1920–1937: The impact of external threats, market forces, and domestic constraints. *Scandinavian Economic History Review*, 50(1), 44–67.

Eloranta, J. (2007). From the great illusion to the Great War: Military spending behaviour of the Great Powers, 1870–1913. *European Review of Economic History*, 11(2), 255–283.

Eloranta, J. (2017). Pro bono publico? Demand for military spending between the world wars. *Essays in Economic & Business History*, 35(2), 99–142.

Eloranta, J., Andreev, S., & Osinsky, P. (2014). Democratization and central government spending, 1870–1938: Emergence of the leviathan? In C. Hanes & S. Wolcott (Eds.), *Research in Economic History* (vol. 30, pp. 1–46). Bingley, UK: Emerald Group Publishing.

Federico, G., & Tena-Junguito, A. (2017). A tale of two globalizations: Gains from trade and openness 1800–2010. *Review of World Economics*, 153(3), 601–626.

Federico, G., & Tena-Junguito, A. (2018a). Federico-Tena World Trade Historical Database: Freights Rates. doi:10.21950/LAFKWD

Federico, G., & Tena Junguito, A. (2018b). Federico-Tena World Trade Historical Database: Openness. doi:10.21950/BBZVBN

Federico, G., & Tena Junguito, A. (2018c). Federico-Tena World Trade Historical Database: World Trade. doi:10.21950/HPW2AK

Ferguson, N. (2001). *The cash nexus: Money and power in the modern world, 1700–2000*. New York: Basic Books.

Findlay, R., & O'Rourke, K. H. (2007). *Power and plenty: Trade, war, and the world economy in the second millennium*. Princeton, NJ: Princeton University Press.

Frank, A. G., & Denemark, R. A. (2015). *Reorienting the 19th century: Global economy in the continuing Asian age*. London: Routledge.

Frankel, J. A. (1982). The 1807–1809 embargo against Great Britain. *Journal of Economic History, 42*(2), 291–307.

Frey, M. (1997). Trade, ships, and the neutrality of the Netherlands in the First World War. *International History Review, 19*(3), 541–562.

Gennaioli, N., & Voth, H.-J. (2015). State capacity and military conflict. *Review of Economic Studies, 82*(4), 1409–1448.

Gilpin, R. (2016). *The political economy of international relations*. Princeton, NJ: Princeton University Press.

Glick, R., & Taylor, A. M. (2010). Collateral damage: Trade disruption and the economic impact of war. *Review of Economics and Statistics, 92*(1), 102–127.

Gøbel, E. (2010). The sound toll registers online project, 1497–1857. *International Journal of Maritime History, 22*(2), 305–324.

Gowa, J., & Hicks, R. (2015). Commerce and conflict: New data about the Great War. *British Journal of Political Science, 47*(3), 1–22.

Häggqvist, H. (2015). On the ocean of protectionism. The structure of Swedish tariffs and trade 1780–1830, vol. 103. Uppsala: Acta Universitatis Upsaliensis; Uppsala University Library.

Halpern, P. (2006). World War I: The blockade. In L. Davis & S. L. Engerman (Eds.), *Naval blockades in peace and war: An economic history since 1750*. New York: Cambridge University Press.

Handel, M. I. (1981). *Weak states in the international system*. London, UK/Totowa, NJ: F. Cass.

Harley, C. K. (1988). Ocean freight rates and productivity, 1740–1913: The primacy of mechanical invention reaffirmed. *Journal of Economic History, 48*(4), 851–876.

Harrison, M. (1998). The economics of World War II: An overview. In M. Harrison (Ed.), *The economics of World War II*. Cambridge, UK: Cambridge University Press.

Hautcoeur, P.-C. (2005). The economics of World War I in France. In S. Broadberry & M. Harrison (Eds.), *The Economics of World War I*. Cambridge, UK: Cambridge University Press.

Heckscher, E. F. (1964). *The Continental System: An economic interpretation*. Gloucester, MA: Peter Smith.

Hedberg, P. (2016). The impact of WWI on Sweden's foreign trade and growth. *Journal of European Economic History, 45*(3), 83–103.

Hedberg, P., & Karlsson, L. (2015). Neutral trade in time of war: The case of Sweden, 1838–1960. *International Journal of Maritime History, 27*(1), 61–78.

Hendrix, C. S. (2010). Measuring state capacity: Theoretical and empirical implications for the study of civil conflict. *Journal of Peace Research*, *47*(3), 273–285.

Hoffman, P. T. (2015). *Why did Europe conquer the world?* Princeton, NJ: Princeton University Press.

Inklaar, R., de Jong, H., Bolt, J., & van Zanden, J. (2018). *Rebasing "Maddison": New income comparisons and the shape of long-run economic development*. Working Paper GD-174, GGDC Research Memorandum from Groningen Growth and Development Centre, University of Groningen.

Jacks, D. S. (2006). What drove 19th century commodity market integration? *Explorations in Economic History*, *43*(3), 383–412.

Jacks, D. S., Meissner, C. M., & Novy, D. (2010). Trade costs in the first wave of globalization. *Explorations in Economic History*, *47*(2), 127–141.

Jacks, D. S., O'Rourke, K. H., & Williamson, J. G. (2011). Commodity price volatility and world market integration since 1700. *Review of Economics and Statistics*, *93*(3), 800–813.

Joenniemi, P. (1998). From small to smart: Reflections on the concept of small states. *Irish Studies in International Affairs*, *9*, 61–62.

Johnson, N. D., & Koyama, M. (2014). Tax farming and the origins of state capacity in England and France. *Explorations in Economic History*, *51*, 1–20.

Ju, C. (2017, July 18). Causes of war: When the unknown creates false optimism. *Chicago Policy Review*. Retrieved from http://chicagopolicyreview.org/2017/07/18/causes-of-war-when-the-unknown-creates-false-optimism/

Kalemli-Özcan, Ş., Reinhart, C., & Rogoff, K. (2016). Sovereign debt and financial crises: Theory and historical evidence. *Journal of the European Economic Association*, *14*(1), 1–6.

Kassimeris, C. (2009). The foreign policy of small powers. *International Politics*, *46*(1), 84–101.

Kennedy, P. (1989). *The rise and fall of the great powers. Economic change and military conflict from 1500 to 2000*. London: Fontana.

Lamoreaux, J. W., & Galbreath, D. J. (2008). The Baltic states as "small states": Negotiating the "East" by engaging the "West". *Journal of Baltic Studies*, *39*(1), 1–14.

Land, J., & Eloranta, J. (2016). Wartime economies, 1939–1945: Large and small European states at war. In N. Doumanis (Ed.), *The Oxford Handbook of European History, 1914–1945* (pp. 461–479): Oxford, UK: Oxford University Press.

Lindert, P. H. (2003). Voice and growth: Was Churchill right? *Journal of Economic History*, *63*(2), 315–350.

Lindert, P. H. (2004). *Growing public: Social spending and economic growth since the eighteenth century*, vol. 1. Cambridge, UK: Cambridge University Press.

Little, D. (1985). *Malevolent neutrality: The United States, Great Britain, and the origins of the Spanish Civil War*. Ithaca, NY: Cornell University Press.

Maass, M. (2009). The elusive definition of the small state. *International Politics*, *46*(1), 65–83.

Marzagalli, S., & Müller, L. (2016). "In apparent disagreement with all law of nations in the world": Negotiating neutrality for shipping and trade during the French Revolutionary and Napoleonic Wars. *International Journal of Maritime History*, *28*(1), 108–117.

Meredith, D. (2016). Review of *British economic growth, 1270–1870*, Stephen Broadberry, Bruce S. M. Campbell, Alexander Klein, Mark Overton & Bas van

Leeuwen (Eds.), *English Historical Review*, *131*(151), 969–970. doi.org/10.1093/ehr/cew141
Milward, A. S. (1977). *War, economy and society, 1939–1945*. London: Lane.
Modelski, G., & Thompson, W. R. (1988). *Seapower in global politics, 1494–1993*. Basingstoke, UK: Macmillan.
Modelski, G., & Thompson, W. R. (1996). *Leading sectors and world powers. The coevolution of global politics and economics*. Columbia: University of South Carolina Press.
Mohammed, S. I. S., & Williamson, J. G. (2004). Freight rates and productivity gains in British tramp shipping 1869–1950. *Explorations in Economic History*, *41*(2), 172–203.
Moreira, C., & Eloranta, J. (2011). Importance of «weak» states during conflicts: Portuguese trade with the United States during the Revolutionary and Napoleonic wars. *Revista de Historia Económica*, *29*(03), 393–423.
Moreira, M. C., Eloranta, J., Ojala, J., & Karvonen, L. (2015). Early modern trade flows between smaller states: The Portuguese–Swedish trade in the eighteenth century as as example. *Revue de l'OFCE*, *140*, 87–109.
Müller, L. (2016). Swedish merchant shipping in troubled times: The French Revolutionary Wars and Sweden's neutrality 1793–1801. *International Journal of Maritime History*, *28*(1), 147–164.
Müller, M. (2009). Coping with barriers to trade: Causes and consequences of the changing competitiveness of Swiss industries (1900–1950). *Paper presented at the EBHA, 12th Annual Conference*, Bergen.
North, D. (1958). Ocean freight rates and economic development 1730–1913. *Journal of Economic History*, *18*(4), 537–555.
O'Grada, C. and Kelly, M. (2017). *Speed under sail, during the early Industrial Revolution (c.1750–1850)* (October 12, 2017). Retrieved from https://ssrn.com/abstract=2412955 or http://dx.doi.org/10.2139/ssrn.2412955
O'Rourke, K. H. (2006). The worldwide economic impact of the French Revolutionary and Napoleonic Wars, 1793–1815. *Journal of Global History*, *1*(1), 123–149.
O'Rourke, K. H., & Williamson, J. G. (2001). *Globalization and history: The evolution of a nineteenth-century Atlantic economy*. Boston, MA: MIT Press.
O'Rourke, K. H., & Williamson, J. G. (2002). When did globalisation begin? *European Review of Economic History*, *6*(1), 23–50.
O'Rourke, K. H., & Williamson, J. G. (2004). Once more: When did globalisation begin? *European Review of Economic History*, *8*(1), 109–117.
Ojala, J., & Eloranta, J. (2015). Sweden and Finland c. 1700–1809, Finland 1809–c. 1850. *Revue de l'OFCE*, *140*, 373–377.
Parchami, A. (2009). *Hegemonic peace and empire: The Pax Romana, Britannica and Americana*. London: Routledge.
Pinilla, V., & Serrano, R. (2008). The agricultural and food trade in the first globalization: Spanish table wine exports 1871 to 1935. *Journal of Wine Economics*, *3*(2), 132–148.
Rauch, C. (2017). Challenging the power consensus: GDP, CINC, and Power Transition Theory. *Security Studies*, *26*(4), 642–664.
Reinhart, C. M., & Rogoff, K. S. (2014). Recovery from financial crises: Evidence from 100 episodes. *American Economic Review*, *104*(5), 50–55.
Rota, M. (2016). Military spending, fiscal caf and the democracy puzzle. *Explorations in Economic History*, *60*, 41–51.
Sabaté, O. (2016). New quantitative estimates of long-term military spending in Spain (1850–2009). In C. Hanes & S. Wolcott (Eds.), *Research in Economic History* (vol. 32, pp. 225–276). Bingley, UK: Emerald Group Publishing Limited.

Salmon, P. (2002). *Scandinavia and the great powers 1890–1940*. Cambridge, UK: Cambridge University Press.

Sarkees, M. R., & Wayman, F. W. (2010). *Resort to war: A data guide to inter-state, extra-state, intra-state, and non-state wars, 1816–2007*. Washington: CQ Press.

Scheltjens, W., & Veluwenkamp, J. W. (2012). Sound Toll Registers online: Introduction and first research examples. *International Journal of Maritime History*, *24*(1), 301–330.

Schroeder, P. (1994). Historical reality vs. neo-realist theory. *International Security*, *19*(1), 108–148.

Singer, J. D., Bremer, S., & Stuckey, J. (1972). Capability distribution, uncertainty, and major power war, 1820–1965. In B. Russett (Ed.), *Peace, war, and numbers* (pp. 19–48). Beverly Hills, CA: Sage.

Stasavage, D. (2002). Credible commitment in early modern Europe: North and Weingast revisited. *Journal of Law, Economics, and Organization*, *18*(1), 155–186.

Stasavage, D. (2011). *States of credit: Size, power, and the development of European polities*: Princeton, NJ: Princeton University Press.

Tilly, C. (1990). *Coercion, capital, and European states, AD 990–1990*. Cambridge, MA: Basil Blackwell.

van Zanden, J. L., & van Tielhof, M. (2009). Roots of growth and productivity change in Dutch shipping industry, 1500–1800. *Explorations in Economic History*, *46*(4), 389–403.

Welling, G. M. (1998). The prize of neutrality: Trade relations between Amsterdam and North America 1771–1817. Dissertation, University of Groningen.

Wohlforth, W. C. (1987). The perception of power: Russia in the pre-1914 balance. *World Politics*, *39*(3), 353–381.

Yun-Casalilla, B., O'Brien, P. K., & Comín, F. C. (2012). *The rise of fiscal states: A global history, 1500–1914*: Cambridge, UK: Cambridge University Press.

Part I

Interplay of trade and conflicts in the long run

2 Trade and the new republic
American trade during the Napoleonic Wars, 1783–1830

Jeremy Land, Jari Eloranta, and Maria Cristina Moreira

Introduction

This chapter analyzes the trading practices and trends for the new, weak republic, the United States, from the beginning of its de fact independence in 1783 through the Revolutionary and Napoleonic Wars all the way to the period of peace in 1830. It taps into an important field of analysis, namely the discussion of the economic impacts of war on trade as well as the role of neutral and/or weaker states in wartime situations. Many scholars have recently investigated the disruptions caused by major conflicts like the world wars, and recent scholarship certainly places the revolutionary wars and the contingent Napoleonic conflicts into the same category. However, these scholars have paid relatively little attention to smaller (often neutral) players, like the Nordic countries, in these wars, assuming that they occupied an insignificant role in the conflict.

Moreover, states that have a large geographic size, but lack political and military power, are either treated the same as great powers or ignored until they gain such status. We want to explore what kinds of changes, including structural, we see in the trade flows between the United States *and* both great powers and weaker states, especially whether the pressure of the war effort allowed more latitude for these states to explore their trade options. Furthermore, we investigate whether there are substantial changes, and what those changes would imply, in the types of goods exchanged over this complex period, hinting at the significance of this trade for both countries. Finally, we analyze whether economic and business concerns overrode political and diplomatic obstacles in these trade relations, thereby opening up opportunities for the smaller/weaker states. Our basic argument is that weak states were able to expand their trade and discover new markets during such large and protracted conflicts, although this was, as in the case of US–Portuguese trade in this period, typically a shorter-term phenomenon. Therefore, longitudinal analysis of US trade flows and behavior over the period of several conflicts will provide a fresh perspective on the role of this new, and oftentimes, weak state.

Our key starting points are as follows: (1) small and medium-sized states have been a much more integral part of world trade than has previously been assumed, particularly during crisis periods; (2) crises tend to accentuate the importance of trade relationships between and with smaller nations, since many of them did not directly participate in the actual conflict, thus providing valuable raw materials and markets for the warring parties; (3) aggregate statistics are likely to understate this role, given that the focus in past scholarship has been mostly on trade between big players in the international system. Our findings support these hypotheses, by and large, even if solely looking at macro statistics. Smaller European states became much more important for US trade during the conflict period, albeit temporarily. We can also see that certain countries became particularly important, since they had the crucial raw materials needed during the age of global war. Moreover, the US also provided much-needed materiél and food to smaller European nations such as Portugal.

In the following chapter we first discuss why the study of smaller/weaker nations is important and review some of the existing scholarship of early American trade. Then we evaluate some broad trends in US trade and take a closer look at the role European nations other than Great Britain, France, and Germany played in this trade. Then we analyze the early 19th century and war years in the context of US trade and discuss US–Portuguese trade as a case in point, to be followed by some preliminary conclusions.

Why study smaller (or weaker) states?

The Revolutionary and Napoleonic Wars were truly total wars based on the methods chosen by the belligerents, which also affect countries outside the direct fighting. The effects of the war spilled over to influence the relations between neutrals as well. Due to the fact that these wars had an impact on the trade relations of *all* nations, many countries scrambled to find new outlets for exports and sources for imports. Respectively, the United States was particularly hard hit by these wars, which forced it to seek alternative trading partners and networks. Therefore, in this situation the bargaining power of weak (like the United States) and/or smaller states (like Portugal which was both weak and small) increased, albeit temporarily.

Scholars have paid too little attention to the smaller players in times of war, often assuming that they occupied an insignificant role in the conflict. "Small power" and "smaller state", typically and erroneously, imply small geographic size. A more fitting definition can perhaps be found in the use of the term "weak state". This concept also applies to countries of considerable area, which were nonetheless weak (political and/or economic) players in the international system.[1] Here we would argue that most European smaller states, like Portugal and Sweden, despite being a war zone for some portions of this period, were indeed such states; a state that increased its international trade and bargaining power due to aforementioned external conditions. The United States was a weak state as well, and for the most part in this period neutral, given its short existence and limited military power.

Neutral states, including the Nordic countries for most of the period (when they were not under occupation), served a vital function during a wartime trading system, when traditional trading networks were disrupted. As Leos Müller has shown, the concept of neutrality evolved in the 17th century, and neutral participation in trade reduced transaction costs among the belligerents, circumventing blockades and other trade restrictions. The ability to use neutral states as trading partners and carriers of goods prevented the wholesale collapse of Atlantic commerce during the era of the Revolutionary and Napoleonic conflicts.[2] Neutral states, often treated differently by the belligerents based on past history and alliances, functioned in a treacherous economic environment, despite their efforts to pressure the great powers to recognize and respect their neutrality status. Some nations formed loose alliances between neutrals. To make this trading environment even more difficult, the British and French effectively instituted blockades on each other after 1802, developing later into the infamous Continental System by Napoleon in 1806.[3] Neutrals, like the United States and Nordic countries, tried to find their niches under these conditions and, while the risks were high, the payoffs too were high. Belligerent nations were desperate for goods and supplies. In fact, the Continental System increased trading opportunities for some nations, increasing the transit trade between neutrals.[4] And, while there have been studies on the trade behavior of some neutral states, including the United States, the networks between the neutrals and great powers have not yet been studied adequately.[5]

Ultimately, it is completely natural to focus most of the analysis on the great empires, like Great Britain and France. After all, it is quite staggering to conceptualize the evolution of an empire like Great Britain, from its humble beginnings in the 16th century, with the building of the navy and its first major victory against the Spanish Armada, to the multicultural, industrialized empire that ruled the world in the 19th century.[6] Additionally, the desire to understand the desperate, global conflict for supremacy from the 1790s to 1815 and Britain's role in this process is again quite understandable.[7] Also, the focus on the naval battles and strategies of these wars, including the building and development of the great fleets, seems quite logical and worthy of intense scholarship.[8] But maybe the intense nature of these rivalries and the total wars between the great powers in fact explains why they had to rely on alliances with lesser powers to complement their war efforts. Therefore, even a great power like Great Britain had to tolerate the activities of the neutral states, sometimes to the detriment of their own war efforts.

Trade and the Early Republic in the historiography

Generally, the majority of books and articles on the Early Republic period of the United States are focused on the political and social changes that appear to dominate the period. However, little is said, other than fleeting mentions, of the importance of European trade in the economic development of the newly formed nation. This is a rather puzzling omission, especially considering the wealth of material available for the study of such factors. Still, there are a few studies that attempt to explain how the early US managed to expand its fledgling economy.

Gordon Wood, a prominent American historian, wrote in his massive study of the Early Republic that American trade with Europe and the rest of the world increased thanks to the wars between the old trading powers. Furthermore, in the 1790s France and Spain threw "open their hitherto closed ports in the Caribbean to American commerce".[9] Americans also profited from the re-export trade, using their neutral ships as the means to transport goods from Europe to other areas of the globe. In addition, Wood maintained that the War of 1812 began because of Britain's refusal to view American ships as neutral, thus limiting American trade to Europe.[10]

Others also have pointed out the connection between trade and the leadup to the War of 1812. Frank Updyke, in his study of diplomacy before, during, and after the war, explained that the ultimately unsuccessful efforts of American politicians and officials to establish neutral status recognition from Britain were a major cause of the war.[11] Yet, Updyke did little more than describe the diplomatic wrangling over neutral trade and offered little detail on how much that trade expanded prior to the war. Alfred T. Mahan argued that the discussion over which ports and countries American ships could trade goods with resulted in many near conflicts prior to the war and, eventually, sparked the war.[12] Still, little has been said of how much those conflicts affected American trade.

Somewhat closer to the topic of this chapter, Joyce Appleby discussed the growth of agriculture during the Early Republic period. She explained that higher prices in the 1790s created demand for more American agricultural products thanks to a variety of issues, including the Napoleonic Wars. However, she argued that it was not the war that drove prices higher, but rather the declining ability of Europeans to produce enough food domestically for the growing populations. Still, she maintains that, by 1820, prices had dropped back to the pre-1790 levels as Europe was finally able to produce enough food for its population, not the end of Napoleonic warfare.[13] Though her argument makes sense on the surface, she does not seem to consider that warfare limits the abilities of nations to produce agricultural products for a variety of reasons, including a lack of manpower and the necessity of feeding large armies and navies.

Several authors have written about the entire American economy and its growth (or decline) prior to 1840. George Taylor argued that the American economy experienced a depression due to the American Revolution and the immediate aftermath from 1775 until 1790. But he also showed how the young economy experienced a surge of growth in the 1790s until 1807 as embargoes and war took a toll on that growth.[14] Though he dealt mostly with standard of living and not trade, his assertions appear to back our hypothesis that the United States experienced an increase in its trade with Europe. Much like Taylor, Diane Lindstrom approached the same topic but with newer evidence. She found, however, that the economy did experience impressive growth, but she contended that it was at a lower level than Taylor argued. Ultimately, Lindstrom succumbed to a common bias in the historiography in viewing the Early Republic period as a precursor to industrialization.[15]

Perhaps the most pertinent study in the historiography, Douglass C. North's *The Economic Growth of the United States, 1790–1860*, explained that foreign trade was key to the overall development of the American economy. Even he was surprised at what he found when he began his research. As he wrote:

> Originally the study was to cover the years 1815 to 1860, on the hypothesis that this had been the critical period in the economy's development. As work progressed it became clear that the previous era of warfare (and particularly the years 1793 to 1808) had played an important role in the country's development.[16]

Though his book incorporated a larger period than this chapter, North argued that the United States benefited greatly from the expansion in trade, both from re-exports and normal exports, to all of Europe, not just the major powers. This was due to the nearly constant state of warfare between the major powers and American neutrality during the period.[17]

Not surprisingly, North's view of the importance of the period of 1790–1808 has drawn criticism. Donald Adams Jr maintained that North overestimated the importance of the exports, arguing that the entire economy's growth did not deviate from the long-run and modest growth experienced prior to the Civil War. He argued that only the re-export trade experienced any growth and "domestic trade exhibited little deviation" from normal trends.[18] Claudia Goldin and Frank Lewis attempted to bridge the gap between Adams and North, staking the middle ground between the two opposing views. They contended that there was evidence to support North's assertion that exports led to the growth of the economy, but not enough to assign exports preeminence over other domestic factors. However, they focused, as did Adams, on income per-capita growth and ignored the population growth of the period.[19] Furthermore, they did not engage much in the export analysis other than allowing it a more important role than Adams claimed. Ultimately, none fully discussed the amount of trade and how warfare affected either the growth or decline. We intend to show how the period of nearly constant warfare in Europe allowed American merchants the opportunity to expand their trade with more than just the major powers.

More recently, historians have begun to ascertain the tremendous importance of European wars on American trade and even state formation. James Fichter made the bold argument that American trade (both prior to and after independence) in the East Indies directly influenced the development of capitalism and states in both the UK and the United States. More importantly, however, Fichter contended that American growth and success in the Indian Ocean as primary carriers of trade was directly related to the wars between France and England during the period 1798–1830.[20]

Not only are historians examining the influence of trade on the American economy and state, but some are examining how American trade forced other, larger nations to adjust their strategies to meet the growing competition that

US traders represented. John Haddad argued that Americans held a comparative advantage in China and the Indian Ocean over European merchants, especially those from England. The United States was such a young nation that very few institutional restrictions forced American merchants into pre-established protocols that British merchants, for example, were forced to follow under the auspices of the East India Company. As a result, both Haddad and Fichter suggested that American success in the Indian Ocean caused the ultimate downfall of the British East India Company's monopoly as British officials sought to compete effectively.[21]

Aggregate trends in US trade, from the 18th century to 1860 (and beyond)

There are few historians who approach the subject of US trade prior to the Civil War and fewer still who are interested in our time period. Some have examined the period from 1770 to 1860 on an even larger scale than we do here, studying the overall American economy with less focus on the foreign trade.[22] Some in the past were seriously interested in the economic trends of the 19th century; as multiple conferences were held in the 1950s and 1960s with this topic in mind. Yet, the authors and academics who are interested in these trends tended to view them via the lenses of the Civil War and industrialization. Most were concerned with finding some piece of key data or analysis that explains how ready, or not ready, the American economy was for industrialization or the horrors of war.[23]

One exception to the others in the historiography was an upper-level textbook that discussed the long-run trends of the period in question. The authors, North among them, explained that the period of 1775–1840 was one of the highest rates of growth ever recorded.[24] Still, there was little discussion of the importance of trade in the context of that expansion, and how European wars affected the American economy.

Unfortunately, we know much less about the aggregate trade before the 1770s, given the typical scholars' preoccupation with the American Revolution. However, we have more information about trade at the state level. As seen in Table 2.1, trade between Massachusetts and England increased rapidly in the 18th century, prior to the Revolution when volatility became very high. In particular, Massachusetts experienced a turbulent period of volatility for its fishing industry in 1770–1810. The American Revolution virtually destroyed the state's commercial fishing, but it experienced a revival very shortly after the end of the Revolution, recovering "more than 70 percent of their pre-Revolutionary levels" by 1790. The average annual amount of codfish exported to Europe in 1765–1775 was 178,800 (hundredweight), whereas it was lower in 1786–1790, at 108,600 (hundredweight). The number of vessels involved, as well as the tonnage, also declined.[25] Once the wars between France and England began in the 1790s, price levels rose quite high. Thus, tonnage for the "state climbed from 19,185 in 1789, to 42,746 in 1798, to 69,306 in 1807."

Table 2.1 Exports to England from the colonies and imports from England to the colonies, 1693–1790

Year	Exports to England	Imports from England	Net balance
1693	113,600	169,381	−55,781
1700	395,021	344,341	50,680
1710	249,814	293,659	−43,845
1720	468,188	319,702	148,486
1730	572,585	536,860	35,725
1740	718,416	813,382	−94,966
1750	814,768	1,313,083	−498,315
1760	761,099	2,611,764	−1,850,665
1770	1,015,535	1,925,571	−910,036
1780	18,560	825,431	−806,871
1790	1,043,389	3,258,238	−2,214,849

Source: Carter et al. (2006a).

Note
Values in pounds sterling, in constant values.

More importantly, average exports of cod per annum expanded from 250,650 (quintals) for the period 1786–1790 to 523,440 for 1803–1807.[26] This is further evidence that the wars in Europe not only expanded American trade, but helped fisheries recover from a destructive war for independence and even exceed prewar levels.

European and American trade, though largely maintained through the larger powers, became a nearly necessary means by which the young republic could solidify its fledgling economy. Nonetheless, some politicians and administrations felt that it could be used as a diplomatic tool. Jefferson's Embargo Act of 1807 was just one example of American trade being used for political purposes. The intention was to pressure France and Britain, through economic hardship, into accepting American neutrality. Unfortunately, it also prohibited trade with nations not named France or Britain. Therefore, it caused widespread domestic hardship and smuggling, and did not affect its intended targets in any meaningful way.[27] Essentially, the embargo ended one of the largest periods of growth in exports in American history as seen in Figure 2.1.

At the end of the 18th century and the beginning of the 19th, American ships became almost exclusive carriers of commerce throughout the Atlantic thanks to major war between France and England. In his diplomatic exertions in 1808, James Monroe justified his attempts to re-establish neutral status for American merchants and ships explained that the "United States were in a prosperous and happy condition", prior to 1808; "as a neutral power, they were almost the exclusive carriers of the commerce of the whole world".[28]

As seen in Figure 2.1, the relative economic weight of both exports and imports has declined over the 19th and 20th centuries. Furthermore, we can see that trade dependence was higher during the years of the Early Republic, and there was

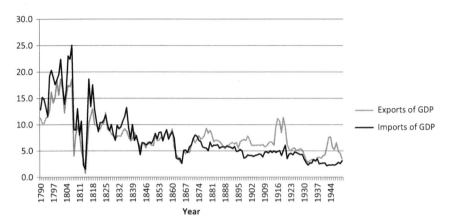

Figure 2.1 US exports and imports as a percentage of GDP, 1790–1950.
Source: Carter et al. (2006a).

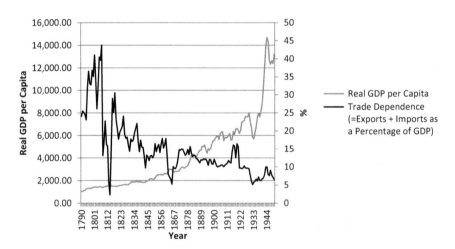

Figure 2.2 US Trade dependence and real GDP per capita, 1790–1950.
Source: Carter et al. (2006a).

much more volatility too. A substantial drop in exports and imports seemed to occur during conflict periods, for example, the Napoleonic wars and the Civil War; however, during the world wars, for example, exports increased substantially.

As displayed in Figure 2.2, over time US trade dependence has declined noticeably, while economic development and standard of living have increased dramatically. This also represents the period during which US became an economic and political superpower, as seen in Figure 2.3. US gained power vis-à-vis the other players in the international system in the late 19th century and was

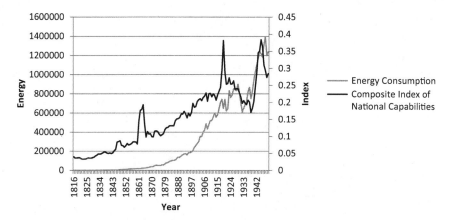

Figure 2.3 US great power status and energy consumption, 1816–1950.

Sources: Singer, Bremer, and Stuckey (1972), data from www.correlatesofwar.org/COW%20 Data/Capabilities/nmc3-02.htm.

Note
Details on the calculation of the CINC score can be found here: www.correlatesofwar.org/COW%20Data/Capabilities/NMC_Documentation.pdf. Energy consumption expressed in thousands of coal-ton equivalents.

finally regarded as a (minor) great power after the turn of the century, although US did not take on the role of a superpower until after World War II.[29] The CINC-index climbs substantially after that point. We can see that energy consumption, perhaps a proxy for economic expansion, developed much more evenly and earlier than the political (or military) power. Typically, most of these types of indices consider US a great power only after 1898, the Spanish-American War. Even then it would be a stretch to call the US a great power, though, given its military weakness.

As seen in Figure 2.4, exports and imports seem to have grown in tandem over the time period from 1790 to World War I, at least when analyzed in real values. Moreover, although exports expanded strongly during the world wars, the net balance was positive for most of this period.

However, as we have already suggested, it would be misleading to analyze US trade simply from the perspective of aggregate trade figures; in particular, let us examine US trade with Europe in more detail, namely what the main trends were over time. First of all, European share of the US exports was over 50 percent for most of the period depicted in the Figure 2.5. The major dips in this share occurred during the war years, the importance of the European markets started to wane in the 20th century, but the aggregate share still remained over or around 50 percent at that point. This suggests that wars tended to involve both parties and induce dramatic volatility in their trade relationships. However, the aggregate trends may, again, be somewhat misleading, since they

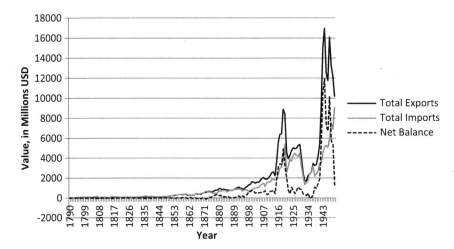

Figure 2.4 Total US exports and imports, and the net balance, in millions of USD, 1790–1950.
Source: Carter et al. (2006a).

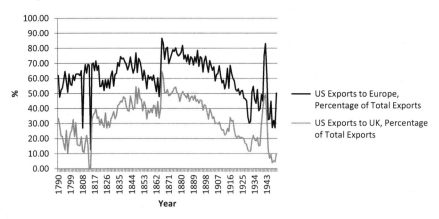

Figure 2.5 US exports to Europe and the UK, 1790–1950.
Source: Carter et al. (2006a).

do not tell us much about the individual countries involved. In fact, did the wars have a similar impact on *all* European countries' trade?

When we expand our analysis to look at the breakdown between the biggest European nations and the "others", a different picture emerges. It seems that the "others" did a lot of business with the United States especially in the beginning of the 19th century and during the world wars. This is the pattern seen in Figure 2.6. This suggests that it would be equally misleading to focus on just the big

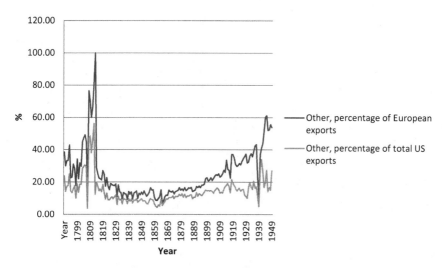

Figure 2.6 US exports to nations other than UK, France, and Germany, 1790–1950.
Source: Carter et al. (2006a).

European nations as America's trading partners, in fact we would argue that that would leave out a big chunk of the trade, especially during crises. In real terms, as seen in Figure 2.7, the volume of imports from nations other than the "big three" increased greatly during the Napoleonic Wars, only to experience a rapid reduction afterwards, with a steady growth trend until 1860. While we do not have the aggregate import figures before 1820, it is quite likely that the imports developed similar to exports during the war years, since they seemed to behave (somewhat) similarly afterwards. On the eve of the Civil War, exports peaked again, with imports showing much more volatility.

We can get a bit more information about trade by looking at the actual tonnage employed in US trade during the Early Republic. As seen in Figure 2.8, foreign vessels were quite important when US entered into world markets as a sovereign nation in the 1780s. Then the share declined to a lower level until 1810, and then there was a sharp spike and a slightly higher level afterwards. Foreign vessels became crucial for the US during the key years of the Napoleonic Wars and, of course, the War of 1812. Therefore, it is important to take a closer look at the war years, and the 1810s in particular. How did the war affect US trade relations, in particular with smaller (or neutral) nations?

US trade in the period 1790 to 1830: the impact of the war years

The Napoleonic Wars, and the War of 1812 in particular, strained former alliances and forced countries like the US to rely more heavily on trade with

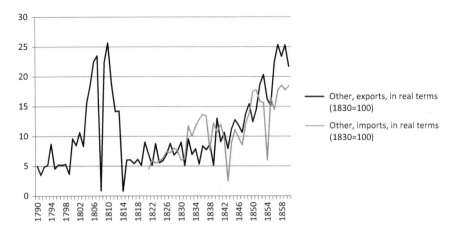

Figure 2.7 US exports to and imports from nations other than UK, France, and Germany, in real USD (1830 = 100), 1790–1860.
Source: Idem.

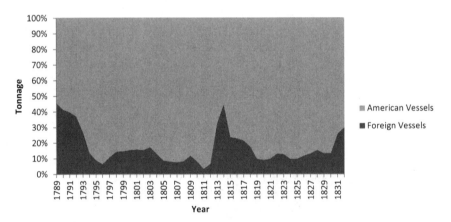

Figure 2.8 American and foreign tonnage employed in US foreign trade, 1789–1832.
Source: Pitkin (1835).

smaller/weaker nations. It is quite noteworthy that the US did a lot of business with Portugal during those years, even though Portugal was an ally of Britain. Necessities of war dictated that countries adopt more practical solutions to their supply problems, sometimes turning a blind eye to violations of sanctions or embargoes.

As seen in Figure 2.9, the share of smaller nations of the total tonnage used in US foreign trade increased first in the 1790s, spiking dramatically during the 1810s. The tonnage of smaller nations proved to be crucial in supporting the US war effort, especially since the American Navy was still in its infancy.

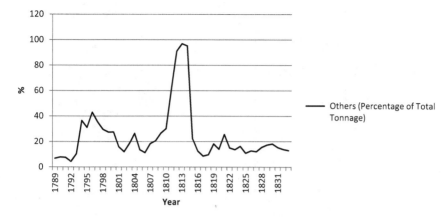

Figure 2.9 Foreign tonnage entering US ports, 1789–1833: percentage share of nations other than Great Britain, France, or Germany.
Source: Pitkin (1835).

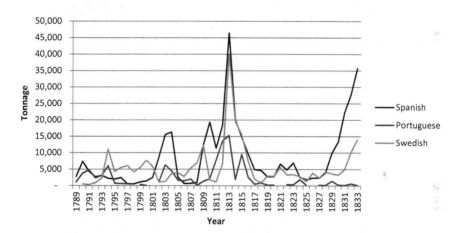

Figure 2.10 Spanish, Portuguese, and Swedish tonnage entering US ports, 1789–1833.
Source: Idem.

Moreover, as seen in Figure 2.10, smaller nations were eager to do business with the US. Spain, which was under Napoleon's rule and partially a war zone, did not have any concerns about trading with the Americans. Portugal, which was on the other side of the Peninsular War, also increased its trade with the US, especially during 1810–1814.

Even smaller nations like Sweden did the same, and in fact matched the Spanish volume of trade (as expressed through tonnage) during the 1810s. Figure 2.11 shows that US exports to European nations other than Britain, Germany, and France were 70 percent of the total in 1810, and typically remained at least

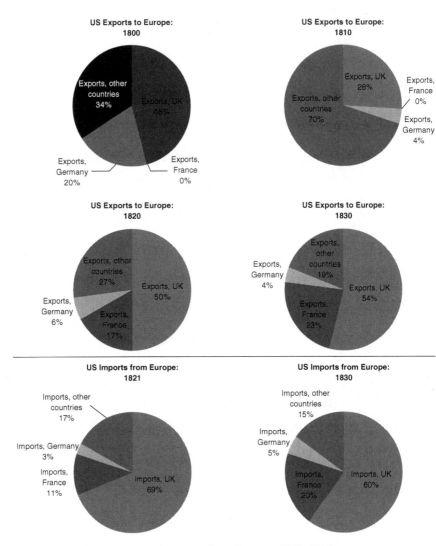

Figure 2.11 US Exports to and imports from Europe, 1790–1830.
Source: Carter et al. (2006).

a quarter of the total trade in this period. As we have indicated, we have data on imports (at this point) only from 1820 onwards, so it is more difficult to examine that dimension of trade. However, all signs, including tonnage figures, point to similar conclusions for the imports.

If we look at Tables 2.2 and 2.3, we can discern the main US export and import products. Agricultural products were initially more important as export products, and by 1830 cotton had become the most important item

Table 2.2 Main US export products, 1790–1830

Year	Total value	Cotton, quantity	Cotton, value	Tobacco, quantity	Tobacco, value	Wheat, quantity	Wheat, value
1790	–	–	–	118	4	1	1
1800	–	18	–	79	–	–	–
1810	27	93	15	84	5	–	–
1820	39	128	22	84	8	–	–
1830	45	298	30	84	6	–	–

Source: Carter et al. (2006a).

Notes
Values in millions of dollars.
Quantities in millions of pounds, wheat expressed as million 60-pound bushels.
The only other product listed in this source is "other wood manufactures", which amounted to 4 million dollars in 1820 and 2 million in 1830.

Table 2.3 Main US import products, values, 1790–1830

Year	Total value	Coffee	Tea	Sugar	Wool manufactures	Cotton manufactures	Iron and steel manufactures
1790	–	–	–	–	–	–	–
1800	–	–	–	–	–	–	–
1810	–	–	–	–	–	–	–
1820*	23	4	1	4	6	8	–
1830	29	4	2	5	6	6	6

Source: Carter et al. (2006a).

Notes
All expressed as values, in millions of dollars.
* = for coffee, tea, and sugar, we used 1821 values, since the previous year numbers were not available. Therefore, the total is also an approximation.

by far, thereby feeding the British Industrial Revolution. However, during the Napoleonic Wars, it seems clear that the US became essential in supplying the foodstuffs that feed armies and civilians alike. In Table 2.4, we can see that, during periods of intense warfare between Britain and France, US wheat and flour exports were at much higher levels than both before and after the Napoleonic Wars, excepting years when the US was at war or attempting trade embargoes. We have more limited information about imports, but coffee, tea, and spices were important, along with some manufactured products.

US trade with Portugal during the war years: small nations mattered

As a consequence of the close relations between the Portuguese and British empires, well established as an ancient alliance and strengthened during that critical period, in the early years of the 19th century England was both the

Table 2.4 US wheat and flour exports, 1791–1816

Year	Wheat (bushels)	Average price per bushel ($)	Flour (barrels)	Average price per barrel ($)	Value of both ($)
1791	1,018,339	–	619,681	–	–
1792	853,790	–	824,464	–	–
1793	1,450,575	–	1,074,639	–	–
1794	696,797	–	846,010	–	–
1795	141,273	–	687,369	–	–
1796	31,226	–	725,194	–	–
1797	15,655	–	515,633	–	–
1798	15,021	–	567,558	–	–
1799	10,056	–	519,265	–	–
1800	26,853	–	653,052	–	–
1801	239,929	–	1,102,444	–	–
1802	280,281	–	1,156,248	–	–
1803	686,415	–	1,311,853	–	9,310,000
1804	127,024	–	810,008	–	7,100,000
1805	18,041	–	777,513	–	8,325,000
1806	86,784	1.33	782,724	8.00	6,867,000
1807	766,814	1.25	1,249,819	7.00	10,753,000
1808	87,330	1.25	263,813	6.50	1,936,000
1809	393,889	1.25	846,247	6.00	5,944,000
1810	325,924	1.50	798,431	7.50	6,846,000
1811	216,833	1.75	1,445,012	9.50	14,662,000
1812	53,832	1.94	1,443,492	10.00	13,687,000
1813	288,535	1.75	1,260,943	11.00	13,591,000
1814	–	–	193,274	9.50	1,734,000
1815	17,634	1.25	862,739	8.00	7,209,000

Source: Pitkin (1835).

main supplier and client of the Portuguese market. This became particularly apparent in 1808 to 1813, as several nations ceased to trade with Portugal, and the English, American, and Spanish traders picked up the slack. In particular, the American market became a pivotal target and source for Portuguese merchants, as other markets were difficult to reach.[30]

As Leos Müller has shown already, American shipping increased dramatically during the Revolutionary and Napoleonic conflicts, with a 300 percent increase in capacity. American shipowners focused heavily on export trade, which meant that they had to find suitable return cargoes. Moreover, as the Napoleonic conquests continued, there were fewer places to do business with in Europe. Therefore, the Nordic markets – Sweden in particular, since it was not conquered – formed important destinations for the Americans.[31] Portuguese trade with the Nordic countries decreased substantially during the war years (see Table 2.5), although there were some years during which trade was curtailed as well. Trade with the other neutrals helped circumvent wartime

Table 2.5 Portuguese Trade with Sweden and Denmark, 1807–1814, *Contos de réis*

Year	Imports from Sweden	Exports to Sweden	Imports from Denmark	Exports to Denmark
1807	733	181	140	87
1808	15	25	16	0
1809	64	130	0	0
1810	0	71	0	0
1811	0	12	0	0
1812	138	18	0	0
1813	510	180	0	0
1814	622	123	47	13

Sources: Portugal's Balance of Trade with Foreign Nations and Portuguese Colonies 1807–1814: Instituto Nacional de Estatística, Lisboa, Portugal: INEG2448, years: 1807, 1809–1814. Instituto Histórico e Geográfico Brasileiro, Rio do Janeiro, Brazil: ARQ 1.5.23, Balança Geral do Commercio do Reino de Portugal com Os Seus Dominios, e Nações Estrangeiras, No Anno de 1808.

regulations and shifting alliances, as well as formed important niche markets for countries like Portugal and the United States.

Based on Maria Cristina Moreira´s research, Portuguese imports were dominated by the key players throughout this period, from 1796 to 1831, as they represented more than 89 percent of the total imports. Of the eight countries that dominated the import flows, the US occupied sixth position as a supplier from 1801 to 1807 (1,185 *Contos*,[32] 6.9 percent); seventh between 1814 and 1820 (711 *Contos*, 3.9 percent), and fell below eighth position from 1796 to 1800 (382 *Contos*, 2.3 percent). It is surprising that, from 1808 to 1813, the United States became the second most important importer and that Portuguese imports from the US peaked, representing around six times the value of the average for the period. In general, these years represented a great boon for the exports and imports to and from the US. Moreira and Eloranta have sustained that, typically, dependence on the Portuguese side on American cereals was quite striking, and these imports kept Portuguese society and English troops alive during the most difficult period of the Peninsular War (see also Table 2.6).[33] The Portuguese market was also important on the American side, often representing a top-three destination for the American exporters.

Conclusions and further challenges

Our key assumptions were that (1) small and medium-sized states have been a much more integral part of world trade than has previously been assumed, particularly during crisis periods; (2) crises tend to accentuate the importance of trade relationships between and with smaller nations, since many of them did not directly participate in the actual conflict, thus providing valuable raw materials and markets for the warring parties; (3) aggregate statistics

Table 2.6 Main US products imported by Portugal, 1796–1820 (percent)

Year	Percentage of total imports	Flour	Corn	Wheat	Rice
1796	14.0	3.3	96.7	0.0	0.0
1797	77.0	24.3	8.0	1.7	65.9
1798	78.7	9.1	42.3	7.4	41.1
1799	78.5	4.3	71.5	6.6	17.6
1800	73.4	19.9	71.4	0.0	8.7
1801	95.2	76.0	23.2	0.3	0.5
1802	86.1	47.8	43.5	3.2	5.5
1803	96.1	46.1	27.7	24.9	1.3
1804	90.0	50.3	35.4	13.4	0.9
1805	69.1	53.5	26.6	19.9	0.0
1806	87.7	79.5	14.4	6.1	0.0
1807	93.9	72.6	17.2	10.2	0.0
1808	94.8	69.0	0.0	31.0	0.0
1809	74.6	69.2	13.4	6.3	11.2
1810	68.0	57.6	24.2	4.3	13.9
1811	82.7	56.2	24.7	11.1	8.0
1812	95.4	69.4	19.9	4.8	5.9
1813	91.0	60.7	16.0	5.3	17.9
1814	40.3	75.8	0.0	16.6	7.6
1815	90.8	25.4	39.4	4.6	30.6
1816	85.8	13.4	70.8	7.1	8.7
1817	79.0	88.3	10.4	1.4	0.0
1818	91.3	14.0	74.7	11.3	0.0
1819	86.3	13.6	38.8	44.7	2.8
1820	19.8	97.6	0.0	0.0	2.4

Sources: Table 4 in Moreira and Eloranta (2011: 408) revised based on Portugal's Balance of Trade with Foreign Nations and Portuguese Colonies 1796–1820: Instituto Nacional de Estatística, Lisboa, Portugal: INEG2448, years: 1796, 1797, 1799 to 1807, 1809 to 1820. Fundação da Biblioteca Nacional, Rio de Janeiro, Brazil: Cód. 11, 4, 11, *Balança Geral do Commercio Do Reyno de Portugal com as Nações Estrangeiras no Anno de 1798* (Arquivo Nacional da Torre do Tombo, Lisboa, Portugal, Projecto Reencontro, Biblioteca Nacional, F0105 P). Instituto Histórico e Geográfico Brasileiro, Rio do Janeiro, Brazil: ARQ 1.5.23, *Balança Geral do Commercio do Reino de Portugal com Os Seus Dominios, e Nações Estrangeiras, No Anno de 1808.*

are likely to understate this role, given that the focus in past scholarship has been mostly on trade between big players in the international system. Our findings support these hypotheses, by and large, although our data are somewhat limited (especially for imports). Smaller/weaker European states became much more important for US trade during the Napoleonic wars, though temporarily. We can also see that certain countries became particularly important, since they had the crucial raw materials needed during the age of global war. Moreover, the US also provided much-needed material and food to smaller European nations.

In this chapter, we wanted to explore what kinds of changes, including structural, we can see in the trade flows between US *and* both great powers and weaker states, especially whether the pressure of the war effort allowed more latitude for these states to explore their trade options. The answer is affirmative – the demands of global war outweighed other (such as alliance) considerations. Economic and business concerns overrode political and diplomatic obstacles in these trade relations, thereby opening up opportunities for the smaller/weaker states. Our basic argument is that weak states were able to expand their trade and discover new markets during such large and protracted conflicts, although this was, as in the case of US–Portuguese trade in this period, typically a shorter-term phenomenon. The networks gained during such conflicts would not last during peacetime, when market conditions changed. Therefore, longitudinal analysis of US trade flows and behavior over the period of several conflicts will provide a fresh perspective on the role of this new, and often weak, state.

Notes

1 Handel (1981). See also Eloranta (2002). On the concept of small states in general, see Joenniemi (1998).
2 Müller (2004, 2008) See also Davis and Engerman (2006). On definitions of neutrality as well as small state challenges, see Ackerman (1983); Karsh (1988). On the American interpretations of neutrality and its implications in this time period, see especially Bukovansky (2003).
3 Davis and Engerman (2006), particularly chapter 2. For an innovative look at the Napoleonic power politics and alliances, see Rosecrance and Lo (1996). For a classic account on the Continental System, see Heckscher (1922).
4 Müller (2004: chapter 7).
5 See the studies listed in Müller (2004). On Denmark, see also Ruppenthal (1943). On American trade history and the impact of the blockades, see Hickey (1981); Keene (1978).
6 The literature on the great empires is massive and cannot be adequately summarized here. Some of it is discussed in an interesting theoretical article about how and why such empires have come about, see Turchin (2009).
7 See e.g. Bell (2007). On the debt burden incurred by Great Britain, reaching at its height over 300 per of GDP, see Ferguson (2001); Stasavage (2003).
8 On the history of the British naval fleet, see especially Kennedy (1976).
9 Wood (2009: 622623).
10 Ibid.: 622–623, 658.
11 Updyke (1915: 59–62).
12 Mahan (1905: 98–100).
13 Appleby (1982: 839–840).
14 Taylor (1964).
15 Lindstrom (1979: 290, 298–299).
16 North (1961: vii).
17 Ibid.: 36–37, 53.
18 Adams Jr (1980: 713–714).
19 Goldin and Lewis (1980).

20 Fichter (2010: 1–4). On state formation, see e.g. Acemoglu, Garcia-Jimeno, and Robinson (2015); Acemoglu and Robinson (2013); Besley and Persson (2009, 2010); Dincecco (2015); Dincecco and Katz (2016).
21 Haddad (2014: 2–4, 80); Fichter (2010: 28).
22 Gallman and Wallis (2007). This collection of articles provides important background information for the entire American economy until the Civil War.
23 Ruggles (1962). This is one example of those that view the Early Republic period as a precursor to American industrialization.
24 Davis et al. (1971: 21–25).
25 Carter et al. (2006: 701).
26 Vickers (1994: 266–267).
27 Watts (1989).
28 As quoted in Mahan (1905: 99).
29 Eloranta (2006).
30 On the trade patterns before 1770, see Fisher (1963).
31 Müller (2006, 2008, 2016).
32 Moreira (2006). *Contos* here means *Contos de réis*, where *réis* were a Portuguese monetary unit of the time: one *Conto* corresponded to one million *réis*.
33 Except for 1796 (staves comprising 66.0 per cent) and two other years, 1814 and 1820, which include different products that represented less than 10 per cent of the total imports, with the exception of butter (14.5 per cent) in 1814 and fish oil (16.1 per cent) in 1820. Moreira and Eloranta (2011).

References

Primary sources

Arquivo Histórico do Ministério das Obras Públicas, Lisboa, Portugal

Fundação da Biblioteca Nacional, Rio do Janeiro, Brazil
Cód. 11, 4, 11, *Balança Geral do Commercio Do Reyno de Portugal com as Nações Estrangeiras no Anno de 1798 (Arquivo Nacional da Torre do Tombo, Lisboa, Portugal, Projecto Reencontro, Biblioteca Nacional, F0105 P)*.

Instituto Histórico e Geográfico Brasileiro, Rio do Janeiro, Brazil

ARQ 1.5.23, *Balança Geral do Commercio do Reino de Portugal com Os Seus Dominios, e Nações Estrangeiras, No Anno de 1808.*

Instituto Nacional de Estatística, Lisboa, Portugal

INEG2448, years: 1796, 1797, 1799 to 1807, 1809 to 1820.

Secondary sources

Acemoglu, D., Garcia-Jimeno, C., & Robinson, J. A. (2015). State capacity and economic development: A network approach. *American Economic Review*, 105(8), 2364–2409.

Acemoglu, D., & Robinson, J. A. (2013). *Why nations fail: The origins of power, prosperity, and poverty*. New York: Broadway Business.

Ackerman, B. A. (1983). What is neutral about neutrality? *Ethics, 93*, 372–390.

Adams, D. R., Jr (1980). American neutrality and prosperity, 1793–1808: A reconsideration. *Journal of Economic History, 40*(4), 713–737.

Appleby, J. (1982). Commercial farming and the "agrarian myth" in the Early Republic. *Journal of American History, 68*(4), 839–840.

Bell, D. (2007). *The first total war: Napoleon's Europe and the birth of warfare as we know it*. New York: Houghton Mifflin Harcourt.

Besley, T., & Persson, T. (2009). The origins of state capacity: Property rights, taxation, and politics. *American Economic Review, 99*(4), 1218–1244.

Besley, T., & Persson, T. (2010). State capacity, conflict, and development. *Econometrica, 78*(1), 1–34.

Bukovansky, M. (2003). American identity and neutral rights from independence to the War of 1812. *International Organization, 51*(2), 209–243.

Carter, S. B., Gartner, S. S., Haines, M. R., Olmstead, A. L., Sutch, R., & Wright, G. (Eds.). (2006a). *Historical Statistics of the United States: Millennial Edition*. Cambridge, UK: Cambridge University Press.

Carter, S. B., Scott, S., Sigmund, G. S., Haines Michael, R., Olmstead Alan, L., Richard, S., & Gavin, W. (2006b). *Historical statistics of the United States: Earliest times to the present*, millennial edition. New York: Cambridge University Press.

Davis, L. E., & Engerman, S. L. (2006). *Naval blockades in peace and war: An economic history since 1750*. New York: Cambridge University Press.

Davis, L. E., et al. (1971). *American economic growth: An economist's history of the United States*. New York: Harper and Row.

Dincecco, M. (2015). The rise of effective states in Europe. *Journal of Economic History, 75*(3), 901–918.

Dincecco, M., & Katz, G. (2016). State Capacity and Long-run Economic Performance. *The Economic Journal, 126*(590), 189–218.

Eloranta, J. (2002). European states in the international arms trade, 1920–1937: The iumpact of external threats, market forces, and domestic constraints. *Scandinavian Economic History Review, 50*(1), 44–67.

Eloranta, J. (2006). Military spending patterns in history. *EH.Net*. Retrieved from http://eh.net/encyclopedia/military-spending-patterns-in-history/

Ferguson, N. (2001). *The cash nexus: Money and power in the modern world, 1700–2000*. New York: Basic Books.

Fichter, J. R. (2010). *So great a profit: How the East Indies trade transformed Anglo-American capitalism*. Cambridge, MA: Harvard University Press.

Fisher, H. E. S. (1963). Anglo-Portuguese trade, 1700–1770. *Economic History Review, 16*(2), 219–233.

Gallman, R. E., & Wallis, J. J. (Eds.). (2007). *American economic growth and standards of living before the Civil War*. Chicago: University of Chicago Press.

Goldin, C. D., & Lewis, F. D. (1980). The role of exports in American economic growth during the napoleonic wars, 1793 to 1807. *Explorations in Economic History, 17*(1), 6–25.

Haddad, J. R. (2014). *America's first adventure in China: Trade, treaties, opium, and salvation*. Philadelphia, PA: Temple University Press.

Handel, M. I. (1981). *Weak states in the international system*. London, UK/Totowa, NJ: F. Cass.

Heckscher, E. F. (1922). *The Continental System: An economic interpretation*: Gloucester, MA: Peter Smith.
Hickey, D. R. (1981). American trade restrictions during the War of 1812. *Journal of American History*, 68(3), 517–538.
Joenniemi, P. (1998). From small to smart: Reflections on the concept of small states. *Irish Studies in International Affairs*, 9, 61–62.
Karsh, E. (1988). *Neutrality and small states*. London: Routledge.
Keene, C. A. (1978). American shipping and trade, 1798–1820: The evidence from Leghorn. *Journal of Economic History*, 38(3), 681–700.
Kennedy, P. (1976). *The rise and fall of British naval mastery*. London: Allen Lane.
Lindstrom, D. (1979). American economic growth before 1840: New evidence and new directions. *Journal of Economic History*, 39(1), 289–301.
Mahan, A. T. (1905). *Sea power in its relations to the war of 1812*, vol. 1. Boston, MA: Little, Brown, and Company.
Moreira, C., & Eloranta, J. (2011). Importance of "weak" states during conflicts: Portuguese trade with the United States during the Revolutionary and Napoleonic wars. *Revista de Historia Económica*, 29(3), 393–423.
Moreira, M. C. (2006). La Importancia del Mercado Español en el Comercio Exterior Portugués (1796–1831), *Hispania Nova Revista de Historia Contemporánea*, 167–191.
Müller, L. (2004). *Consuls, corsairs, and commerce: The Swedish consular service and long-distance shipping, 1720–1815*. Uppsala: Uppsala Universitet.
Müller, L. (2006). The Swedish consular service in southern Europe, 1720–1815. *Scandinavian Journal of History*, 31(2), 186–195.
Müller, L. (2008). Swedish–Portuguese trade and Swedish consular service, 1700–1800. *A Articulacão do sal português aos circuitos Mundiais. Antigos e novos consumes [The articulation of Portuguese salt with worldwide routes. Past and new consumption trends]* (pp. 93–104). Porto: University of Porto.
Müller, L. (2016). Swedish merchant shipping in troubled times: The French Revolutionary Wars and Sweden's neutrality 1793–1801. *International Journal of Maritime History*, 28(1), 147–164.
North, D. C. (1961). *The economic growth of the United States, 1790–1860*. New York: W. W. Norton.
Pitkin, T. (1835). *A statistical view of the commerce of the United States of America: Including also an account of banks, manufactures and internal trade and improvements*. New Haven, NJ: Durrie & Peck.
Rosecrance, R., & Lo, C. C. (1996). Balancing, stability, and war: The mysterious case of the Napoleonic international system. *International Studies Quarterly*, 40(4), 479–500.
Ruggles, R. (1962). Trends in the American economy in the nineteenth century.*Conference on Research in Income and Wealth, Studies in Income and Wealth*, vol. 24. Princeton, NJ: Princeton University Press.
Ruppenthal, R. (1943). Denmark and the Continental System. *Journal of Modern History*, 7–23.
Singer, J. D., Bremer, S., & Stuckey, J. (1972). Capability distribution, uncertainty, and major power war, 1820–1965. In B. Russett (Ed.), *Peace, war, and numbers* (pp. 19–48). Beverly Hills, CA: Sage.
Stasavage, D. (2003). *Public debt and the Birth of the democratic state: France and Great Britain 1688–1789*: Cambridge, UK: Cambridge University Press.

Taylor, G. R. (1964). American economic growth before 1840: An exploratory essay. *Journal of Economic History*, *24*(4), 427–444.

Turchin, P. (2009). A theory for formation of large empires. *Journal of Global History*, *4*(2), 191–217.

Updyke, F. A. (1915). *The diplomacy of the War of 1812*. Baltimore, MD: Johns Hopkins University Press.

Vickers, D. (1994). *Farmers and fishermen: Two centuries of work in Essex County, Massachusetts, 1630–1850*. Chapel Hill: University of North Carolina Press.

Watts, S. (1989). *The republic reborn: War and the making of liberal America, 1790–1820*. Baltimore, MD: Johns Hopkins University Press.

Wood, G. S. (2009). *Empire of liberty: A history of the early republic, 1789–1815*. Oxford, UK: Oxford University Press.

3 The United States and the Mediterranean during the French Wars (1793–1815)

Silvia Marzagalli

Introduction

In the 18th century, the Thirteen Colonies became increasingly integrated in Atlantic, Southern European and Mediterranean economies. As John J. McCusker has shown, these represented an essential element in the Colonies' balance of trade. This situation was beneficial to British imperial interests.[1] The North Americans sold non-enumerated products and Newfoundland codfish to Southern Europe, where they charged a cargo of Mediterranean products and remitted the balance to London, before sailing to Great Britain to deliver this cargo and embark on the voyage home. Mediterranean trade, in other words, made it possible for North Americans to buy more British manufactured goods.

Whereas American captains sailing to the Mediterranean had in colonial times enjoyed British protection for their ships, as citizens of the United States they experienced new challenges. First, they were excluded from the British Empire and thus became subject to British Navigation Acts, which prevented United States ships from carrying Mediterranean products to Great Britain. This forced American ship-owners to conceive new entrepreneurial strategies and trade flows, including infra-Mediterranean trade and tramping. Second, they were repeatedly confronted with the difficulty of protecting their shipping from Barbary privateering, since the Barbary states considered themselves at war against the United States, for lack of peace treaties. Thus, in order to make its shipping and trade competitive, the United States was obliged to learn the existing diplomatic rules and options within the Mediterranean. Third, they had to face the contingencies of the Revolutionary and Napoleonic Wars, termed here 'the French Wars' (1793–1815), in which their neutrality was many times seriously challenged by all belligerents.

European warfare, however, led also to a dramatic increase in neutral shipping and trade. Whereas small states in Europe lost their neutrality in the course of the conflict, the United States was able to preserve theirs longer than anybody else. Historians considering United States trade statistics and the increase in American shipping as the era proceeded have rightly stressed the importance of the European wars in fostering American growth.[2] This trend was, however, the result of adding many different and partially integrated trades, each with a specific port and region and each presenting its own particularities and chronology. The presence of different belligerents within the Mediterranean and on its shores, the alternate phases of British mastery at sea in the region, the changing alliances of Spain and the Italian States over this span of time, and the ups and downs of bilateral relations between the United States and each of the Mediterranean countries, created a unique configuration in this area. Based upon United States consular and business records, this chapter reconstructs the modality of American shipping and trade in the Mediterranean during the French Wars and shows how the navigation of a small power such as the United States could take advantage of European warfare in order to penetrate the complex trading in this area. American neutrality, however, was fragile.[3]

By looking at the case of the United States in the Mediterranean, this chapter suggests two elements which may be useful for a general understanding of what neutrality then meant to small states. Trade at the time was based on complementarities and mutual recognition between small, mostly neutral countries and major mercantile, often mutually hostile empires.[4]

First, this chapter advocates contextualizing neutrality precisely in space and time, moving away from the tendency to conceive of it purely as a juridical notion,[5] or to examine it mainly as an element of political governance and diplomatic action.[6] It is argued here that the benefits of neutrality for the United States were different in different times and places. Comparing the chronology of American shipping and trade in other areas – such as Asia, the West Indies or Bordeaux – shows their substantial differences from the Mediterranean region. In practice, neutrality for a given country meant different things in different places, even though the state was theoretically neutral everywhere.[7] This chapter, thus, suggests that the opportunities that Americans – and neutral merchants and ship-owners everywhere – enjoyed during the French Wars were shaped by local conditions, and their advantages were determined by the relative positions of other neutral competitors in the area, just as much as by the changing latitude that belligerents granted to different neutral carriers, according to their power and willingness to prevent the neutrals from sailing in a given region. America's presence in the Mediterranean, moreover, was affected by its capacity to give support to neither of the two major European belligerents and also by its relations with the Barbary states – an element that may possibly suggest the necessity of conceiving of different degrees of neutrality, according to the respective might of the states with which one was at peace, at war, or at "quasi-war" with it.

Second, in penetrating Mediterranean trade, Americans largely trusted agents on the spot. American captains and supercargoes, just like the United States' consular system, entrusted a consistent part of their interest to preexisting merchant networks. It looked to other countries' agents in general to negotiate the peace treaties and naval escorts from which it benefited. It is contended here, thus, that the capacity to take advantage of neutrality depended, in the Mediterranean case, on the capacity to rely on local agents, some of whom were subjects of belligerent states. The understanding of the American presence in the Mediterranean, therefore, should relinquish a strictly national perspective, and move toward a systemic approach, in which the clear-cut definitions of national allegiance, and of neutral versus belligerent, are blurred in the everyday intercourse of merchants and agents in situ. The second element found in this paper, then, concerns the usefulness of moving away from a state-centered perspective and looking more closely at merchants' behavior to better understand how markets and trade flows were reconfigured in times of war through the agency of both neutral and belligerent merchants.[8]

Securing United States shipping and trade in the Mediterranean: a small power in troubled waters

After its independence, the United States faced the challenge of promoting trade and shipping through effective diplomatic action, in order to compensate for the protection they had lost from Britain as subjects. Enlightenment ideology, which considered trade a powerful means to promote and regulate smooth international relations, concurred with merchants' interests in sustaining American attempts to promote United States trade and shipping around the world. Bilateral trade treaties and a strict politics of neutrality were conceived as the pillars supporting the United States in international relations and defending its interests as a small state – and a republican one. Although Jefferson and Madison had divergent views on the ultimate role of neutrality, the willingness to implement conditions favoring trade and shipping abroad were consistently similar – and as a matter of fact, the means did not radically differ from those of absolutist or parliamentary European monarchies.[9] In order to promote American commerce and navigation, the United States had recourse to commercial treaties, and established consulates in major ports. They also tried to secure peace with the countries that could threaten their neutrality.

Despite the attempts to generalize bilateral treaties with European countries on the basis of 'most favored nation' and the implementation of the "free ships free goods" principle, in the 1780s the United States managed to ratify treaties only with France, Sweden, Prussia and Morocco. The Spanish government in Morocco had obtained the release of the crew of the *Betsy*, taken in October 1784 by the emperor, whose 1779 peace offer had been answered in May 1784 by Congress, without being associated with the customary presents.[10] Shortly afterwards, in 1786, Thomas Barclay managed to secure a treaty offering very favorable conditions with the assistance of the Genoese brothers Francesco and Giuseppe Chiappe, who remained in charge of American interests in the following years. Francesco was recommended to Thomas Barclay in 1790, when the latter was dispatched to Morocco to renew the peace treaty after the death of the former emperor.[11] Temporary difficulties arose once more in the mid-1790s, when Morocco experienced a civil war, and an American ship was seized for provisioning the enemy.[12]

Relations with the Barbary regencies were considerably more problematic. Whereas Roman law required a declaration of war to start a conflict, Muslim law demanded a peace treaty with Christian states to initiate peace. Once independent, United States merchant ships were no longer shielded by British diplomacy, though this, it must be admitted, might even have encouraged Barbary privateering against a former British colony. When Spain ratified peace with Algiers in 1785, after a series of fruitless or disastrous military campaigns, the Spanish navy ceased to patrol the Strait and protect Western ships against privateers.[13] The Algerians captured two American ships in October 1785 and reduced their crew to slavery. The negotiations of the Connecticut merchant John Lamb to rescue them ended in total failure, and he was unable to initiate negotiations for a peace treaty which could secure future American shipping in the Mediterranean. From 1787 to 1793, United States merchant ships were protected by the Portuguese squadron when passing the Strait. In 1793, however, the sudden and unexpected peace between Portugal and Algiers – favored by the British consul at Algiers – provoked the departure of the Portuguese navy from the Strait. Algerian privateers thereupon ventured into the Atlantic and took a dozen American ships.[14] This prompted political action: within a few years, the United States had signed peace treaties with the Barbary regencies. Negotiations in Algiers involved the American agent Joseph Donaldson Jr., the brother of the Swedish consul Per Eric Skjoldebrand, the French government and the American agent Joël Barlow.[15] Together they produced a treaty which cost almost a million dollars and remained fragile because of the United States' difficulties in honoring its financial clauses, including an annual tribute and naval stores. Consul Richard O'Brien, a former American captive and since 1797 United States consul in Algiers, negotiated peace with the regency at Tripoli through the intermediation of the dey of Algiers. Two truces, the second of them handled by the French agent Joseph Etienne Famin, led finally to the ratification of the peace treaty with Tunis. The payment of tributes and ransom money was handled through the Sephardic merchant house Bacri.[16]

In the absence of a commercial treaty, the conditions met by American captains entering European ports were handled and negotiated on the spot by consignees, and United States consuls, a minority of whom were American citizens. The decision to establish consular posts reflected contemporary perceptions of the value of a port as a destination for American ships. In 1785, John Jay, in his capacity as the Secretary for Foreign Affairs, submitted to the Congress a report mentioning three Mediterranean ports only as potential locations for American consulates, namely Malaga, Alicante and Barcelona,[17] thus confining to the Iberian Peninsula the opportunities for men of New England to trade in fish and cereals.

The first United States consulate in the Mediterranean was established in Marseille in 1790 and after the French Revolutionary wars began in 1792–93 the consular system expanded significantly. Before the turn of the century, United States consuls had been appointed also in Morocco, Malaga, Alicante,

Gibraltar, Leghorn, Algiers, Tripoli, Tunis, Naples, Genoa, Venice, Rome, Trieste and Barcelona. That the American consular service was extended to the Adriatic Sea and the existing network in the Western Mediterranean made more dense in the late 1790s and the 1800s reflected the relevant growth of United States shipping and trade during the French Wars, when the increased demand for neutral transport services sustained American business. With a total of 15 posts, the Mediterranean in the late 1790s represented a quarter of all American consulates.[18] Consuls provided various services to facilitate American activities, assisted the ships' captains in case of trouble, registered their sea protests and informed them about risks at sea. They also corresponded with the Secretary of State and provided useful information on local and regional contingencies. They were considered necessary to secure American shipping, especially when it was threatened by conflict in the international context.

Despite Congress's resolution of 16 March 1784 converting consulate and vice-consulates to national agents, the United States consular system in the Mediterranean before 1815 relied largely on foreign merchants on the spot, such as the Frenchman Etienne Catalan (Marseille 1790), the Irish Michael Murphy (Malaga 1793), or his successor, the Scottish William Kirkpatrick.[19] Two were already consuls of another state when they were appointed as United States consul: James Simpson, an English subject, at Gibraltar (1794, consul of Russia); and Conrad Frederick Wagner, at Trieste (1797, consul of Sweden). In Leghorn, a non-American consul (the Italian Filippo Filicchi, 1794), was replaced in 1798 by the American citizen Thomas Appleton.[20] The opposite case could also be found: in Sicily, two British subjects succeeded the American consul Joseph Barnes. It must be confessed that the appointment of American citizens as consuls was not necessarily welcomed by the appointee. Out of the 15 tenants of United States consulates established before 1815 on the northern rim of the Mediterranean, seven were American citizens, but only three of them actually resided at their posts and served as consuls.[21] In comparison, of their eight foreign colleagues, seven accepted their post. If the tendency to employ American citizens increased over time (before 1815, 12 out of 17 successors to consular posts on the northern rim of the Mediterranean were American citizens), foreigners still proved more amenable to accepting this position (100 percent versus 66 percent). Having in general resided in the city for many years, they were also better connected with local authorities and with other Mediterranean ports through their business networks. Some of them may have conceived the position of United States consul that they had lobbied for as a potentially useful protection against belligerents' hostile attitudes – thus taking advantage of American neutrality to foster their own personal and business interests.[22]

After signing peace treaties with the Barbary states in the mid-1790s, the United States appointed American citizens as consuls there, the only exceptions to the British Simpson in Morocco, formerly consul at Gibraltar, and the Swedish Per Eric Skjoldebrand, who served in Algiers from 1795 to 1797. Consular posts in the Barbary regencies required high negotiation skills because there was no plenipotentiary minister on site, these states formally being dependencies of the Ottoman Empire. The fact that none of the American consuls was a merchant, thus, did not represent a major inconvenience for the interests of the scant American trade in these ports.[23] Their collective lack of diplomatic experience was by far more problematic. Moreover, neither Cathcart nor Eaton was particularly eager to reach their post; they waited 19 months from their appointment before sailing to their post. The frequent and increasing difficulties with the Barbary states in the late 1790s and 1800s may be conceived as a result of the United States relying on its own agents, without taking much advice or assistance from pre-existing local agents, who were often suspected by United States agents of conspiring against American interests.[24]

Securing safe shipping conditions through peace treaties and consular efforts was essential in order to take advantage of neutrality during the French Wars. International tensions directly affected United States shipping and the demand for American shipping. At the end of 1784, when rumors of Algerian privateering against American ships spread in London, the insurance premium on American bottoms increased to 16–20 times higher than on their British counterparts.[25] Only two weeks after the French declaration of war against Great Britain, the United States consul at Marseille regretted the absence of American ships in his port, and incidentally confirmed that the situation depended on the defined danger at sea, rather than on the theoretical state of neutrality with European belligerents:

> I could freight here fifty americans vessels, and the Shippers or their Insurors here would make a very trifling difference of your Colours, with the Swedish or danish ones on account of your war with algiers, Thirty Dollards Freight per Ton only to Go to Philadelphia are offered to me, on American Bottom. It is a Pity that in this Circumstance a Treaty Could not be made yet between you and algiers, or Two or Three Frigates fitted out to Protect your Flag in the Mediteranean Sea.[26]

Relations with the Barbary states have attracted consistent scholarly attention,[27] but they represented only one of the possible threats to American shipping interests in the Mediterranean. The number of prizes taken by European belligerents during the French Wars was in fact 15 to 20 times greater than those made by Barbary privateers. From a shipowner's standpoint, European belligerents were in economic terms considerably more dangerous for North American interests than Barbary privateers.

In the 1790s, Americans were repeatedly faced by hostile attitudes to neutral shipping from European belligerents. During the Quasi-War against the United States (1797–1800), France largely controlled the Western Mediterranean and most Italian ports. French privateers infested the Italian, French and Spanish coasts. In only two months – April and May 1797 – 15 American ships were captured and seized as enemy property by French consuls at Malaga, Alicante and Cartagena.[28] Ulane Bonnel records 134 American ships taken in the Mediterranean and in the Strait of Gibraltar and sentenced by the *Conseil de Prises* in Paris, a court entrusted with the judgment of neutral prizes.[29] This figure underestimates the total, both because the sources of this court are uncomplete, and because the tribunal was created in 1800, and therefore did not judge all the appeals of the ships condemned as enemy property during the Quasi-War.[30] It should be stressed that "French" privateer means in this context a privateer with a French letter of marque. Their crews, in fact, were composed of sailors of all possible nations, including those of neutral states.[31] The same applies to the cruisers of the Barbary states, which were partly manned by Christian renegades: the brig *Franklin* of Philadelphia under Morris as captain – the only American merchant ship which was taken during the war against Tripoli on the voyage from Marseille to Martinique – was captured in 1802 near Cartagena by Robert Lisle, a British renegade.[32] With regard to British prizes, the Vice-Admiralty in Minorca judged only one American ship, but the island was under British control for only three years, from 1799 to 1802.[33] Malta and Gibraltar Vice-Admiralty courts were active over a longer period of time. The registers of the decrees of the Vice-Admiralty court at Gibraltar make it possible to identify a total of 19 United States vessels which were sentenced during the Revolutionary Wars (1793–1801), resulting in eight ships and cargoes being considered as good prizes, three cargoes being confiscated as enemy property but the ships restored, and eight instances of full restoration.[34] The number of ships sentenced in Gibraltar during the Napoleonic era, before the United States entered into war against Great Britain (and notably after July 1805, when the British became less tolerant of neutral trade), was consistently greater, despite some gaps in the sources. Before June 1812, 30 ships and their cargo were condemned as good prize; 7 others had at least a part of the cargo confiscated, whereas 25 others were released.[35] Some of the United States ships confiscated at Gibraltar were, however, captured off Cadiz, and thus were not directly involved in Mediterranean trade.[36] Admiralty reports from Malta to London, finally, mention approximately 40 ships which were likely to be American (without specifying a flag), which were confiscated between 1803 and 1815.[37] Contrary to those judged at Gibraltar, they were all involved in Mediterranean trade. Possibly just as many were captured and released. Both Admiralty sources in London and American consular correspondences point to a peak of British seizures in 1807. This was also the year in which American trade in the Mediterranean reached its highest level. In all, different belligerents may have captured 250 to 300 American ships in the Mediterranean, some of which were confiscated. Neutrality did not mean impunity, but merchant ships were not entirely helpless.

American captains relied on several different strategies to reduce the risk of being stopped and seized by privateers or belligerent navies. Some of them took a consistent crew, carried guns, and did not hesitate to make use of them. The Salem merchant Elias Hasket Derby Jr. proudly reported to his father that, after running into a French fleet and being shot, all hands were active in Clearing Ship for action for our surprise had been compleat . . . & in a quarter of an hour gave him our broad side in such a stile as evidently sickend him . . . I was mortified at not having it in my power to return him an equal number without exposing myself to the rest of the fleet.[38]

A second possibility consisted in sailing together with other merchant ships, so as to deter small isolated privateers. Both strategies might prove effective, and in September 1798, David Humphreys, the United States Minister to Spain, noticed that "the French Privateers have as yet kept at a respectful distance from our armed merchant vessels in the Mediterranean".[39] However, taking risks increased insurance premiums, and led merchants to prefer other flags. Finally, merchant ships occasionally took advantage of a convoy. American captains in the Mediterranean resorted to whatever escort they might find, neutral or belligerent. In the late spring of 1797, the captains of 14 American ships dispatched a captain and a supercargo to Gibraltar to seek for a convoy, because the United States consul in Malaga had Nelson's promise that two English frigates would assist them. They had been retained for a considerable time in Malaga, where the French consul had warned that he had given instructions to all French privateers to detain indiscriminately and carry into the closest Spanish port every American vessel they met. All but one of the 14 American merchant ships nevertheless managed to leave and to pass the Strait safely.[40] Neutral escort was occasionally available, as well. Shortly after the beginning of the maritime war in 1793, France had fostered an armed neutrality project that included Sweden, Denmark, Turkey, Poland, Venice, Genoa and the United States, but to no effect.[41] In 1798, Humphreys asked his Swedish counterpart in Madrid to require his government in Stockholm to instruct Swedish officers to protect and convoy American merchant ships sailing in the Mediterranean, as they occasionally had done in the past.[42] But it took three more years to produce an efficient collaboration between American and Scandinavian navies for convoying their merchant ships around the Strait of Gibraltar and along the Spanish, French and Italian coasts. In December 1801, the Swedish commander Cederström proposed to Commodore Dale, in command of the United States squadron in the Mediterranean, that he would take under his protection American and Swedish merchant ships from Barcelona to Sicily, following the coasts; he asked for American escort services for those who passed the Strait of Gibraltar to and from Barcelona.[43] Such cooperation increased the protection offered to merchantmen, at a time when the United States and the Scandinavian fleets were too weak to protect their own merchant shipping in the Mediterranean without help. Such cooperation, however, worked only when European neutral states shared common enemies or concerns.

Before 1801, United States merchant ships did not use any naval protection in the Mediterranean. The United States government had reluctantly agreed to finance a naval fleet to protect Mediterranean trade in 1794, but by the time the first three units were ready to sail (1797), the United States had ratified peace with all the Barbary states. It was, however, still involved in a Quasi-War with France. It was therefore only after signing the treaty of Mortefontaine with France that the United States squadron passed the Strait of Gibraltar.[44] In the meanwhile, the bashaw of Tripoli, who had repeatedly warned that the excessive American delay in respecting the clauses of the peace treaty would lead to a conflict, declared war against the United States. This rupture, however, was also linked to the fact that the United States had underestimated Tripoli – consul Cathcart having received no instructions from the State Department in almost a year – and that the bashaw had settled his differences with Sweden without receiving the customary presents from the American consul.[45]

If Tripolitan privateers captured only one American merchant ship during the war against the United States – their major booty consisting of the 307 men of the United States frigate *Philadelphia*, who were dearly rescued in 1805 – the conflict against the Barbary states affected American shipping, as it increased its protection costs. Meanwhile other neutral flags which were not at war against the Barbary states provided competing transport services in the Mediterranean. This was particularly annoying when the demand for neutral transport services increased anew after the short-lived peace of Amiens (1802–3) came to an end. Only two years after the end of the Tripoli War, the British contested neutral shipping in this region. In spring 1807, 20 American ships were carried to Malta to be mostly confiscated as good prizes.[46] By 1808, neutral shipping had become virtually impossible due to the clashing legislation of the European belligerents, and to Jefferson's embargo. Tensions continued in the following years, notably from the expansion of the French Empire, and by 1812 the United States were no longer neutral.

A strong commercial American presence in the Mediterranean required the United States government to establish peaceful relations with Mediterranean countries and to maintain them. As we have seen, however, the security of its trade depended above all on the evolution of multilateral relations among European powers, the Ottoman Empire, the Barbary states and the United States. These relations, among other things, determined whether the Americans could benefit from the protection offered by European navies against privateering in the Strait of Gibraltar, and from the mediation of men on the spot in favor of American interests. The effectiveness of American Mediterranean policy was thus affected by factors which were sometimes beyond the reach of the United States government, its bilateral relations with a foreign country, and its conception of neutrality. In only a very few years during the French Wars could American ships sail more or less unmolested in the Mediterranean. This situation contrasts with other areas or ports, where United States shipping had dominated neutral trade since the very beginning of the conflict between France and Great Britain in 1793. Nevertheless, despite the long series of crises which affected the potential benefits of neutrality for the United States in the Mediterranean, the number of American ships trading in this region during the French Wars increased considerably.[47]

The Mediterranean within global United States trade and shipping growth

During the French Wars, the United States experienced an immense increase in trade and shipping. This growth was closely related to their capacity to penetrate world markets and take advantage of neutrality, which they were able to preserve longer than most European states. Neutrality, however, was a fragile attribute. American shipping to the Mediterranean, as we have seen, was affected by persisting conflicts with Barbary states, and the temporarily hostile attitudes of European belligerents. This situation may have been particularly frustrating to American merchants, given the value of the Mediterranean for American shipping and trade interests in colonial times. Trade to the Mediterranean after the French Wars broke out, therefore, did not require a radical reconfiguration of merchant networks, nor a need to set up entirely new ones, as trade in other regions did. To substantiate both the peculiar difficulties for the United States of Mediterranean shipping and trade, and the suggestion that the benefit of neutrality for smaller states ought to be contextualized in time and space, we should bring up quantitative evidence on United States trade and shipping in the Mediterranean over time.

Unfortunately, the task of producing such data is extremely delicate, if not impossible. American authorities recorded export values according to the country of destination rather than specific geographical areas, such as the Mediterranean. In the 1790s, official statistics aggregated import and export values for French and Spanish ports. In 1802, "in obedience to the resolution of the House of Representatives", the Secretary of the Treasury Albert Gallatin "respectfully report[ed] that the documents in the Treasury do not discriminate the Exports of the United States to Spanish and French ports, in the Mediterranean, from those to ports of the same nations respectively on the Atlantic".[48] This proved frustrating for contemporary American policy-makers, who during the war against Tripoli were trying to assess how important the Mediterranean was. It is just as frustrating for today's historians. Gallatin confined himself, therefore, to providing the value of trade with Italian ports and Gibraltar. The evolution of trade to the Italian peninsula (Figure 3.1) shows the positive impact of war upon American Mediterranean trade, especially at the end of the Quasi-War against France. The nature of the trade had also consistently changed within a few years, as re-export trade boomed. American ships visited Mediterranean ports with goods from the West and East Indies, which Marseille, a traditional importer of sugar and coffee, could no longer provide, not only because of the risk for French ships of running into British privateers, but also because slavery had been abolished in the French colonies in 1794, and sugar production had shifted to the British, Spanish and Portuguese colonies after the success of the 1791 revolt of Haitian slaves.

From 1803 onwards, the United States statistics introduced a distinction between French and Spanish Atlantic and Mediterranean ports. Figure 3.2 shows the evolution of United States exports to the "Mediterranean". The bulk was

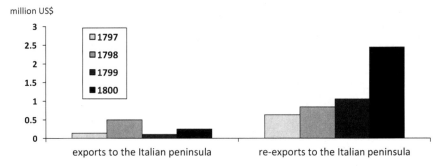

Figure 3.1 American exports and re-exports to the Italian peninsula, 1797–1800.

Source: Letter and report from the Secretary of the Treasury accompanying a statement of the value of the exports of the United States to the ports of Italy, Gibraltar and the Barbary powers, for each of the five years preceding the 30th of September, 1801 . . . (Washington, 1802) [Early American Imprints. Series II. Shaw-Shoemaker].

clearly headed to Italian ports. In 1806, American ships introduced US$5.3 million worth of goods into Leghorn, consisting mainly in West and East Indian products. This figure corresponded to almost 9 percent of total United States re-exports for the year. American ships cleared occasionally on ballast, and quite often with a cargo worth less than the imported one. Exports from Leghorn, consisting of silk, soap, wine, marble, and a vast array of manufactured goods, or silver species, amounted to US$2.5 million in 1806.[49] The balance was in general remitted on London.

United States imports and exports to and from Mediterranean countries, however, represented only part of the business that American ships were carrying in the Mediterranean. In fact, they were increasingly involved in tramping and in multi-polar trades, linking Northern Europe, Asia, the West Indies and the United States to Mediterranean ports. A ship clearing New York to Lisbon, heading thereafter to the Italian peninsula to sell its cargo, and sailing thence to Copenhagen before returning to the United States, would not be computed into the balance of trade as an element of Mediterranean trade, although a substantial part of its profit was generated there. In order to assess the benefit of United States neutrality for American interests in the Mediterranean, we should therefore look more closely at the number of ships involved in this area and at the kind of trade they engaged in. Assessing the importance of Southern Europe and the Mediterranean before American independence, Thomas Jefferson estimated that the Mediterranean had absorbed about one-sixth of the total exports of wheat and flour from the Thirteen Colonies, a quarter of the exported fish, and some rice.[50] This trade required, according to the data he could collect, 80 to 100 ships a year. The report stated that "Our navigation . . . into the Mediterranean, has not been resumed at all since the peace", but in fact American exports to "Southern Europe" – a category which included the whole Iberian Peninsula, but not France – averaged

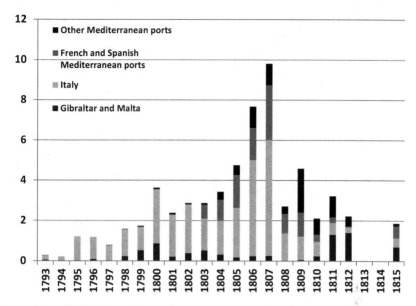

Figure 3.2 Official values of United States exports to identified Mediterranean destinations, 1793–1815 (million US $).

Sources: *American State Papers, Commerce and Navigation*, vol. 1. French and Spanish Mediterranean ports are singled out from total French and Spanish ports from 1803 onwards. "Other Mediterranean ports" include Austrian Adriatic ports, Morocco, the Barbary states, and the Levant (Ottoman Empire).

US$4 million from 1790 to 1793, or 15 percent of all United States exports, a figure corresponding to John McCusker's estimate of the relative importance of Southern Europe for the Thirteen Colonies in 1768–1772,[51] but representing twice as much in absolute values, because of the general growth in trade.

In order to assess the extent of American Mediterranean shipping, I examined the records of the United States consulates. Consuls had to keep a register of incoming American ships and record their clearance. They were also supposed to keep a register of American crew members and cargo manifests. These registers, unfortunately, have not been systematically repatriated by the National Archives Record Administration (RG 84). Moreover, the lists of American ships that consuls had to send twice a year to the Secretary of State seem to have been preserved among consular correspondence (RG 59) only when they were sent in duplicate. Documentary evidence, thus, is far from being complete.[52]

The most important Mediterranean port for American interests was Leghorn. The number of United States ship entrances increased from 27 in 1799 to 144 in 1807, when it represented 124 different ships.[53] The same year, the number of entrances in Leghorn alone thus was higher than the total number of North American ships to the entire Mediterranean in colonial time, or in the early 1790s. By crisscrossing the data for Marseille, Palermo, Tunis, Malaga and Naples, I identified 240 different United States flagged ships sailing in the Mediterranean in 1807. Barcelona, which ranked in second or third place, has no consular records for this year, nor do other Spanish Mediterranean ports, where American shipping was traditionally significant. Given the documentary gaps, I estimated that 500 different ships might have sailed in Mediterranean waters in 1807.[54] If this proxy is acceptable, American shipping in the Mediterranean increased by five to six times between the early 1790s and 1807. This growth was higher than those of other neutral carriers, such as the Danish or the Swedish.[55] As mentioned, American ships were increasingly taking part in inter-Mediterranean trade: 40 percent of United States ships entering Marseille in the first semester of 1807, for instance, came from another Mediterranean port. Whereas in 1804 only one ship in four left Leghorn for another Mediterranean port, one ship in two did so in 1807.[56]

Commercial correspondence and shipping papers point to the coexistence of different kinds of business carried in American bottoms: in addition to direct import–export for the account and risk of United States merchants, a considerable proportion of American captains tramped from port to port, in the Mediterranean alone, or between the Mediterranean and Northern Europe or Asia. This trade was either on behalf of Americans or belligerents, for American citizens provided them with false papers protecting the property from the risk of being captured by enemy forces.

The following commercial adventure provides a good example of the commercial strategies of one of the most important American merchant houses, the Derby, of Salem, Massachusetts. On 1 August 1800, the captain Elias Hasket Derby Jr. of the *Mount Vernon* proudly announced to his father and ship-owner that he had arrived at Gibraltar after an extremely short passage of 17 days. The market being dull – "nothing is to be done here to advantage but the obtaining of information from above" – he decided to sail to Naples, and eventually to look for better markets in Venice or Constantinople. He finally disposed of his cargo in Naples and sailed from there to Manfredonia (Apulia) together with two English prizes he had bought in Palermo after their confiscation. He gave the command of these 290- and 310-ton polacres to his first and second mate. The three ships took on a cargo of wheat in Manfredonia, which he sold in Leghorn. In the meanwhile, Derby's agents in Naples prepared his return cargo. The price of the cargo in Leghorn brought young Derby US$160,000, part of which he remitted to Philadelphia. The equivalent of US$6,753 was shipped in cash, and the rest invested in an assorted return cargo, which was shipped on board the *Mount Vernon* and the two polacres. The latter were sold in Gibraltar together with their cargo, at a 20 percent profit.[57]

Part of the trade carried by United States ships in the Mediterranean was on behalf of belligerents. The *Joshua Potts*, captain Buell, was captured and carried to Malta while sailing from Gallipoli (Apulia) to Marseille under false papers to Lisbon. The attempt to cover the property of the cargo belonging to a person residing in Marseille was discovered, and the cargo seized.[58] Up to

1807, such business was relatively sure. When a ship was captured, the cargo was held and the freight lost, but the ship and the captain's private venture, as well as all sufficiently proven neutral property on board, were restored, unless the vessel had tried to enter a blockaded port.[59] Because of the high freight rates, American merchants and captains were tempted to cover trades which belligerents might consider illegal. Commercial realities blurred traditional concepts of national allegiance and affiliation. In condemning the *Fortuna* on appeal, the British Admiralty judge, Sir William Scott, stressed a "series of falsehoods . . . : false property, false destination, and false description of the national character". The case was peculiar, notably because this vessel had been freighted in 1796 by the American agent in Algiers, Joël Barlow, to ship rescued American crews from Algiers to Leghorn. Moreover, once the *Fortuna* arrived at Marseille, the American agent Joseph Donaldson Jr. agreed to have it sailing under the American flag on the account of Jacob Bacri, a member of one of the most important Mediterranean Sephardic houses which had helped the United States to pay its debts to the Barbary regencies.[60] The facility with which United States agents and merchants agreed to cover belligerents' property undermines the very notion of neutrality, which we might conceive to stem from a constantly evolving system of relations and balances of power in a given region, rather than designating a clear-cut legal status to define the maritime trading rights of a given flag.

From the Mediterranean, American ships sailed to Northern Europe, Asia or America. The *Prudent*, a ship belonging to Nathaniel West, Benjamin Crowninshield master, sailed from Salem to Leghorn, which she left a few days later bound first for Messina, then Mahon and London. The ship, which was insured in November 1800 in Salem for one or more voyages from England to the Mediterranean, with an optional stop at Gibraltar, was probably serving British interests. On her way southward, she was captured and carried to Algeciras, where she was detained from December 1800 to July 1801. After being released, she sailed to Madeira and back to Salem before being dispatched to the East Indies.[61] Approximately 5 percent of American ships clearing Leghorn sailed directly from the Mediterranean to the East Indies. In Leghorn, captains and supercargoes could easily procure species, or remit their balance to London or elsewhere. Even when they sailed back to the United States with a cargo, American ports were often nothing more than intermediary calls connecting globalizing markets. In order to avoid difficulties with European belligerents, a ship could safely avoid a direct voyage between two enemy ports, discharge the cargo and load a new one. Drawback registers for Baltimore show that imports from Leghorn between April 1800 and June 1802 were reshipped to the French West Indies, Havana and New Orleans, whereas shipments from Baltimore to Leghorn included products that had previously been imported into the United States from Batavia, Canton, Cuba and Jacmel. John Carrère, a Saint-Domingue refugee who had settled in Baltimore and been naturalized, used the schooner *Polly* to ship to New Orleans the oil imported on 29 September 1800 from Leghorn to New York on board the brig *Neutrality*, Eric Schroeder master, together with 200 boxes of soap imported from Leghorn on the *Hercules Courtenay*.[62] A cargo might take many different directions after its arrival. The brig *Ann*, Brown junior master, sailed from Trieste to Newburyport on 4 August 1804 with a cargo which was reshipped on 25 different ships bound for the East Indies (including Cape of Good Hope; Île de France, or today's Mauritius; India; Surinam), Demerara, and the West Indies (Guadeloupe, Havana, Santiago de Cuba, Ance à Vaux) between 13 August 1804 and 27 February 1805.[63] Imports and exports to and from the United States thus represented a part only of a much more complex web of business connections.

Despite the difficulties they met from belligerent powers during the French Wars, American captains seized the opportunity to expand their presence in the Mediterranean and to venture farther east, to the Adriatic and the Levant, as well as along the North African coast. Between spring 1809 and spring 1810, 24 American merchant ships entered Smyrna, while 26 had entered in Tunis in 1809.[64] In extending their presence in the Mediterranean, Americans largely relied on pre-existing merchant networks. French expansion in Europe did not entirely disrupt British networks in the Mediterranean. In Leghorn, for instance, the British merchant Webb still handled most of the American trade in 1800 and succeeded in staying in the city and in business despite the three successive French occupations of Leghorn, and its annexation to the French Empire in 1808.[65] In some Mediterranean ports, the United States consul monopolized the bulk of the trade carried by American ships. After he became the American consul in Palermo in 1805, British-born Abraham Gibbs, a naturalized subject of the King of Naples, was the consignee of almost all the American ships arriving at the Sicilian port.[66]

Conclusion

The growth of American shipping and trade in the Mediterranean during the French Wars relied on agents on the spot who were selling and buying cargoes, freighting and handling credit. A tiny minority of these agents were American citizens. Neutral trade and shipping opportunities in wartime, thus, should be conceived as a part of a system which relied for its efficiency on cross-national networks, and employed ships of different flags, according to the degree of security they offered. Security, however, changed rapidly in times of war, since the relative advantage of a flag and international demand for transport services were determined by a dense web of constantly shifting international relations. Even the capacity of the United States to establish a consular service, to initiate diplomatic relations with the Barbary states, and to smooth the payment of due tributes, depended on men who were familiar with the Mediterranean world and who shared multiple identities. Conceiving national belongings as fixed and clearly defined categories can, in some instances, notably in times of war, mislead those who wish to understand how trade was carried on.

The Mediterranean was an area which was particularly characterized by the presence of a multiplicity of intertwined actors with different national adherence and multiple identities. No hegemonic power dominated this region, and beside the critical balance between the European powers on the one side, and the Ottoman Empire and Barbary states on the other, the opportunities for captains and merchants of any given country depended also on the position of actual and potential competitors.

While the United States government resorted to diverse means to secure American trade (peace treaties, military deterrence, naval protection, consular posts and diplomatic action), the effectiveness of these means depended on constant interactions with networks of agents on the spot, who were often not American citizens. The United States' difficulties in protecting its economic interests in the Mediterranean during the French Wars affected the political history of the country, by encouraging the move to a federal government which could deal with the Barbary states and initiate a national navy.[67] The increase of East Indian trade can also be conceived as a response to the peculiar difficulties met in the Mediterranean. The American case suggests the opportunity not only to conceive neutrality as a negotiable and changing configuration, produced by specific conditions at given times, in given areas and given contexts, rather than as a clear-cut status defined by legal categories, but also to think of trading to a region as part of a world system.

Notes

1 McCusker (2010).
2 North (1960); Clauder (1932).
3 For a general introduction to the American presence in the Mediterranean, see Field (1991).
4 The small-state perspective was central to the session on "The Impact of warfare on global trade development. A small-state perspective, 1756–1815, 1914–1918, and 1939–1945" that Leos Müller organized at the 16th World Economic History Congress, Stellenbosch, South Africa. On the 18th-century structural complementarity between major colonial powers, steadily involved in conflicts, and neutral small-state shipping, see Marzagalli (2016b).
5 On the intellectual history of neutrality and its emergence as an element of international relations, see Stapelbroek (2011).
6 Belissa (2015).
7 Fichter (2010); Covo (2013); Marzagalli (2015).
8 Marzagalli and Müller (2016), addressed specifically the issue of neutrality "in practice". The five contributions of the Forum, based on specific cases of neutral shipping, illustrate the complementarity of neutral and belligerent trade and shipping, as well as the significance of neutrality for the continuity of commerce in wartime. They also suggest the existence of vast grey zones which enabled merchants and captains to negotiate their maritime trade. Neutral shipping is not conceived as determined by the abstract mechanical enforcement of the belligerents' rule, but rather as the result of a contingent balance of powers between a given belligerent and a given neutral agent in a given area.

9 Belissa (2015: 410) contrasts Jefferson's conception of neutrality as a means to promote peaceful international relations with Hamilton's view of its readiness to favor American economic development. See also Lambert (2005: 22–30).
10 Wilson (1982: 124–125).
11 "We think that Francisco Chiappe has merited well of the United States by his care of their peace and interests": Barclay's letter of appointment dated Philadelphia 13 May 1791, in *Naval Documents* 1939, I, 31. On Barclay, see Roberts and Roberts (2008).
12 *Naval Documents* 1939, I, 167–168, United States Minister at Lisbon David Humphreys to the Secretary of State, Lisbon, 18 July 1796.
13 Lambert (2005: 45–48).
14 See "A List of American Vessels Captured by the Algerines in October & November 1793": *Naval Documents* 1939, I, 56, and Lambert (2005: 74–76), on the friendly Portuguese attitude to the United States and rumors of British influence on the unexpected peace with Algiers.
15 Ross (1935).
16 Lambert (2005: 79–95). *Naval Documents Related to the Quasi-War*, 1935, I, 121–122, 158, 210–214. On Famin's personal interests, Allison (1995: 165–166).
17 *Journal of the Continental Congress*, vol. 29, 831–833, Jay to Congress, 13 October 1785.
18 Kennedy (1990: 20).
19 Barnes and Morgan (1961: 33–34); Allen (2012); National Archives and Record Administration (College Park, MD) (henceforth NARA), RG 59 and RG 84. On Cathalan: Carrière (1973: II, 926). On Murphy: "Memorandum from Thomas Jefferson, 28 February 1793", *Founders Online*, National Archives, last modified February 21, 2017, http://founders.archives.gov/documents/Washington/05-12-02-0174 (consulted 1 March 2017). At the time he became consul, Murphy had been living in Spain since 1753. On Kirkpatrick: Carlin (2011).
20 Antonucci (2010).
21 One refused the position, another obtained a more important post, a third was so slow in reaching his post that by the time he finally reached Trieste, the United States government had already named his successor. James Anderson provides a good example of scanty willingness to accept the appointment when the personal economic interest in doing so was low. Anderson was informed in March 1802 of his appointment as United States consul in Sète, but it took him three years to move there from Paris, and three months only to decide to quit: "From a firm persuasion of the impossibility of paying my expenses by residing at Cette, I have taken the resolution of going to Marseille, where I hope to be more fortunate." NARA, RG 59 Cette (Sète), James Anderson to James Madison, 7 September 1805, available at http://founders.archives.gov/documents/Madison/02-10-02-0283 (consulted 5 August 2016).
22 A few examples thereof in Marzagalli (2016a).
23 Among the first appointed consuls, ship's captain Richard O'Brien (Algiers) and sailor James Leander Cathcart (Tripoli, and later Tunis) had been captives in Algiers for ten years, William Eaton (Tripoli) had served in the army.
24 *Naval Documents*, 1939, I, passim.
25 Lambert (2005: 16).
26 NARA, RG 59, Marseille, Stephen Cathalan to Thomas Jefferson, Jr., 17 February 1793, *Founders Online*, http://founders.archives.gov/documents/Jefferson/01-25-02-0190.
27 Lambert (2005). On American difficulty in understanding the nature of Barbary diplomacy, see Folayan (1972); Kitzen (1996); Ross (1935).
28 See Marzagalli (2016a).

29 On the changing jurisdiction in France concerning neutral prizes, see Le Guellaff (1999).
30 Le Guellaff (1999: 620–626).
31 Williams (2009: 24).
32 NARA, RG 59, Gibraltar, 29 June 1802, John Gavino to the Secretary of State, http://founders.archives.gov/documents/Madison/02-91-02-0403; NARA, RG 59, Marseille: Copy Circular by Richard O'Brien to the Consul of the US, Algiers, 26 June 1802.
33 The National Archives, Kew, HCA 49/84 and 49/85. The proceedings of the capture of the *George*, Isaac Howland master, in HCA 49/68 and the ship's papers in HCA 49/75.
34 National Archives, Gibraltar. Admiralty Court, Registers of Neutral Decrees, 1796–1801.
35 National Archives, Gibraltar. Admiralty Court, Registers of Neutral Decrees, 1803–1806, and Registers of Decrees, 1806–1808, and 1811–1815. Data for 1808–1811 have been completed with consular reports; NARA, RG 59, Gibraltar, reel 3, but some consular letters are missing.
36 On the contrary, American ships coming back from the Mediterranean might have been seized in the Atlantic or in the Indian Ocean and condemned in some other British court. Out of the 21 printed appeals concerning Mediterranean trade judged by the High Court of Admiralty in London that I located, two were condemned outside the Mediterranean in the first instance (Vice-Admiralties in Jamaica and New Providence). New York Public Library, *Great Britain. High Court of Appeals for Prizes. Prizes causes, 1803–1811*, London, n.p., 7 bound volumes; Philips Library, Salem, MA, *Admiralty Court records of Essex County vessels captured by British Men-of Wars and privateers, 1806–1811*, London, n.p., and *Admiralty Court records of vessels captured by British Men-of War and privateers, 1776–1808*, London, n.p., 9 vols.
37 The National Archives, Kew, HCA 49/100. I have not been able yet to identify and consult sources in Malta.
38 Derby Family Papers, MSS 37, Phillips Library, Peabody Essex Museum, Salem, MA, vol. 15, Letterbook, Gibraltar, 1 August 1799.
39 *Naval Documents Related to the Quasi-War*, 1935, I, 419, David Humphreys to the Secretary of State, Madrid, 18 September 1798.
40 *Naval Documents Related to the Quasi-War*, 1935, I, 27, Extracts from the Consular letters respecting captures by the French; NARA, RG 59, Gibraltar, reel 2, letter no. 69, 31 May 1797, Simpson to the Secretary of State.
41 Bemis (1918).
42 *Naval Documents Related to the Quasi-War*, 1935, I, 484–485, David Humphreys to the Secretary of State, Madrid, 2 October 1798. *Naval Documents*, 1939, I, 70–71, United States consul Michael Murphy to the Secretary of State, 3 April 1794, reporting a Swedish convoy protecting an American ship.
43 NARA, RG 59, Malaga, 7 January 1802, Kirkpatrick to the Secretary of State at Washington, available at http://founders.archives.gov/documents/Madison/02-91-02-0250.
44 *Naval Documents*, 1939, I, 364–365, Secretary of State to John Quincy Adams, United States Minister to Berlin, Washington, 24 July 1800: "Until the differences between the United States and France shall be so far accommodated as that actual hostilities shall cease between them, to station American frigates in the Mediterranean would be a hazard, to which our infant navy ought not perhaps to be exposed."
45 Kitzen (1996).

46 *Newbury Herald*, 29 September 1807. The maps of the intended voyage of the ships carried to Malta in Marzagalli (2010: 57).
47 Marzagalli (2010) and Clauder (1932).
48 *Letter and report from the Secretary of the Treasury accompanying a statement of the value of the exports of the United States to the ports of Italy, Gibraltar and the Barbary powers, for each of the five years preceding the 30th of September, 1801*... (Washington, s.n., 1802) [Early American Imprints. Series II. Shaw-Shoemaker].
49 NARA, RG 59, Leghorn, T 214, reel 1. North (1960).
50 *American State Papers*, Foreign Relations, vol. 1, no. 44, Report of Secretary of State Jefferson to the House of Representatives.
51 McCusker (2010).
52 Mediterranean port records, when they exist, do not systematically state the flag of incoming and clearing ships.
53 NARA, RG 84, Leghorn, vol. 138 (microfilm), Arrivals and departures of American Vessels 1798–1817. On Leghorn, see Keene (1978).
54 I estimated the representativeness of these 240 ships from other sources (lists of ship-entries in New York and lists of ships captured by the British and carried to Malta): Marzagalli (2010).
55 Müller (2011); Andersen and Pourchasse (2011).
56 NARA, RG 84, Leghorn, Entrances and clearances of American ships.
57 Derby Family Papers, MSS 37, Phillips Library, Peabody Essex Museum, Salem, MA, Box 5 folder 7 and 8, Box 13 folder 1, and vol. 15.
58 Derby Family Papers, MSS 37, Phillips Library, Peabody Essex Museum, Salem, MA, Box 13 folder 4, letter of Ja. Chabot to Derby dated Malta, 4 June 1807.
59 Evidence based on prize cases judged by the British Vice-Admiralties and appeals judged by the High Admiralty court in London. In some instances, the cargo might be condemned but the freight due was restored, as in the case of the *Aurora*, captain Hall, and the *Humbird*, captain Stewart: NARA, RG 59, Gibraltar, reel 3, John Gavino to the Secretary of State, 4 November 1805 and 10 March 1807. The cargo of the latter was condemned on account of two letters found on board which gave room to suspect it was Genoese property.
60 The case is reviewed in detail in Marzagalli (2016a).
61 Benjamin Crowninshield Family Papers, MH 16, Phillips Library, Peabody Essex Museum, Salem, MA, Box 1, folder 1–3.
62 New York Historical Society, Custom House Records, Baltimore, folder 4.
63 Newburyport Custom House, 282, Philips Library, Peabody Essex Museum, Salem, MA, vol. 211.
64 Morison (1928: 215). NARA, RG 84, Tunis, vol. 51. Data for Tunis are available in the online database: http://navigocorpus.org.
65 D'Angelo (2004: 22); John Carter Brown Library, Brown Papers, European correspondents, Box 109, Webb, Holmes & Co. to Brown & Ives, circular letter dated Leghorn, 17 November 1800.
66 NARA, RG 84, Palermo, vol. 144, Shipping Register, 1806–1835.
67 Lambert (2005: 53, 71–72).

References

Allen, Debra J., 2012. *Historical Dictionary of U.S. Diplomacy from the Revolution to Secession*, Lanham, MD, Scarecrow Press.
Allison, Robert J., 1995. *The Crescent Obscured. The United States and the Muslim World*, New York, Oxford University Press.

Andersen, Dan H. and Pierrick Pourchasse, 2011. "La navigation des flottes de l'Europe du Nord vers la Méditerranée (XVIIe–XVIIIe siècle)", *Revue d'histoire maritime*, 13, 21–44.

Antonucci, Anthony, 2010. "*Consuls & Consiglieri*: United States relations with the Italian States, 1790–1815", in Silvia Marzagalli, John McCusker, and Jim Sofka (eds.), *Rough Waters. The United States Involvement in the Mediterranean (18th–19th c.)*, St. John's (Newfoundland), International Maritime Economic History Association (Research in Maritime History, 44), 77–99.

Barnes, William and Morgan, John Heath, 1961. *The Foreign Service of the United States. Origins, Development, and Functions*, Washington, Government Printing Office.

Belissa, Marc, 2015. "Faire la guerre pour avoir le droit d'être neutre? Les enjeux politiques de la neutralité américaine", in Eric Schnakenbourg (ed.), *Neutres et neutralité dans l'espace atlantique durant le long XVIIIe siècle (1700–1820). Une approche globale [Neutrals and Neutrality in the Atlantic World during the long eighteenth Century (1700–1820). A global approach]*, Bécherel, Les Perseides, 405–429.

Bemis, Samuel Flagg, 1918. "The United States and the Abortive Armed Neutrality of 1794", *American Historical Review*, 24, 26–47.

Carlin, Colin, 2011. *William Kirkpatrick of Málaga Consul, Négociant and Entrepreneur, and Grandfather of the Empress Eugénie*, Glasgow, Grimsay Press.

Carrière, Charles, 1973. *Négociants marseillais au XVIIIe siècle*, Marseille, Institut historique de Provence, 2 vols.

Clauder, Anne, 1932. *American Commerce as Affected by the Wars of the French Revolution and Napoleon, 1793–1812*, Philadelphia.

Covo, Manuel, 2013. "Commerce, empire et révolutions dans le monde atlantique La colonie française de Saint-Domingue entre métropole et États-Unis (ca. 1778 – ca. 1804)", PhD thesis, École des Hautes Études en Sciences Sociales.

D'Angelo, Michela, 2004. *Mercanti inglesi a Livorno, 1573–1737. Alle origini di una British Factory*, Messina, Istituto di Studi Storici Gaetano Salvemini.

Fichter, James R., 2010. *So Great a Proffit. How the East Indies Trade Transformed Anglo-American Capitalism*, Cambridge & London, Cambridge University Press.

Field, James A., 1991. *From Gibraltar to the Middle East. America and the Mediterranean World, 1776–1882*, Chicago, Imprint Publications.

Folayan, Kola, 1972. "Tripoli and the War with the USA, 1801–05", *Journal of African History*, 13(2), 261–270.

Keene, C. A., 1978. "American Shipping and Trade, 1798–1820: The Evidence from Leghorn", *Journal of Economic History*, 3, 681–700.

Kennedy, Charles Stuart, 1990, *The American Consul. A History of the United States Consular Service, 1776–1914*, New York, Greenwood Press.

Kitzen, Michael, 1996. "Money Bags or Cannon Balls: The Origins of the Tripolitan War, 1795–1801", *Journal of the Early Republic*, 16(4), 601–624.

Lambert, Frank, 2005. *The Barbary Wars. American Independence in the Atlantic World*, New York, Hill and Wang.

Le Guellaff, Florence, 1999. *Armements en course et Droit de prises maritimes (1792–1856)*, Nancy, Presses Universitaires de Nancy.

Marzagalli, Silvia, 2010. "American Shipping into the Mediterranean from the Independence War to the end of the French Wars (1776–1815)", in Marzagalli, Silvia, John McCusker, and Jim Sofka (eds.), *Rough Waters. The United States Involvement in the Mediterranean (18th–19th c.)*, St. John's (Newfoundland), International Maritime Economic History Association (Research in Maritime History, 44), 43–62.

Marzagalli, Silvia, 2015. *Bordeaux et les États-Unis, 1776–1815: Politique et stratégies négociantes dans la genèse d'un réseau commercial*, Geneva, Droz.

Marzagalli, Silvia, 2016a. "Études consulaires, études méditerranéennes. Éclairages croisés pour la compréhension du monde méditerranéen et de l'institution consulaire à l'époque moderne", *Cahiers de la Méditerranée*, 93, 15–23.

Marzagalli, Silvia, 2016b. "Was Warfare Necessary to the Functioning 18th-Century Colonial Systems? Some Reflections on the Necessity of Cross-Imperial and Foreign Trade in the French Case", in Cátia Antunes and Amelia Polónia (eds.), *Beyond Empires. Global, Self-Organizing, Cross-Imperial Networks, 1500–1800*, Leiden, Brill, 253–277.

Marzagalli, Silvia and Leos Müller (eds.), 2016. "'In Apparent Disagreement with all Law of Nations in the World': Negotiating Neutrality for Shipping and Trade during the French Revolutionary Wars", *International Journal of Maritime History*, 28(1, February), 108–192.

McCusker, J., 2010. "Worth a War? The Importance of Trade between British America and The Mediterranean", in Silvia Marzagalli, John McCusker, and Jim Sofka (eds.), *Rough Waters. The United States Involvement in the Mediterranean (18th–19th c.)* St. John's (Newfoundland), International Maritime Economic History Association (Research in Maritime History, 44), 7–24.

Morison, S. E., 1928. "Forcing the Dardanelles in 1810: With Some Account of the Early Levant Trade of Massachusetts", *New England Quarterly*, 1(2, April), 208–225.

Müller, Leos, 2011. "Commerce et navigation suédois en Méditerranée à l'époque moderne, 1650–1815", *Revue d'histoire maritime*, 13, 45–70.

Naval Documents Related to the Quasi-War between the United States and France, vol. I, *Naval Operations from February 1797 to October 1798*, Washington, 1935.

Naval Documents Related to the United States Wars with the Barbary Powers, vol. I, *Naval Operations Including Diplomatic Background from 1785 through 1801*, Washington, 1939.

North, Douglass C., 1960. "The United States Balance of Payments, 1790–1860", in *Trends in American Economy in the Nineteenth Century*, Princeton, NJ, Princeton University Press.

Roberts, Priscilla H. and Richard S. Roberts, 2008. *Thomas Barclay (1728–1793): Consul in France, Diplomat in Barbary*, Bethlehem, Lehigh University Press.

Ross, Frank E., 1935. "The Mission of Joseph Donaldson Jr., to Algiers, 1795–1797", *Journal of Modern History*, 7(4), 422–433.

Stapelbroek Koen (ed.), 2011. *Trade and War: The Neutrality of Commerce in the Inter-State System, Collegium: Studies Across Disciplines in the Humanities and Social Sciences*, vol. 10, available at www.helsinki.fi/collegium/journal/volumes/volume_10/index.htm

Williams, Greg H., 2009. *The French Assault on American Shipping, 1793–1813: A History and Comprehensive Record of Merchant Marine Loss*, Jefferson, NC, McFarland and Co.

Wilson, Gary E., 1982. "American Hostages in Moslem Nations, 1784–1796: The Public Response", *Journal of the Early Republic*, 2(2), 123–141.

4 Commercial relations between Portugal and Russia
Neutrality, trade, and finance (1770–1850)

Maria Cristina Moreira, Rita Martins de Sousa, and Werner Scheltjens

Introduction

The aim of this chapter is to examine the trade patterns and finance between Portugal and Russia as they related to diplomatic relations. The analysis is focused on the Baltic Sea region in a context of the major international changes during 1770–1850, a period of new global wars, neutrality, and peace, in particular due to the American War of Independence and the Napoleonic Wars. Portugal and Russia should be analyzed in the context of the changed trading conditions of both empires.

This chapter is related to the broader Portuguese debate on the role of conflicts and institutions in shaping trade flows during the early 19th century, as discussed in such studies as Moreira and Eloranta (2011), Cruz (2011) and Eloranta, Moreira and Karvonen (2015), which is also an important field of larger debate among economic historians in the last two decades.[1]

We argue that the commercial relations between these two markets can be explained on the basis of the role of Russia as a large trade nation determined to impose its neutrality status in Europe, at least until the end of the 18th century. Besides that, we point out that the bilateral trade between Portugal and Russia should be analyzed considering how the market conditions, conflicts, and other factors changed the relationship between the two empires.

The primary sources used in this study comprised Portuguese yearly manuscripts on trade balance, namely in 1776, 1777, 1783 and 1796–1831,[2] which provide data on exports and imports of products, values, quantities, and prices for each market. Furthermore, evidence on the Portuguese-Russian trade was extracted from the Danish Sound Toll Registers Online (known as STRO).[3] Based on a recent conversion into metric tons of the detailed cargo descriptions in STRO,[4] the volume of Russian exports to Portugal and Portuguese imports to Russia was estimated for the period 1770–1850. Both sources provide information to evaluate the bilateral trade and assess the consequences of the Napoleonic Wars in Portugal, considering that trade was cut between Portugal and Russia in 1808 and 1811.

In the following section, we examine the most important changes in the diplomatic relations between Portugal and Russia. Then we review the three main avenues of commercial interaction, including detailed analysis of certain key products. Russian hemp and flax exports to Portugal and Portuguese sugar exports to Russia were the key products. The fourth section points out that the difficulties of navigation, like the organization and finance of Portuguese trade, are important variables to explain the lack of presence of Portuguese merchants in the commercial transactions with the Baltic Sea region. After that, we will offer some conclusions.

Overall trends in the diplomatic relations between Portugal and Russia

The American War of Independence (1776–1783), the wars after the French Revolution (1789), the First (1792–1797), Second (1799–1801), Third (1804), Fourth (1806), and Fifth Coalition (1809), the Peninsular War (1807–1814), the Russian Campaign (1812–1814), and the end of the Napoleonic Wars (Waterloo, 1815) were events that altered the geopolitics of Europe, with clear consequences on the commercial relations between Portugal, Russia, and Great Britain. The conflicts that followed from Anglo-French rivalry affected the conditions of world trading severely. This contributed to the erosion of the alliance between the belligerents and nations like Portugal. For instance, between 1775 and 1783, England saw its North American colonies fight for independence. This contributed to the crumbling of the alliance between Portugal and England. Besides the opposition towards England in Europe, this power no longer secured Portuguese interests in South America. It was in this context that Portugal readjusted its foreign policy in order to achieve a larger degree of autonomy. In order to counterbalance the reduction of British imports, Portugal began to establish commercial relations with other markets such as the United States, Sweden, and Russia.[5] The main products imported from these markets were, respectively, grain, timber and iron, and flax.[6]

However, the commercial exchanges in these markets were linked to power policy conditions. For this reason, diplomatic considerations became part of the commercial issues. In this chapter, our focus is on the Portuguese-Russian trade, which is of special interest for several reasons. Russia was not only one of the largest trading nations in the world, it was also a great naval and military power.[7] Russia and Portugal established official diplomatic relations in the 18th century. In 1769, Russia assigned its first consul in Lisbon,[8] strengthening the pre-existing informal liaisons between these empires. There are records of contacts between Portugal and Russia since the 15th century.[9] In the beginning of the 18th century, there was a gradual increase in the contacts between the two nations, due to the advantageous geographical position of Portugal and the role of Brazil in the Portuguese empire.

It was from 1765 onwards that further contacts led to the establishment of diplomatic and direct commercial relations between Portugal and Russia. In that year, the Portuguese representative granted the Russian authorities permission to send a ship to Lisbon with a few goods like, wax, leather, linen cloth, iron, copper, and flax to engage a few Russian traders. The Portuguese representative, Martinho Melo e Castro, was hopeful that this would show the Portuguese that there would be profit in trading directly with Russia.[10] As a consequence of these contacts, in 1766 Empress Catherine II issued an order (*Regulamento*) reducing the custom duties on Portuguese wine imported by Russia from 80 to 10 per cent.[11] The main goal of this document was to establish a treaty of trade (in order to decrease the costs arising from the fact that commerce between Portugal and Russia was done by third parties) and nominate representatives (*Ministros*) in both countries.

The commerce between Russia and Portugal was done by third parties, because it was not dynamic enough to justify direct trade. To trade directly with Russia, the Portuguese ships had to go in ballast to Russia to bring their products to Portugal (and vice versa for the Russian vessels), which was economically unviable. Furthermore, the Portuguese sailors were better accustomed to sailing the southern seas. Sailing to the north would be a risky challenge from which there was no apparent profit.[12]

In order to change this state of affairs, it was necessary to strengthen existing commercial and diplomatic relations. This was partially achieved in 1769, when Catherine nominated a consul of Russia in Portugal, Johannes Anton Borchers, a Hamburg-born banker[13] who arrived in Portugal in 1770[14] and would stay there until 1794.[15] Subsequently, in 1779 Portugal sent its first official consul to St Petersburg, Horta Machado (Table 4.1).[16]

When Horta Machado was nominated, he received an essay about the trade with Russia written by the Portuguese ambassador in London, Luis Pinto de Sousa Coutinho. These *instructions* constituted a thorough description of the expectations about trading with Russia.

As far as Russian flax and linen were concerned, Sousa Coutinho made quite an interesting conclusion, describing the possible ways to best take advantage of those items. He stated that the best flax came from Riga, Narva, and Reval (now Tallinn) (cities in present-day Latvia and Estonia) and that Portugal's chances were to be found there. However, he thought it a good idea to invest in flax seeds. Coutinho claimed that the Russian seeds were adaptable to any soil. Portugal could import them to develop a flax culture in its mainland or in the southern areas of Brazil in order to extinguish Portuguese dependence on foreign flax. By doing so, Portugal would not have to import flax from abroad, while at the same time it would free mainland areas to produce products other than flax. Be that as it may, one thing was absolutely needed: lower duties on Russian goods.

These *instructions* Coutinho provided went on for 200 pages more. In them, Coutinho described other products available in Russia that could serve the Portuguese agenda and also which Portuguese items could be of interest to the Russians. This document thus became yet another building block in the establishment of official commercial agreements between Russia and Portugal.[17]

By this time, Russia was determined to impose its neutrality status in Europe. For this purpose, Russia had formed the First League of Armed Neutrality.[18]

Table 4.1 List of treaties between Portugal and Russia

Treaty	Place and date
Maritime Convention of Armed Neutrality between the Queen of Portugal Mary I and the Empress of Russia Catherine II	St Petersburg, July 13 and 24, 1782
Treaty of Friendship, Navigation and Commerce between the Queen of Portugal Mary I and the Empress of Russia Catherine II	St Petersburg, December 20, 1787
Main products included in this treaty:	
Portuguese products: Brazilian *anil*, Brazilian tobacco, olive oil, salt, wine	
Russian products: iron (arches, anchors, artillery and bullets), linen cloth, rigging, wood	
Treaty of Friendship, Navigation and Commerce between the Queen of Portugal, Mary I, and the Emperor of Russia, Paul I (renewal)	St Petersburg, December 16 and 27, 1798
Treaty of Defensive Alliance between the Prince Regent John and the Emperor of Russia, Paul I	St Petersburg, September 7 and 18, 1799
Declaration, renewing the 1798 Treaty of Friendship, Navigation and Commerce between the courts of Portugal and Russia	Vienna, March 29, 1815
Declaration, renewing the 1798 Treaty of Friendship, Navigation and Commerce between the courts of Portugal and Russia*	St Petersburg, May 29 and June 10, 1821

Source: based on Ministério dos Negócios Estrangeiros (MNE; 2004: 755)

Note
* For the purposes of this chapter, we focused on the 1787 treaty. The results of the analysis of the subsequent renewals (1799, 1815, and 1821) are not included in this chapter, for this is ongoing research. The same thing happens with the 1799 treaty, which is also a part of our ongoing research.

This was a coalition of countries led by Russia with the objective of protecting the freedom of commerce, threatened by the British Royal Navy's blockade policies on the high seas. In order to impose neutrality, Empress Catherine II in 1780 sent Russian naval forces to the Sound, the Mediterranean Sea, and the longitude of Lisbon in the Atlantic Sea.[19] Shortly after, the Portuguese queen confirmed the neutral status of Portugal in a war and, in 1782, Portugal agreed to join the League.[20] As a member of the League, Portuguese trade was formally empowered with the right to call at open ports and sail in the shores of belligerent nations while her ships, carrying merchandise belonging to warring powers, were regarded as free on board, apart from contraband.[21] This meant that the preconditions for a Portuguese–Russian *rapprochement* increased. As Eloranta, Moreira and Karvonen (2015: 12) have pointed out, increased neutrality "was a typical boon for trade".

Both Russia and Portugal depended on foreign demand for their growth. Portugal depended on imports of commodities like linen cloth and flax, which was of great strategic importance since the domestic production was insufficient. Such products were produced in the Baltic Sea area – especially by Russia. In addition, the wine merchants of Porto had been looking for alternative markets rather than the British to buy its wine since the 1750s but faced opposition from the British. From a Portuguese perspective, the Baltic Sea area was a market of great potential. For this reason, the Portuguese–Russian attempts to strengthen the diplomatic connections were crucial and thus of benefit for both countries. These two dimensions (commercial and diplomatic) were clearly regarded a valuable asset, for this would render easier the transportation of goods, without interference from France or Britain.[22] However, as we will see in the "Portuguese merchants and trade finance" section, the organization and finance of this trade did not permit an escape to this intervention.

As a result, negotiations continued during the 1780s.[23] Even though both countries would benefit from an expanded trade, they had difficulties to achieve it. The main issue was related to Russian reluctance to reduce custom duties.[24] Negotiations did, however, result in a treaty in 1787, but flax was not included in the agreement.[25] We argue that this happened mainly for two reasons: (1) the Portuguese royals were more interested in purchasing linen cloth in order to satisfy the needs of the colonies and the kingdom for linen cloth; (2) to Russia, it was preferable to export linen cloth (which was favoured in the treaty, with a 50 per cent reduction of its custom duties in Portugal) instead of raw material. As far as Russian export commodities were concerned, only timber, including masts, iron (arches, anchors, artillery and bullets), and rigging used in naval construction were exempted from customs fees (50 per cent reduction on customs duties).[26] This was a Russian concession. Portugal, in turn, obtained the same privilege regarding wine (not higher than 4 *rubles* and 50 *copecks* per hogshead of Portuguese wine, or wine produced on Madeira or the Azores),[27] salt, olive oil, Brazilian *anil* (indigo), and tobacco (50 per cent reduction on customs duties for all these products), provided that the merchandise was carried by Portuguese or Russian vessels (Table 4.1).[28]

The treaty of 1787 was renewed in 1798, in 1806, 1810, 1815, and in 1816 after the Napoleonic Wars[29] and again in 1821.[30] These agreements, alongside the Defensive Alliance of 1799, seem to have consolidated the relations between the empires. At the same time, however, it is clear from the changes made to the agreement that Russian–Portuguese trade went into a new phase during the Napoleonic Wars, when the trade treaty was temporarily put on hold.

Commercial relationships between Portugal and Russia

The shifts in international power politics as well as the changing of market conditions influence the bilateral trade flows between Portugal and Russia. The relative importance of Portuguese–Russian trade is presented in Figures 4.1 and 4.2 using the cover rate, which measures the relationship between the value of exports and the value of imports. The yearly cover rate for the

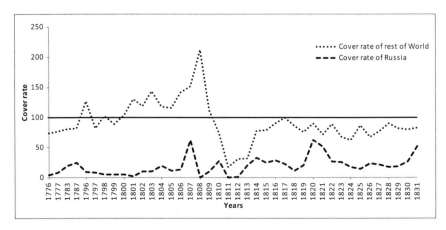

Figure 4.1 Cover rate of Portuguese external trade with Russia and the rest of the world (1776–1831).

Source: PBT.
Cover rate of rest of World = (Exports rest of World/Imports rest of World) * 100
Cover rate of Russia = (Exports Russian/Imports Russian) * 100

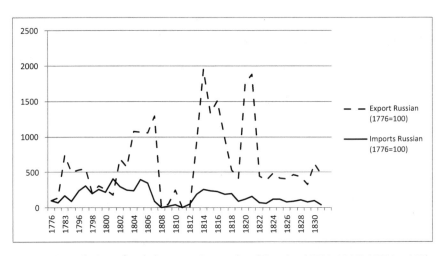

Figure 4.2 Evolution of trade between Portugal and Russian (1776–1831) (1776 = 100).
Source: PBT.

trade between Portugal and Russia for the period between 1776 and 1831, interrupted in 1808 and 1811, was always below 100. The weight of Russia in Portugal's trade was not very substantial. In terms of annual exports value, its maximum value was only 5.6 per cent of the overall Portuguese exports in 1821; in this year, the most exported product was sugar. In fact, the

Portuguese imports share of Russia in overall Portuguese imports in the foreign market amounted to a bit more than 10 per cent; during 10 years of the period of study, it varied between 10.2 per cent and 14.6 per cent (1776, 1783, 1796, 1797, 1801–1803, 1805 and 1806), mainly due to the imports of flax mostly through Porto. This happened in nine of the 10 years, except in 1801 – that is when wheat was the most imported product from Russia, followed by flax.

According to STRO data (Figure 4.3), between 1770 and 1850, the volume of Portuguese imports to Russia was highly irregular. After a short period of growth in the 1770s, the volume reached a peak in 1780 and then went into a long phase of decline, which was interrupted only during the years 1783–1784, 1792–1793, and 1797. In contrast, during the last two decades of the 18th century, the volume of Russian exports to Portugal went upwards, reaching a peak at the turn of the 19th century.[31] During the Continental Blockade, Russo-Portuguese trade collapsed. When trade was resumed in 1814, Portuguese imports to Russia took their former, rather irregular course, which was still marked by sudden short-lived upswings and long periods of decline. During the immediate post-Napoleonic period, Russian exports to Portugal jumped up to late 1790s levels, but declined from 1818 onwards.

Portuguese exports to Russia

The rise of Portuguese exports to Russia was characterized, on one hand, by the increasing Russian demand for Portuguese wine and 'exotic' commodities, in which the opening of a branch of the *Companhia Geral da Agricultura e Vinhos do Alto Douro* in St Petersburg (1781) may have played a stimulating, but not decisive, role.[32] The take-off of Portuguese-Russian trade was consolidated in the 1787 commercial treaty (confirmed in 1798) and the establishment of a Russian consulate in Porto in 1789. On the other hand, the course of Portuguese-Russian trade was often disturbed by Portugal's and Russia's differing positions during the French Wars (1793–1813), the effects of the Portuguese civil war (1828–1834), and the long-term impact of the Latin American independence movement during the first three decades of the 19th century.[33]

The development of Portuguese sugar exports to Russia illustrates the latter point (Figure 4.4). Between 1772 and 1825, there was a more or less steady rise of Portuguese sugar exports to Russia, which was interrupted by the French Wars (1793–1813). Between 1814 and 1819, the sugar trade resumed its former course before reaching unprecedented levels between 1820 and 1830. In general, the modest volumes of sugar exported to Russia indicate that these exports always possessed a secondary importance compared to the volumes exported by other nations; on average, Portuguese sugar exports to Russia accounted for 8 per cent of all sugar arriving in Russia between 1772 and 1831. Their decline might be explained by two factors. First of all, due to internal conflicts, the loss of Brazil as a colony and increasing international competition from the

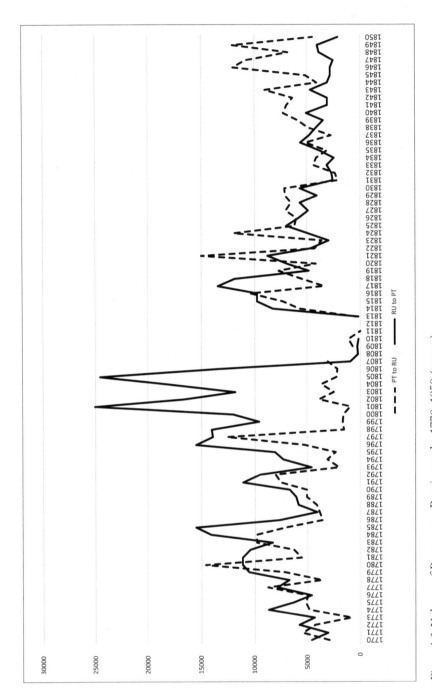

Figure 4.3 Volume of Portuguese–Russian trade, 1770–1850 (tonnes).
Source: STRO.

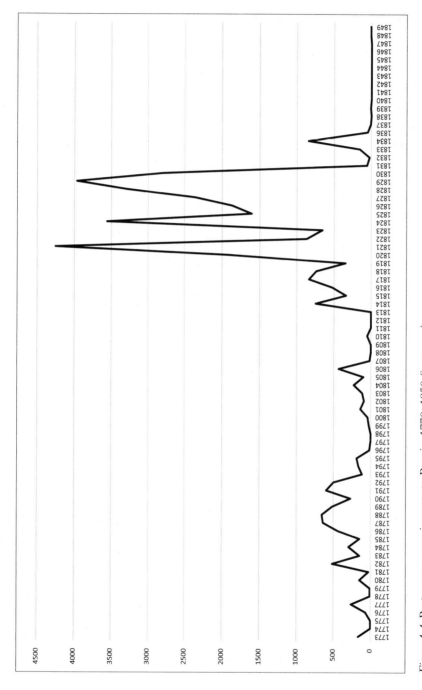

Figure 4.4 Portuguese sugar imports to Russia, 1770–1850 (in tonnes).
Source: STRO.

United States, Portuguese sugar exports to Russia could no longer be sustained. Second, the closely related independence movement in the South Americas and the Caribbean was an incentive for the Russian government to establish direct transatlantic trade relations. Thus, even though much more research is needed on the structure of sugar imports to the Baltic during the first half of the 19th century, it may be assumed that the temporary upswing in sugar exports from Portugal to Russia in the 1820s was supported by the political positions held by either party during that period. As soon as direct sugar imports from Havana took off around 1830, Portuguese exports to Russia disappeared.

Russian exports to Portugal

The volume of direct Russian exports to Portugal experienced a significant rise in the second half of the 1770s, which continues until the mid-1780s, after which the volume fell back in two years' time from 17,230 tonnes in 1785 to 4,289 tonnes in 1787. In the early 1790s, direct Russian exports to Portugal started to recover and – typically large annual fluctuations notwithstanding – their volume rose from 7,657 tons in 1790 to 28,458 tonnes in 1805. Most of this rise followed on account of a dramatic increase in the volume of grain exported from Russia to Portugal, whereas hemp and flax exports hardly changed during the same period. During the early phase of the French Wars, i.e. until 1805, due to its neutral status Portugal probably became a popular choice for grain shipments with a different final destination.

At a much lower level, the same export pattern prevailed after the Napoleonic Wars, at least until about 1820. Afterwards, grain disappeared completely as a commodity exported directly from Russia to Portugal, which may in part be due to the rise of Russia's Black Sea trade. Like before, the volume of hemp and flax exports to Portugal underwent little changes after the Napoleonic Wars – flax continued to be the main product imported from Russia by the Portuguese (Figure 4.5).

Considering the Portuguese sources, the main periods of Portuguese imports of Russian linen products were 1783, 1796–1806, 1813–1816 and 1821. In these years, the value of these imports varied between 1,000 and 1,800 Contos (Table 4.2).[34]

In addition, besides flax, Russia was Portugal's main supplier of hemp and oakum, except in 1809–1811 (when Britain was the main supplier), 1818, 1820 and 1822, when Prussia was the main supplier (Table 4.3).

The analyses of the quantities of flax, hemp, and oakum imported from Russia allows us to conclude that the most important period in these trade relations was before the Peninsular War (mainly in 1796–1806), with values between 50,000 and 139,000 *quintais*.[35] The years of highest values of imported linen raw material coincided with the years of highest quantities imported, clearly associated with the trade (1797 and 1806) and the military treaties (1782 and 1799) between the two empires. Those quantities varied, respectively, between 129,000 and 139,000 *quintais*. According to Alexandre (1994) and

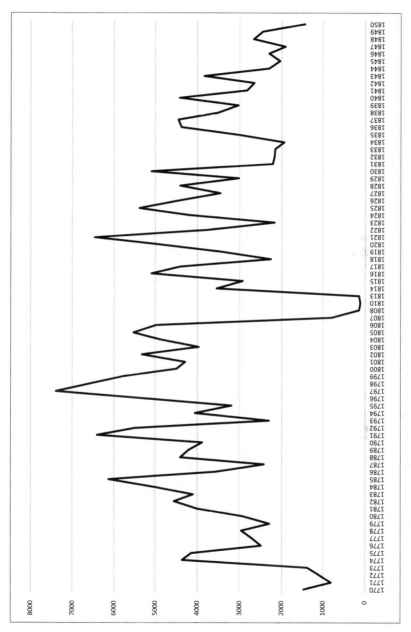

Figure 4.5 Hemp and flax exports from Russia to Portugal, 1770–1850 (in tonnes).
Source: STRO.

84 *Moreira et al.*

Table 4.2 Portuguese imports of Russian flax, hemp, oakum and linen (1776–1831)

Year	Total (Contos)	Russian imports (%)	Year	Total (Contos)	Russian imports (%)
1776	572	83	1813	1,115	83
1777	384	74	1814	1,421	81
1783	957	83	1815	1,100	68
1787	519	82	1816	1,124	72
1796	1,375	84	1817	610	47
1797	1,780	84	1818	304	22
1798	1,188	89	1819	490	81
1799	1,295	72	1820	763	91
1800	1,009	67	1821	987	89
1801	1,045	37	1822	455	90
1802	1,449	72	1823	339	75
1803	1,299	77	1824	653	78
1804	904	55	1825	769	92
1805	1,538	56	1826	415	79
1806	1,572	66	1827	559	87
1807	430	69	1828	706	94
1809	59	43	1829	490	93
1810	252	94	1830	611	88
1812	285	78	1831	220	80

Source: PBT.

Note
1 *Conto* = 1,000,000 *réis*, because the *Real* was the name of the Portuguese national currency from 1435 until 1911.

Pedreira (1994), this was also a period of sizable exports of linen cloth to the overseas Portuguese colonies, namely to Brazil.

Portuguese domestic flax production was not enough to provide for the needs of the linen manufacturers. It was the imports from abroad (mainly from Russia) that permitted an increase in the linen production. After 1806, this kind of annual trade declined to less than 50,000 *quintais*, with the exception of the years 1814, 1815, 1821, and 1825 as the quantities imported were in the range of 50,000–91,000 *quintais*.[36] Between 1808 and 1811, the commercial and diplomatic relationships with Russia were suspended, due to the war and commercial blockades. In fact, in 1808 Spain was Portugal's sole supplier of flax, though the imports were rather modest. In 1810 and 1811, Portugal began buying its flax from England. Nonetheless, in 1812, despite the Napoleonic invasion of Russia, it reclaimed its place as the most important linen raw material supplier of Portugal.

During the Peninsular War there was a contraction of the imported quantity of flax, hemp, and oakum from Russia due to the high price of these products during the period of conflict. The decrease of flax imports and, of course, the

Table 4.3 Main suppliers of flax, hemp, and oakum to Portugal

Year	Total Value (Contos)	Russia (%)	Prussia (%)	England (%)	Others (%)
1776	588	95.2	0	0	4.8
1777	375	95.0	0	0	5.0
1783	881	95.1	0	0	4.8
1787	508	88.7	0	0.4	10.9
1796	1,114	76.9	0.6	16.3	6.2
1797	1,431	93.4	3.0	0.1	3.5
1798	952	90.2	5.6	0.6	3.6
1799	699	87.7	3.8	0.6	7.9
1800	878	79.2	10.7	1.2	8.9
1801	725	93.0	3.8	0.4	2.9
1802	1,033	90.6	0	0	9.4
1803	1,310	91.2	6.1	0.2	2.5
1804	951	91.6	2.0	0.6	5.9
1805	1,074	92.4	0.6	0	7.0
1806	1,414	98.8	0	0	1.2
1807	339	66.0	0	0.6	33.3[a]
1808	0	0	0	0	[b]
1809	189	0	0	42.0	58.0[c]
1810	922	15.1	0	78.4	6.5
1811	927	0	0	95.0	5.0
1812	278	73.5	0	14.8	11.7
1813	608	92.5	0	2.4	5.1
1814	1,640	62.8	11.3	19.5	6.4
1815	1,334	53.0	28.2	14.2	4.6
1816	976	80.0	7.0	7.8	5.3
1817	787	58.3	38.3	0.0	3.3
1818	503	34.8	59.9	0	5.2
1819	905	47.9	43.6	4.3	4.2
1820	861	33.7	50.8	11.6	3.9
1821	1,772	49.6	45.5	2.5	2.4
1822	907	45.8	50.9	0	3.3
1823	498	61.4	29.8	1.5	7.3
1824	1,079	58.7	34.9	0	6.4
1825	898	81.5	15.8	0	2.7
1826	422	90.9	5.2	0	4.0
1827	573	93.4	3.8	0	2.8
1828	829	83.6	11.4	2.2	2.7
1829	523	86.0	3.4	2.2	8.5
1830	622	95.3	2.1	0.5	2.2
1831	223	89.9	0.8	6.3	3.0

Source: PBT

Notes
a Denmark achieved a quota of 21.0 per cent.
b The sole supplier in this year was Spain, even though with a rather low export of 0.21 *Contos*.
c Besides England, the second supplier of this raw material in this year was Spain, with a quota of 41.6 per cent. Italy was also an important supplier, with a quota of 15.8 per cent.

war was very harmful to Portuguese linen production.[37] The linen raw material trade between these two nations was not only important for the civilians, but especially for the Army (for example, textile materials for army uniforms and material used in artillery) and Royal Navy Arsenal (for instance, flax and hemp for maritime activities, such as linen for ropes).

As we have previously mentioned, the official bilateral relations between Portugal and Russia began in 1779, and in 1782 an official diplomatic agreement was signed. We do not have data for this four-year period (1779–1783), but in 1776 and 1777 it is possible to gauge that Portugal was already importing linen raw material from Russia (560 *Contos* in 1776 and 356 *Contos* in 1777). However, in 1783, one year after the signing of the Maritime Convention of Armed Neutrality between the Queen of Portugal Mary I and the Empress of Russia Catherine II, we can observe an important increase in the value of flax imports (838 *Contos*). The value of flax imports would continue to be very high in the following years until the Napoleonic invasions of Portugal. This treaty was renewed in 1798. These agreements, alongside the treaty of 1799 (see Table 4.1), seem to have consolidated the relation between the empires, despite some fluctuations in the values imported from Russia. A further analysis of the 1787 trade commerce renewals (1798, 1815, and 1821) and the Defensive Alliance of 1799, in addition to our analysis here, reinforces the role of linen raw material in the diplomatic and commercial relations between Portugal and Russia.

The importance of Russian linen raw material in Portuguese imports was also confirmed via qualitative sources such as the official correspondence of Portuguese and Russian diplomats. According to Carvalho, almost all Russian ships that arrived in Portugal carried flax. In a document dated 1793, Portugal asked to expedite from Riga to the Royal Navy Arsenal in Lisbon 5,000 to 6,000 *quintais* of first-quality hemp and, in another letter of that same year, 20,000 *quintais* of hemp were ordered.

Portuguese merchants and trade finance

The treaty signed in 1787 increased Portuguese merchants' weight as a percentage of the total value of St Petersburg's overseas commodity trade, despite the fact that this percentage was relatively insignificant (less than 1.5 percent) (Table 4.4).

Why did the Portuguese merchants have so little direct trade with Russia? Three factors need to be highlighted: the difficulties of navigating the Baltic, the bad governance of commercial organizations, and the absence of a financial structure.

Navigation in the Baltic for the Portuguese was conditioned by the weather, since the ice did not permit it all year. Moreover, trade in the Baltic was carried out with large boats and numerous crews, which led to high freight costs. Insurance contracted in London, Amsterdam, and Hamburg was expensive. Portuguese ships had to pay 11 to 12.5 per cent, in contrast

Table 4.4 Total exports and total imports as a percentage of the total value of St Petersburg's overseas commodity trade by merchants nationals

Years	British EXP	British IMP	Russian EXP	Russian IMP	Dutch EXP	Dutch IMP	Danish EXP	Danish IMP	Austrian EXP	Austrian IMP	French EXP	French IMP	Spanish EXP	Spanish IMP	Portuguese EXP	Portuguese IMP
1768–1779	61.2	24.5	11.1	40.1	4.5	8.0	0.2	0.2	0.1	1.4	3.3	2.0	0.7	0.7	n.a.	n.a.
1781–1792	50.0	14.1	38.5	71.7	0.9	1.7	2.5	2.4	0.3	1.0	2.8	1.2	0.9	0.5	0.7	1.3
1795–1798	63.0	29.2	34.0	61.6	0.1	0.5	0.3	0.6	0.6	2.4	.2	1.4	0.3	0.2	0.7	1.0
1800–1801	56.7	29.0	39.7	69.0	n.a.	n.a.	1.1	0.4	0.1	0.2	n.a.	n.a.	n.a.	0.3	0.9	0.6

Source: Kaplan (1986: 93, 94; adapted).

Note
n.a. – no trading activity.

to the 4–5 per cent paid by the ships of other nations.[38] Therefore, even after the signing of the treaty, transport continued to be performed almost exclusively by foreign ships.[39]

Taking into account the organization of commerce, which we underscored in the "Commercial relationships between Portugal and Russia" section, the Portuguese Trading Company was established in St Petersburg in 1781.[40] Perhaps this is why Portuguese trade only started to be registered in St Petersburg Customs records from 1781 (Table 4.4). This Trading Company sought to centralize imports and exports of goods, however it struggled throughout its existence on account of numerous disagreements among its directors. The *A Companhia de Vinhos do Alto Douro* had accumulated huge losses between 1782 and 1802, and the difficulties for Portuguese traders in Russia increased at the beginning of the century.[41] They were forced to trade with so-called upper-class Russian businessmen, who were few in number but were able to control wine prices.[42]

After 1808, when Brazilian ports were opened to direct foreign trade, several products reached the Russian market from Brazil.[43] During the period of the continental blockade of Napoleon, Russia abandoned bilateral trade agreements and implemented the Tariff Act of 1816 that established a uniform regime of protective tariffs. This decision prejudiced direct Portuguese trade with Russia, as shown by the statistic that the number of Portuguese merchant vessels entering the port of St Petersburg decreased every year: from between 18 and 20 prior to 1816, to 8 during 1817, and only to 3 and 2 during 1818 and 1819, respectively[44] (Figure 4.2).

We have scarce information about the financing of trade between Portugal and Russia; however, it would appear that the financing of Portuguese trade was undertaken in the two most important financial centres of the 18th century – Amsterdam and London. The debts of Russian merchants to English firms and the methods of paying custom duties explains the considerable influence of British merchants.[45] Since 1766, England was the only country that could pay half of its custom duties in our own currency, as all countries were obliged to pay the totality of custom duties in *rixdollars*.[46] This is why this English privilege was extended during the 1780s to all countries that signed treaties with Russia, including Portugal. However, the treaty signed 10 years later implied again the payment of custom duties in *rixdollars*. The payment in *rixdollars* confirms the dominance of Dutch finance and the role of the Amsterdam *Wisselbank* in international trade and finance.[47] In spite of this dominance, the increased importance of London can be seen as, after 1763, direct exchange quotations from St Petersburg to London were regular.[48]

Considering the trade of precious metals, Portuguese ships were forbidden to export gold in bars, but were allowed to export gold coins with "low duties". The Sound Toll accounts did not record either currency, neither gold bars nor in an unminted form.[49]

In spite of there being no direct exchange quotations during the 18th and 19th centuries in Portugal, bills of exchange were more important. London

Portuguese–Russian commercial relations 89

and Amsterdam were the clearing centres and it was difficult to avoid using these centres. The Commercial Treaty did not change this state of affairs. The par value in 1790 was one Russian rouble of 100 *copecks* to 720 Portuguese *réis*, and then this par value changed and Portuguese merchants chose the most advantageous transaction.[50] If we compare the evolution of nominal exchanges rates, we can see that Amsterdam was the most flat (Figures 4.6 and 4.7).

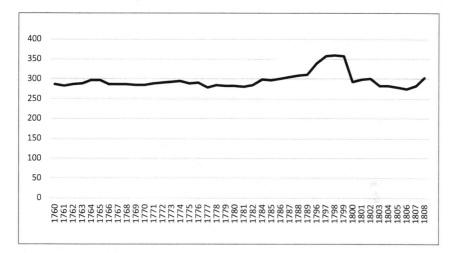

Figure 4.6 Guilders per 100 *Mil réis*.
Source: Denzel (2010).

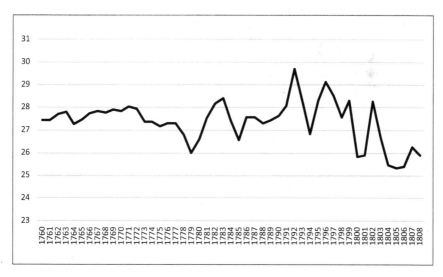

Figure 4.7 Pounds sterling per 100 *Mil réis*.
Source: Denzel (2010).

The behaviour of English pound-sterling exchange rate shows more volatility, probably as a result of more transactions throughout the London market.

If we consider the acquisition of commodities for the Portuguese Navy, this implied payments by the State. In a document written in 1791,[51] we can follow the road map. Payment to Russian exporters was made in cash, on presentation of a letter of credit from London and Amsterdam. The same conclusions are reached if the analysis is carried out from the Russian perspective.[52]

To sum up, in spite of the existence of treaties and conventions signed between Portugal and Russia, commerce faced some difficulties. The practices of trade with the Baltic would have required another type of answers. Factors which made life difficult for Portuguese traders based in St. Petersburg included delays in the instructions received from Lisbon, problems with the office of the Portuguese Trading Company, and the lack of a direct exchange rate between the two countries.

Some final remarks

It is beyond doubt that the Portuguese-Russian trade was an important issue, as both the treaties and the consular bilateral correspondence maintained by the empires testifies. By cross-checking quantitative and qualitative sources, we can conclude that the main reason for the trade between Portugal and Russia was indeed flax, imported from the Russian market mainly through Porto. Nevertheless, flax was not included in the 1787 treaty. We argue that this was so mainly for two reasons: (1) Portuguese rulers were more interested in purchasing linen cloth in order to satisfy the needs of the colonies and the kingdom for linen cloth; (2) for Russia, it was preferable to export linen cloth (which was favoured in the treaty with a 50 per cent reduction of its custom duties in Portugal) instead of raw material.

This research also underlines that the other Russian commodities mentioned in the 1787 trade treaty did not have a clear impact on the Portuguese imports until 1831. This reinforces just how important flax was for the imports of Portugal from Russia. In terms of the Portuguese exported products mentioned in the 1787 treaty, wine, sugar, and salt are the most important products with the trade with Russia, although their values were not significant.

The most important period for the import of linen raw material from Russia occurred before the Peninsular War (mainly in 1796–1806). Russia supplied the vast majority of flax, hemp, and oakum that entered Portugal. Prussia and England were also important partners, but their importance in this trade was not even close to Russia's. Be that as it may, Russia would become the most important commercial partner to Portugal when it came to dealing with linen as a raw material.

The diplomatic negotiations were a lever to the development of trade in the context of neutrality and belligerence. They allowed the nullification of the previous triangular trade (Russia – Britain/Netherlands – Portugal and vice versa) and the fostering of a direct trade relation between Portugal and Russia, with clear benefits for both empires. Nevertheless, these benefits would have been higher for Portuguese merchants if the organization of trade had not been plagued by institutional problems. The navigation difficulties, the distance between Lisbon and St Petersburg, and the intermediation of London and Amsterdam in trade financing were variables that also explained the low level of direct trade. In effect, the conflicts and the institutions were crucial in shaping the trade of these two nations.

Notes

1 See studies listed in Eloranta, Moreira, and Karvonen (2015).
2 BTP´s sources do not allow us to extend the analysis until 1850 given that in a context of political instability, namely two civil wars, only the Portuguese Trade Balance for the years of 1843 and 1848 were produced but with a different methodology. See Moreira (2013, 2015).
3 Scheltjens and Veluwenkamp (2012).
4 The method is described in Scheltjens (2009) and more recently in Scheltjens (2015).
5 Al'perovič (1988).
6 Pedreira (1994).
7 Kaplan (1986).
8 Carvalho (1979).
9 MNE (2004).
10 MNE (2004: 74).
11 MNE (2004: 21).
12 MNE (2004: 61–62, 288).
13 Bantyš-Kamenskij (1897).
14 Pereira and Sá (1990); MNE (2004: 97).
15 Bantyš-Kamenskij (1897).
16 Carvalho (1979).
17 MNE (2004: 155, 159).
18 Neutrality was a concept gradually developed during the 16th century. In this century treaties defined that a country did not assist an enemy of the other in case of war. During the 18th century the First Armed Neutrality was the earliest organized attempt by a group of neutral powers to extort from belligerents in the name of neutrality greater security for their maritime commerce see Roxburgh (1919).
19 MNE (2004: 185–186). For further research on historical relations between Portugal and Russian in 1780, see Pereira and Sá (1990).
20 MNE (2004: 232–234).
21 MNE (2004: 247–250).
22 MNE (2004: 61–62).
23 Fox (1971).
24 MNE (2004: 287–291).
25 For the full text of the treaty, see Polnoe Sobranie Zakonov (1830) (henceforth PSZ), XXII, Nr. 16594.
26 PSZ, XXII, Nr. 16594 (article 7.3).
27 PSZ, XXII, Nr. 16594 (article 6.2).
28 MNE (2004: 318–320).
29 PSZ, XXXIII, Nr. 26276.
30 MNE (2004: 755).

31 Šarkova (1998); Fomičev (2003, 2005).
32 Komissarov (1987); Silva (2004).
33 Bartley (1978); Božkova (1999, 2012).
34 1 *Conto* = 1 million *réis*.
35 One *quintal* equal to around 59 kg. Silveira (1868).
36 The pricing of imports is registered as c.i.f. (cost, insurance and freight) and exports prices are registered as f.o.b. (free on board). For more detail about BPT source see Moreira (2015).
37 For further details on Portuguese linen production in mentioned period see Pedreira (1994).
38 Carvalho (1979).
39 Grinman (2002).
40 Carvalho (1979); Sousa (2008).
41 Sousa (2008).
42 MNE (2004: 606–608).
43 MNE (2004: 622–624).
44 Bartley (1976).
45 Grinman (2002).
46 This is a unit of account that played a great role in the financial and commercial transaction in the Baltic region, fixed at 25.98 grams of silver. From the 1650s onwards, a sharp distinction was drawn in Holland between domestic circulation and the coins that can be exported.
47 Riley (1980);Van der Wee (2012).
48 Denzel (2010).
49 Attman (1981, 1983).
50 Carvalho (1979).
51 Order by the Secretary of State, Martinho de Melo e Castro, addressed to José Pedro Celestino Velho, giving him instructions about the trading activities that were to be developed in Russia, in his role as the Portuguese naval Commissariat in this country, in Carvalho (1979: 246–248).
52 MNE (2004: 511–512).

References

Al'perovič, M. S. (1988), U istokov russko-portugal'skich otnošenij (vtoraja polovina XVIII načalo XIX v.), *Novaja i novejšaja istorija*, 1, 65–82.

Alexandre, V. (1993) *Os Sentidos do Império. Questão nacional e questão colonial na Crise do Antigo Regime Português*, Porto: Afrontamento.

Attman, A. (1981), The Russian Market in World Trade, 1500–1860, *Scandinavian Economic History Review and Economy and History*, 29(3), 177–202.

Attman, A. (1983), *Dutch Enterprise in the World Bullion Trade, 1550–1800*, Gothenburg: Kungl. Vetenskaps- och Vitterhets-Samhället.

Bantyš-Kamenskij, N. N. (1897), *Obzor vnešnich snošenij Rossii (po 1800 god)*, part 3. Moscow.

Bartley, R. N. (1976), The Inception of Russo-Brasilian Relations, 1808–1828, *Hispanic American Historical Review*, 56(2), 217–240.

Bartley, R. N. (1978), *Imperial Russia and the Struggle for Latin American Independence*, Austin: University of Texas Press.

Božkova, S. G. (2012), Rossijskij general'nyj konsul v Rio-de-Žanejro Ju.A. Vallenštejn: u poroga mnogoletnej služby, *Latinskaja Amerika*, 10, 63–77.

Božkova, S. G. (1999), F.F. Borel' i razvitie otnosenij Rossii s Portugaliej i Braziliej v pervoj treti XIX veka, St Petersburg, PhD dissertation, St Petersburg State University.
Carvalho, R. (1979), *Relações entre Portugal e a Rússia no século XVIII*, Lisbon: Sá da Costa Editora.
Cruz, M. A. (2011), *A Neutralidade portuguesa na Europa da revolução Portugal (1792– 1807)*, Lisbon: Tribuna da História.
Denzel, M. A. (2010), *Handbook of World Exchange Rates, 1590–1914*, London: Routledge.
Eloranta, J., Moreira, M. C., and Karvonen, L. (2015) Between Conflicts and Commerce: The Impact of Institutions and Wars on Swedish–Portuguese Trade, 1686–1815, *Journal of European Economic History*, 3, 9–50.
Fomičev, P. E. (2003), Rossijsko-portugal'skie torgovo-ėkonomičeskie otnošenija v XVIII–načale XIX v., *Latinskaja Amerika*, 8, 69–76.
Fomičev, P. E. (2005), Rossijsko-portugal'skie torgovo-ėkonomičeski i diplomatičeskie otnošenija v XVIII–načale XIX v, PhD dissertation, St Petersburg State University.
Fox, F. (1971), Negotiating with the Russians: Ambassador Segur's Mission to Saint-Petersburg, 1784–1789, *French Historical Studies*, 7(1), 47–71.
Grinman, A. (2002), A Aproximação entre Portugal e a Rússia na Segunda Metade do Século XVIII, mimeo, master's thesis.
Kaplan, H. H. (1986), Observations on the Value of Russia's Overseas Commerce with Great Britain during the Second Half of the Eighteenth Century, in *Slavic Review*, 45(1), 85–94.
Komissarov, B. N. (1987) *Peterburg – Rio de Janeiro = S. Petersburgo – Rio de Janeiro: Stanovlenie otnošenij*, Leningrad: Izd-vo LGU.
Ministério dos Negócios Estrangeiros (ed.) (2004), *Relações Diplomáticas Luso-Russas. Colectânea Documental Conjunta (1722–1815)*, Lisbon: Instituto Diplomático.
Moreira, Cristina and Jari Eloranta (2011) Importance of "Weak" States During Conflicts: Portuguese Trade with the United States During the Revolutionary and Napoleonic Wars, *Revista de Historia Económica – Journal of Iberian and Latin American Economic History*, 29(3), 393–423.
Moreira, M. C. (2013) *Relaciones comerciales luso-españolas, 1774–1860*, Madrid: Editorial Académica Española.
Moreira, M. C. (2015) Portugal, 1775–1831, in Charles Loïc and Daudin Guillaume (eds.), special issue of the *Revue de l'OFCE Eighteenth-Century. International Trade Statistics*, 140(4), 319–333.
Pedreira, J. M. (1994), *Estrutura industrial e mercado colonial Portugal e Brasil (1780–1830)*, Linda-a-Velha: Difel.
Pereira, G. M. and Sá, V. (1990) *Do Porto ao Báltico, 1780: Achegas para a história das relações entre Portugal e a Rússia*, in *Revista da FLUP: História*, series 2, vol. 7. Porto: FLUP, 219–254.
Polnoe Sobranie Zakonov Rossijskij Imperii (1830), *Poveleniem gosudarja imperatora Nikolaja Pavloviča sostavlennoe. Sobranie pervoe, s 1649 po 12 dekabrja 1825 goda*, St Petersburg: Tip. 2 otd-nija Sobstv. E.I.V. kanceljarii.
Riley, J. C. (1980), *International Government Finance and the Amsterdam Capital Market, 1740–1815*, Cambridge: Cambridge University Press.
Roxburgh, R. F. (1919), Changes in the Conception of Neutrality, *Journal of Comparative Legislation and International Law*, 1(1), 17–24.
Šarkova, I. S. (1998), Russko-portugal'skie torgovye otnošenija v poslednej treti XVIII v., in B. N. Komissarov (ed.), *Portugalistika v Sankt-Peterburge. Materialy meždunarodnoj*

konferenciii, posvjaščennoj 100-letiju so dnja roždenija prof. O.K. Vasil'evoj-Švede (13–15 September 1995), St Petersburg.

Scheltjens, W. (2009), The Volume of Dutch Baltic Shipping at the End of the Eighteenth Century: A New Estimation Based on the Danish Sound Toll Registers, *Scripta Mercaturae: Zeitschrift für Sozial- und Wirtschaftsgeschichte*, 43(1–2), 83–110.

Scheltjens, W. (2015), Maße und Gewichte: Konvertierungsmöglichkeiten am Beispiel der Sundzollregister, in Peter Rauscher and Andrea Serles (eds.), *Wiegen – Zählen – Registrieren: Handelsgeschichtliche Massenquellen und die Erforschung mitteleuropäischer Märkte (13.–18. Jahrhundert)*, Innsbruck/Vienna/Bozen: StudienVerlag, pp. 455–479.

Scheltjens, W. and Veluwenkamp, J. W. (2012), Sound Toll Registers Online: Introduction and First Research Examples, *International Journal of Maritime History*, 24(1), 301–330.

Silva, Francisco Ribeiro da (2004), Os ingleses e as circunstâncias políticas do negócio dos vinhos do Porto e Douro, *Douro: estudos e documentos*, 9, 18, 93–111.

Silveira, Joaquim Henriques Fradesso da (1868), *Mappas das medidas do novo systema legal comparadas com as antigas nos diversos concelhos do reino e ilhas*, Lisboa: Imprensa Nacional.

Sousa, F. (2008), A Rússia e a Companhia do Alto Douro. Um Balanço Dramático de Três Décadas de Relações Comerciais (1805), in *A Companhia e as relações económicas de Portugal com o Brasil, a Inglaterra e a Rússia*, CEPESE Porto: Ed. Afrontamento.

Van der Wee, H. (2012), The Amsterdam Wisselbank's Innovations in the Monetary Sphere: The Role of Bank Money, in John H. Munro (ed.), *Money in the Pre-Industrial World: Bullion, Debasements and Coin Substitutes*. London: Pickering & Chatto.

5 Taxation in Brazil in the Napoleonic Wars

Neutrality, economy and the outcomes of a royal court in transit

Rodrigo da Costa Dominguez and Angelo Alves Carrara

Over the last three decades, Brazilian historiography has testified the growing and development of Economic History studies. Regardless of chronology, topics, original databases and new methodologies utilized, its recent "boom" carries out the great influence of classic and traditional approaches, as well as the latest contribution of native scholars, especially concerning relevant themes such as economic growth and policies, dependence and development during the nineteenth and twentieth centuries, different forms of credit, banking history, economic activities and so on. Conventional methods and data have been recently challenged by innovative perspectives regarding the sources previously known by economic historians, as well as some new data brought up by this new generation's work. In this recent historiographical scenario, colonial economic aspects have been privileged, with trade and taxation occupying a prominent place.

In this chapter, the authors' goals are to bring out a Brazilian historiographic panorama that has influenced these "new" economic history schools of thought, as well as to summarize some important economic studies recently developed during this period regarding these topics. Moreover, it aims to outline the impact of opening Brazilian ports in 1808, with regard to Brazilian economic growth so far and the contrast between the *Alfandegas* (customs) movement in Brazil (Rio de Janeiro) and Portugal (Lisbon), in order to verify the paradigm shift which meant (in terms of revenues and taxation) the transfer of the Portuguese court to Brazil within the context of the Napoleonic Wars.

Brazilian economic history and the historiography

Any historian would have a hard time trying to point out a milestone for the origins of Brazilian economic history. It is something complex and controversial, as well, to propose an overall view, due to the polarization around the schools of economic thought. Moreover, it gets particularly hard when considering the topics we intend to discuss here. In general terms, some scholars suggest – as a fundamental and first chronological reference – the first essays of José da Silva Lisboa, Viscount of Cairu, in his *Princípios de economia política*

(Principles of political economy) and the *Observações sobre a franqueza da indústria, e estabelecimento das fábricas no Brasil* (Comments on the openness of the industry, and the establishment of factories in Brazil), both edited at the beginning of the nineteenth century.[1]

Others would propose, historically and in a stricter sense, the classic and pioneering work of Francisco Adolfo de Varnhagen,[2] Viscount of Porto Seguro, edited in the 1850s. Nevertheless, Varnhagen is considered by many historians as the "Brazilian Herodotus",[3] concerning both the background of the Brazilian Historical and Geographical Institute (IHGB) and the implications regarding the implementation and institutionalization of scientific and historiographic thought during the first decades of Pedro II's reign (1840–1889).

Curiously (or not), both Silva Lisboa and Varnhagen bring us a metropolitan point of view, in the sense that their contribution to the construction of Brazilian national identity comes from an "ode to the Portuguese" and to colonization,[4] and both merge towards an institutional perspective. This point of view contrasts with the work of Capistrano de Abreu and his *Capítulos de História Colonial* (Chapters of colonial history), produced and edited during a whole different context of the Brazilian monarchical regime, "shaken after the Paraguay War, and at stake, like slavery, seeking for new political, economic and intellectual references".[5]

Regardless of this debate about the origins and protagonists of Brazil's economic history, Varnhagen and the IHGB influenced the first generation of Brazilian historians who dedicated their efforts to economic and social topics between the 1930s and 1960s, such as Gilberto Freyre, Sérgio Buarque de Holanda, Nelson Werneck Sodré, Celso Furtado and Caio Prado Junior, and who still have a great influence on the recent generations of economic historians.

Yet other important reference is Roberto Simonsen's work on the economic history of Brazil, first edited in 1937, which served as an essential landmark.[6] Despite his academic formation as an economist and engineer, he developed a much more complete description, utilizing a great deal of sources with a profound depiction of the economic processes of colonial Brazil.[7] In fact, Caio Prado Junior would use a lot of Simonsen's theories for his own research[8] related to the formation of contemporary Brazil, as well as a particular vision for an economic history of Brazil, combining both economist and Marxist approaches, very much in vogue in the 1940s and 1950s.[9] Celso Furtado also followed his guiding lines, inspired by Simonsen's meticulous work, in order to mature his own studies while he was in Cambridge,[10] which provided the basis for one of his most important publications[11] and still a great reference for Brazil's economic history. In summary, Simonsen's work provided, to a great degree, the basis for a scientific methodology concerning the study of Brazilian economic history and correspondingly influenced the first generation of historians who would become authentic references for the all-time Brazilian historiography.

In terms of fiscal history, although the Church and ecclesiastical taxation is a fundamental part of this puzzle, it is important to highlight the fact that analysis is centered on the State's point of view. Nevertheless, it is also fundamental to emphasize the lack of recent bibliography about this topic.[12] Furthermore, the fragmentary and specific character of Brazil's fiscal dynamics, composed by a number of different units, the Captaincies[13] (the *capitanias*), each one with its own commercial activities and interests, characterizes the Brazilian territory as a space of economic and fiscal diversity.[14] The former province of Minas Gerais (nowadays one of Brazil's states) holds a whole particular chapter regarding the taxation's complexity and the importance of gold extraction and its remittance to Portugal.[15]

Much of what has already been written on this topic is due, on the one hand, to the historians previously mentioned, but on the other hand, and largely, to the *Brazilianists* such as Charles R. Boxer, Stuart Schwartz, Kenneth Maxwell, A. J. R. Russell-Wood, Arno Wehling and many others who, somehow, addressed those subjects in their respective works. Primary sources and collections of legislation[16] comprised the essential elements for that development, such as the documents of *Arquivo Histórico Ultramarino* (Ultramarine historical archive), laid up at the *Torre do Tombo* (Portuguese National Archives), and the data stored at the National Library of Rio de Janeiro, combined with relevant bibliography written by the twentieth century's important Portuguese scholars,[17] would complete that scenario. The new methodology applied by those authors with Portuguese economic history sources would be reflected in a whole generation of historians yet to come.

That "new generation", encouraged and stimulated by new/other type of sources, such as the Portuguese trade balance sheets – which contains all the relevant detailed information about the commercial dynamics involving different regions of Brazilian territory and Lisbon – would pave the way to another level of the historiographic debate concerning the economic history of colonial Brazil. Part of this same context begins with José Roberto do Amaral Lapa.[18] As one of Sergio Buarque de Holanda's disciples, he provided a fundamental basis for the economic historians, with new "inter-colonial perspectives".[19] Yet, the 1970s would be a very important time for colonial trade and economy history, due to a set of groundbreaking Ph.D. theses[20] submitted at the University of São Paulo by Carlos Guilheme Mota, Virgílio Noya Pinto, Fernando Novais and José Jobson de Andrade Arruda, scholars who would establish one of the groups regarding economic thought within the new Brazilian economic history. The first two address economic and social topics related to two of the most important secessionist movements, with a very important contribution concerning the sources' interpretation, and relations with the Portuguese commerce and their partners, such as England. The second two were based on that documentation (Portugal's trade balance sheets), bringing innovative perspectives regarding quantitative methods, which constitute Arruda's thesis subtitle.

By that time, and moving towards the 1980s, economic history was entering the mainstream, residing on the "top three" topics[21] related to social sciences in Brazil. Other scholars were also seduced by this subject, such as Ciro Flamarion Cardoso,[22] who was originally worked in ancient and medieval history.

His efforts opened up space for a new debate. His motivation was to oppose the Marxist perspective, an outdated debate, in his point of view.[23] Such different perceptions would be fundamental to drawing the lines that would separate the two main schools of economic thought: one in Rio de Janeiro, the other in São Paulo. Indeed, Francisco José Calazans Falcon followed the same path,[24] more concerned and focused on the economic, juridical and ideological perspectives, and also strongly critic of that Marxism.[25] Then, the Brazilian context regarding the political process towards the restoration of democracy, combined with the economic challenges faced by the country, and the development of many graduate and postgraduate programs in history,[26] provided a rich environment for the growth not only of historiography in general, but also of economic history studies.

Regarding the colonial fiscal history of Brazil, within the same context, Tarquínio J. B. de Oliveira wrote about some very important features of the Portuguese Royal Treasury (Erário Régio) and its administration's dynamics.[27] It is a personal interpretation of eighteenth-century sources and offers an important contribution to fiscal organics in Minas Gerais and its relationship with local secessionist movements.[28] Graça Salgado also contributed significantly to this topic,[29] with a broad view of the management organization created by the Portuguese and its operation, which resulted from pioneering methodical research concerning the structure and the officers in charge, and with a chapter devoted to fiscal matters. In fact, its importance can be measured by the utilization of the volume's data to the research project called MAPA (Memory of Brazilian Public Administration),[30] created and coordinated by the Brazilian Bureau of Justice (Ministério da Justiça) in cooperation with the National Archives of Rio de Janeiro.

The 1990s brought a very different scenario to Brazil's economic historiography. All the conditions were created by the previous generation for a "third wave" of economic historians, who were much more specialized, up-to-date and familiar with new methods and approaches, such as New Institutional Economics,[31] supported as well by florescent production of social and cultural history research projects and postgraduate programs. At that moment, two different historiographic streams were established. In Rio de Janeiro, a path more devoted to an agrarian/slavery approach concerning the local economy was established, which resulted in important contributions from scholars such as João Fragoso,[32] bringing to light important features of that relationship. Other important aspects of the Brazilian colonial economy, such as land tenure structures and organization of economic activities in the hinterland, were advanced by other relevant studies[33] submitted in 1997.

During the 1960s in São Paulo, the establishment of some of the previous generation's historians at the local university opened space for new perspectives in Brazilian economic history. At that time, a new set of scientific researches was in progress, on all kinds of topics, relating to fiscal history and separatist movements, including 1800s banking history, to the occupation of the more provincial portion of Brazil and the struggle with native and slave communities.[34] During the following decade, a breakthrough work by Luiz Felipe de Alencastro would emerge.[35] This established a new paradigm for colonial and economic studies, based primarily on his Ph.D. thesis submitted 14 years before, in Paris, and supervised by Frédéric Mauro, one of the Brazilianists' group. Greatly influenced by him, his Atlantic system theory of the slave trade as a fundamental support for Brazil's structuring and Portugal's economy was an innovation, as the new millennium came out with different visions and approaches for colonial economic history. It also opened up space for an intense historiographic debate about conceptual differences involving the colonial pact.[36]

Furthermore, the celebration of 500 years of the discovery of Brazil, combined with the creation, in Portugal, of the National Commission for the Commemoration of the Portuguese Discoveries (CNCDP), fostered a greater contact with a refreshed Portuguese historiography. Many research projects, as well as important research centers, were now being financed, and a new generation of historians devoted to economic history within Brazilian topics was blooming, supported by important historians such as Joaquim Romero Magalhães[37] and José Luís Cardoso.[38] From this greater exchange, we can highlight a scientific production focused very much on seventeenth- and eighteenth-century colonial trade and gold economics.[39]

More recently, a brand-new group is brewing, with different approaches for Brazil's economic development, and focusing on the *capitanias*' local perspectives and the analysis of the importance of each case within the Brazilian colonial economy.[40] Regarding taxation, a similar process took shape in Minas Gerais, where a group of economic studies and quantitative methods were structured,[41] focused in fiscal history, and which provided a set of recent MAs and Ph.D. theses, combining forces with São Paulo and Rio de Janeiro. Based on these efforts, we can pinpoint the approach of important topics such as credit, financial administration, taxation, and its relationship within a war context of. The results can be seen, from 2001 onwards,[42] in a series of research projects financed by the Brazil's national institutes for science funding (CAPES and CNPq), and at regional level (such as FAPESP and FAPEMIG), as well as a series of recent studies and collective publications.[43] New research centers devoted to economic and fiscal history are also blooming in other regions, with examples in Pernambuco and Bahia. From this perspective, recent works have broadened the field of fiscal history studies to Colonial Brazil.[44]

Observing the recent development of Brazil's historiography as it relates directly to economy and taxation, we can see a prosperous picture, with a synthesis of past and present historiographic debates, combining old and new theories, methods and different perspectives. Indeed, recent work on political administration by scholars originally dedicated to other topics, such as Laura de Mello e Souza,[45] is an example of how these subjects are in vogue and how that kind of fusion, testified by this intense debate between different points of view, has contributed to the recent historiographic production. This same portrait was not so sumptuous a few decades ago, but the openness of Brazilian historiography to new approaches, mixed with Portuguese influence and a strong Marxist tradition, proved to be a unique combination, in the sense that it provided an important starting point to the improvement and growth of an economic and fiscal history of colonial Brazil.

Napoleonic Wars and the Portuguese Empire

The Napoleonic Wars exerted a strong impact on the Portuguese Empire: the Portuguese Court moved in 1808 from Lisbon to Rio de Janeiro, the center of its colonial dominions in South America. It was a unique phenomenon in history – a European metropolis moved its governance to the colony. This strategic option, considering all economic and geopolitical conditions motivated by the Continental Blockade from 1806 onwards, enabled Portugal to better play its neutral role within the war scenario. Moreover, it kept Portugal's economy alive by granting open access to Brazilian ports and its colonial commodities – cotton in particular, due to the embargo imposed to Britain by the United States[46] – for all Portuguese economic partners in a key period[47] in which the Atlantic seaports in Europe were under Napoleon's scope of action. This fact was obviously accompanied by absolutely essential measures for the State's maintenance, especially the establishment of administrative structures for tax collection. This took place on June 28, 1808, when a letter signed by the Prince Regent created the Brazilian Royal Treasury and Board of Finance.[48] In practice, the trials carried out previously by the Board of Finance abroad began to center on the new organ. Thus, all matters related to the extraction, distribution and administration of the Royal Treasury in the Portuguese dominions in America, Africa and Asia, the Azores and Madeira passed into the jurisdiction of the Royal Treasury in Rio de Janeiro. The results were immediate and very unlike what generally occurred in times of war. By 1809, the revenues of the captaincy of Rio de Janeiro soared.

From the beginning of the fourteenth century until at least the first two decades of the seventeenth, the State of India (Estado da Índia) was the major direct source of revenues of the Portuguese Empire: in 1607 it yielded about 60 percent, and in 1620 it represented 45 percent of the total Crown's revenues.[49] After decades facing a number of difficulties caused by military pressure, the Portuguese Empire was experiencing a change in the fiscal/economic relevancy of each of its colonies scattered overseas. The production of gold in Brazil was responsible for this radical transformation.

Taking into account Brazil's structure of revenues and expenditures, it is possible to talk about two "fiscal logics" in force within Portuguese America: one prevailing during the sixteenth and seventeenth centuries; and another, completely different one in the eighteenth century. Until gold effectively arrived at the port of Lisbon, the State of Brazil (Estado do Brasil) was able to solely generate revenues to meet their expenses – and this even with some difficulty – rarely being possible to send net remittances to the metropolis. A drastic shift took place in the eighteenth century's early years, when Brazil became responsible for bulky net remittances of pure gold. There is no doubt about the importance of this contribution to Portuguese finances, i.e., mining producing the first and rapid effects on the imperial economy. Apart from gold, these revenues were generated by tobacco monopolies, Brazilian wood, diamonds, and by customs duties (export and import taxes). Notwithstanding this, when gold production began to decay in the 1760s, the Brazilian economy was already entering a new phase. According to Jorge Pedreira, shipments of gold began to decline, especially after 1766.[50]

The eighteenth century's overall framework still needs further research. However, equally, we do know of Portugal's difficulties caused by the natural disaster of 1755, strains with the Atlantic traffic, as well as a decline in gold mining in Brazil.[51]

Among the problems emerging from this new situation for the Portuguese authorities – especially financial tightness in the metropolis and insufficient money offered for international payments – the most important became the chronic trade deficit. When gold lost its importance, two commodities replaced it:

> sugar and cotton formed the two most important Brazilian products reaching the European markets through Portuguese ports. These commodities made up 85 percent of the re-exports of merchandise from Brazil in 1796–1800. The only other staples having a sizeable part in those shipments were hides (6.5 percent), tobacco (3.5 percent) and cocoa (3 percent).[52]

But a major consequence of decades of gold prominence was the change in Brazil's economic gravity axis – from the northeastern ports of Salvador and Recife to that of Rio de Janeiro.

The captaincy of Rio de Janeiro at the end of the eighteenth century

The first problem one is confronted with when studying the finances of the ancient captaincy of Rio de Janeiro is the disturbing scarcity of sources from its Treasury (*Casa dos Contos*).[53] This fact is indeed more relevant than the idea put forward by Adrien Balbi of a "policy of secrecy" in fiscal and financial matters by the Portuguese government. According to Italian geographer and statistician Pombal's obsession regarding the protection and state secret about the empire's revenues, punishment for high treason for disclosing such documents, as well as the levels of independence and secrecy within the structuring process of the new Royal Treasury after 1761, comprises the source of waste and disorder introduced into the kingdom's finances.[54]

One century before the transfer of the Portuguese Court to Brazil, the captaincy of Rio de Janeiro, more than any other, bore the impact of the new phase generated by gold production. Until the final years of the sixteenth century, it was affected by strong deficits, but since the first moments when gold began to come into light and start circulating, the revenues of its Royal Treasury grew astonishingly. But this growth was only felt in commercial activity. Agricultural production measured by the tithe records, together with whaling, kept the same income levels as the previous century. In 1712, the total amount of customs duties equaled almost 18 *Contos de réis*. Ten years later, 66 *Contos*, and in 1724 the customs duties reached 100 *Contos de réis*.[55]

Compared to the values of the tithes, customs duties make clear the importance of commerce to the captaincy of Rio de Janeiro, as shown in Figure 5.1.

Figure 5.1 shows that the strong growth trend in international trade during the first half of the eighteenth century did not exert any influence on rural activities. Apart from customs duties, other important source of revenue was the Mint of Rio de Janeiro.

During the last three decades of the eighteenth century, and despite the regrettable scarcity of fiscal sources, a relative stability of the total amounts collected seems to prevail (summarized by Table 5.1). During the last years of the 1790s, other important captaincies in terms of fiscal income were Minas Gerais (still the captaincy, where the Portuguese Crown gathered the highest revenues – more than 500 *Contos de réis*), Bahia (420 *Contos*) and Pernambuco (244 *Contos*). The total income collected by the Royal Treasury in Rio de Janeiro was around 450 *Contos de réis*.[56]

The data in Table 5.1 show clearly that the fiscal structures of Rio de Janeiro were firmly anchored in the taxes levied on foreign trade and its Mint. This changed completely in 1808.

To Portugal, the second half of the eighteenth century corresponds to a period of fiscal stability, and customs duties were by far the most important

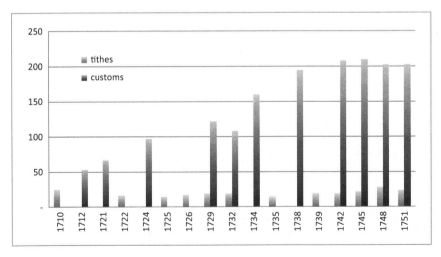

Figure 5.1 Total amount of tithes and customs duties in Rio de Janeiro, 1710–1751, in *Contos de réis*.

Source: Carrara (2009a: 50–53).

Table 5.1 Revenues of the captaincy of Rio de Janeiro in 1785, in *Contos de réis*

Items	Amount collected	%
Taxes collected by Customs House (inclusive of Coast Guard)	148.82	33.49
Mint	114.41	25.75
Duties on salt	38.45	8.66
Subsidies levied on wines, brandies and olive oil	31.22	7.03
Tithes	30.53	6.87
Other taxes	24.30	5.47
Whaling	19.20	4.32
Duties on export of slaves to the mining regions	13.34	3
Taxes on tobacco	12.98	2.92
Tolls levied on persons traveling to the mining regions	11.10	2.5
Grand total	*444.34*	*100*

Source: Arquivo Histórico do Tribunal de Contas de Lisboa, livro 4044, 1785.

source of fiscal resources.[57] This stability was suddenly broken by military pressure during the Napoleonic times. At the end of 1796, Portugal resorted to a loan for the first time – indeed, the first officially taken by this country – totaling 4.000 *Contos de réis* in bonds, at a 5 percent yearly interest rate.[58]

Fiscal impacts related to the transfer of the Portuguese Court to Brazil

The most important issue in the list of preoccupations of the metropolitan authorities regarding the transfer of the Portuguese Court to Brazil was obviously the financial cost of the undertaking, especially the expenditure for the Royal House and infrastructure works in the new capital, Rio de Janeiro. Between 1808 and 1820, the Royal House alone took around 20 percent of the total expenditures of Brazil.[59] Besides, the speed of these changes immediately provoked another effect: the incapacity to promptly face the payment of such costs.

When finally established in Brazil, the Portuguese Crown put into effect four measures to finance the state expenses (in chronological order):

1 the institution of the Royal Treasury in Brazil, origin of the late Brazil's Ministry of Finance; as a consequence of this measure, the shift of the net remittances of all captaincies (hitherto sent to Lisbon) to Rio de Janeiro, by far the most important expedient;
2 the establishment of new taxes;
3 the drainage of all gold dust available in Minas Gerais through its exchange for paper notes and silver and copper coins;
4 creation of the Bank of Brazil, a little later converted into the state's main lender.

The first measure converted Rio de Janeiro into the receiver of the fiscal surplus generated by all Brazilian captaincies – a role until then performed by Lisbon. Until 1818, more than half of all extraordinary resources available to the State corresponded to these provincial leftovers. This shift of the financial flows constitutes the more significant landmark of a new fiscal organization, and even the core of a debate around the fiscal constitution of the new state. This meant an important move to deal with new routines, due to the creation of a Royal Treasury (Erário Régio) in Brazil, by Royal Charter, on June 28, 1808. To every Brazilian province, the institution of a Royal Treasury in Rio de Janeiro solely implied the establishment in Brazil of an office responsible for the management of revenues and expenditure of the Portuguese overseas territories, separated from its equivalent installed in Lisbon in 1761. So, from the standpoint of the other provinces, it just changed the address of the recipient of their financial remainders. From 1808 onwards, what happens in Brazil is the reproduction of the model prevailing since 1761 in Portugal.

The second measure consisted in the creation of new taxes, without any significant change in the pre-existing fiscal base: it purely added another major set of taxes to the prior system.[60] Still in Salvador, Prince Regent D. João decreed the opening of Brazilian ports in 1808 to direct trade with all countries in peace with Portugal,[61] whose impact was immediately felt by the provincial treasuries: between 1810 and 1818 the revenues increased more than 50 percent. In 1817, German naturalist Spix observed that Rio de Janeiro was the "scale-deposit for all little ports along the Brazilian coast, from Bahia until Montevideo".[62] This role as a hub performed by the port of Rio de Janeiro explains the disproportion of fiscal revenues generated mainly by its Customs, in comparison with the other provinces.

Beside the new rates levied by Customs, between 1808 and 1810 the following taxes were created:

a) 1 percent over the market value of each urban real estate;[63]
b) 5 percent over the selling price of slaves born in Brazil;[64]
c) an inheritance tax of 10 or 20 percent depending on the degree of parenthood (decree of June 17, 1809);
d) a sealed paper tax (decrees of June 17, 1809 and November 10, 1810);
e) a 10 percent tax over the marketing of real estate (decree of June 30, 1809).

The third measure acted as a financial expedient: the exchange of gold dust for paper notes, as well as silver and copper coins.[65] The immediate consequence of that act could be observed in 1809: the royal fifths (*quintos reais*) increased by almost 20 percent in comparison with the previous year.[66] This sudden growth did not relate to an increase in production, but to the law's effectiveness. It explains why, in the following years, gold production resumed its downward trend. An example extracted from the Mint of São João del Rei helps to understand the limited effects of this measure (see Figure 5.2).

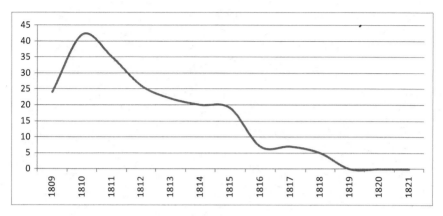

Figure 5.2 Gold dust exchanged for paper notes and silver/copper coins in São João del Rey Mint, 1809–1821, in *Contos de réis*.
Source: Coleção Casa dos Contos de Ouro Preto/Série permuta do ouro em pó de faisqueira and Carrara (2005: vol. 2, 83–87).

Finally, the loans taken from the Bank of Brazil were a powerful extraordinary fiscal resource to finance the State's various expenditures.[67] If, between 1810 and 1813, the issue of paper notes was offset by their redemption, from 1814 to 1821 the amount of paper money in circulation increased considerably, as seen in Figure 5.3.

In Brazil, the total spending of the Royal Household between 1810 and 1818 grew, whilst military and naval expenditures remained stable. The extraordinary expenditure, however – the most relevant item in this

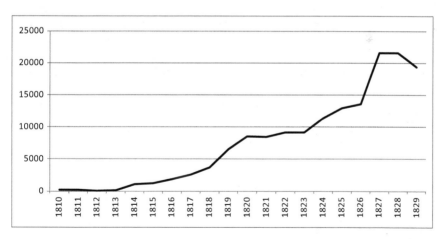

Figure 5.3 Paper money issued by the Bank of Brazil, 1809–1829, in *Contos de réis*.
Sources: (a) from 1810 to 1828: Franco (1983: 17–18); (b) for 1829: Cavalcanti (1893: 34–35).

account – was indeed just a zero-sum simple operation: the re-coinage of provincial currencies and purchase of Spanish pesos and copper bars. Between 1816 and 1818, the Treasury bought 5,219 *Contos de réis* in Spanish silver pesos and its shipment to the Mint of Rio de Janeiro; however, an extraordinary income corresponding to 5,523 *Contos de réis* in the same period as a result of such an operation. On the income side, despite the undeniable growth of the role performed by the Customs of Rio de Janeiro after the opening the ports to friendly nations, the most important item was the transfer of surplus resources from all provinces to the Royal Treasury.[68] During the Napoleonic Wars, taxes and other revenues collected by the Public Treasury of Rio de Janeiro grew rapidly, and the political disturbances in 1820–1821 caused only a sudden, but equally brief, impact on this trend, as seen in Figure 5.4.

To sum up, the period that opened with the arrival of the Portuguese Court in Brazil is characterized by the consolidation of the central role performed by Rio de Janeiro, which in the middle of the eighteenth century replaced Salvador (in Bahia) and Recife (at the Brazil's northeast), as the colony's most important economic region during the sixteenth and seventeenth centuries.[69] More than that, it changed the geography of powers responsible for decision making all over the Portuguese empire. The main impact occurred through intra-imperial financial flows: the revenues of the ancient captaincy of Rio de Janeiro, which in 1807 were about 825 *Contos de réis*, grew to more than 2,000 *Contos de réis* in 1808, and are what clarifies its strengthened role as the main Brazil's commercial and fiscal reference from 1808 onwards.[70]

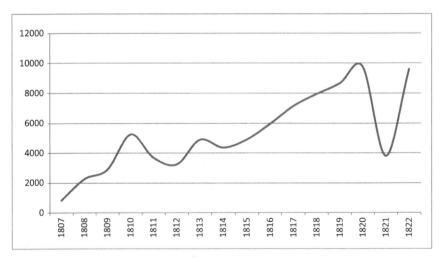

Figure 5.4 Total revenues of Brazil, 1807–1822, in *Contos de réis*.
Source: Freycinet (1827: vol. 1, part 1, 297–313).

Conclusions

Considering the traditional explanation of a standard level of economic development brought by the first generations of economic historians in Brazil, the text presented here largely distances itself from the usual narrative of the events found within the Brazilian historiography on the subjects addressed here. The progress of economic anthropology in the last two decades – in particular, the work of Karl Polanyi – and the micro-history can be invoked to explain the most commonly adopted perspectives. Simultaneously, the Spanish-American economic history, to which this study is affiliated, experienced a remarkable growth, in which a key element is the tax perspective. In the recent years, however, the interest in fiscal history has gained a greater number of researchers, which augurs a promising field for the Economic History produced in Brazil.[71]

The good news is that Brazil's own historiography, after all, in itself, has been able to gradually see the multiple benefits of both a more general and paradigmatic approach,[72] as much as a "ginzburgian" methodology. That is, the various monographic studies, under a local standpoint, which have been recently developed across the country, have been fundamental in helping to compose a new big picture and, at the same time, confirming or challenging a number of concepts, sources, statistical data and methodologies. These have been taking place largely because of two very constructive situations: the first, as discussed earlier, the openness and receptivity of that historiographic school; and the second, the resumption of a highly positive debate for the Brazilian – and international – historiography, about a supposed "death"[73] of Economic/Quantitative History during the 1990s. Such phenomena, according to some scholars,[74] suffered some setbacks when it came to international historiography and its influences in Brazil, but it must be observed and analyzed, according to each specific context. These days, regarding the Brazilian case, it goes steady and strong in its intention to help review and rethink some situations, when it comes to production of an increasingly dynamic Economic History, and with a broader horizon.

Notes

1 Novais and Arruda (2003: 225–226).
2 Varnhagen (1956).
3 Reis (1999: 23–24).
4 Reis (1999: 25–33).
5 Reis (1999: 89).
6 Mantega (1989: 29).
7 Carone (1971: 25).
8 See Junior (1942, 1945).
9 Reis (1999: 178–179).
10 Mantega (1989: 34–35).
11 See Furtado (1972).
12 Carrara (2009a: 10–11).

13 Captaincy: a single political/economical/administrative division of a viceroyalty in Spanish or Portuguese colonial administration; hereafter, we are following the translation given by Leslie Bethell, The Cambridge History of Latin America, 1985, Vol. 3, p. 165, 171, etc.
14 Cardoso in Linhares (2000: 107–109); Alencastro in Bethencourt and Curto (2010: 120–121).
15 Gouvêa in Vainfas (2000: 18–19).
16 Carneiro (1818); Silva (1828–1844); Falcão (1859).
17 See Azevedo (1922); Macedo (1951); Godinho (1955).
18 See Lapa (1968, 1973).
19 Erbereli Júnior (2012: 1–11).
20 See Mota (1972); Pinto (1979); Novais (1979); Arruda (1980).
21 Lapa (1982: 155–156).
22 See Cardoso (1984, 1985).
23 Elias and Garcia (2012: 18–19); Silva (1992: 18–19).
24 See Falcon (1982).
25 Gonçalves and Gontijo (2011: 366–367).
26 Martins (2011: 211–212).
27 See Oliveira (1976).
28 Resende (1999: 75–76).
29 See Salgado (1985).
30 http://linux.an.gov.br/mapa/
31 See North (1990).
32 See Fragoso (1990, 1992).
33 See Sanches (1997); Carrara (1997).
34 See Figueiredo (1996); Furtado (1999); Puntoni (1999); Guimarães (1997).
35 See Alencastro (2000).
36 Bicalho (2001: 271–273).
37 Mata and Valério in Garrido, Costa and Duarte (2012: 17–18).
38 See Cardoso and Lains (2010); Cardoso, Monteiro and Serrão (2010); Cardoso (2013: 87–104).
39 See Costa (2002); Costa, Sousa and Rocha (2013).
40 See Lopes (2008); Gil (2009); Menz (2009).
41 One of the research groups established in Minas Gerais is the Grupo de Pesquisa em História Econômica – História Quantitativa e Georreferenciada (Research Group of Economic History – Quantitative and Georeferenced History), at the Federal University of Juiz de Fora (UFJF): www.ufjf.br/hqg/
42 National Council for the scientific and technological development: http://cnpq.br. Other regional/state-level foundations also provide funding for science in Brazil, in each state, such as FAPEMIG (Minas Gerais' Foundation for scientific research supporting), FAPESP (São Paulo's Foundation for scientific research supporting), as well as other private foundations.
43 See Carrara (2009a, 2009b, 2010); Carrara and Sánchez Santiró (2012).
44 See Araújo (2002); Ferreira (2011); Costa (2013); Lenk (2013); Pereira (2014).
45 See Souza (2006).
46 Macedo (1990: 38–39).
47 Lima (2009: 136–137).
48 Martins (2007: 119–120).
49 Falcão (1859: 19–45); Oliveira (1804: 329–355).
50 In his words: "gold remittances from Brazil, which had been for some decades the most important financial resource in the empire and had become the major driving force

behind its integration into the Atlantic economy, began faltering. The decline, which could already be felt in 1760, became very serious after 1766". Pedreira (2000: 840).
51 See Macedo, Silva and Sousa in Bordo and Cortés-Conde (2001: 187–228). For the gold production, see Costa, Sousa and Rocha (2013).
52 Alden in Bethel (1987: 312).
53 Carrara (2009a: 9).
54 Balbi (1822: vol. I, 302).
55 Carrara (2009: 49, note 1).
56 Alden (1968: 317–323). Regarding the absence of fiscal documents, especially balance sheets of income and expenditure, Alden regretted also not having found "not a single specimen of these balances". In 1795, the total amounts grew from 445 *Contos de réis* (expenditure) to 479 *Contos de réis* (income). See Arquivo Histórico do Tribunal de Contas de Lisboa/Cartórios Avulsos, caixa 77, "Mapas demonstrativos da receita e despesa que tiveram as capitanias do Rio de Janeiro, Bahia, Pernambuco, São Paulo, Maranhão, Pará, Minas Gerais. Goiás, Moçambique, Goa, Ilhas dos Açores, Ilha da Madeira".
57 See Mont Serrath (2013).
58 See Almeida (1989–1990); Bulhões (1867).
59 Simonsen (1969: 420–428; Balbi (1822: vol. 1, see appendix 3); this item equaled around 14.5 percent of the total revenues between 1762 and 1776. See Tomaz (1988: 380).
60 Costa in Chaves and Silveira (2007: 134).
61 Martins (2007: 117–118); Lima (2009: 135–137).
62 Spix (1981: 70, 78).
63 See Carrara (2001).
64 See Araújo (1820: vol. 1, 156–158).
65 For a detailed description of this documental series see Carrara (2005: vol. 2).
66 Eschwege (1922: 398).
67 The archival sources available about the first Bank of Brazil, created in 1808 and extinct in 1829 are "scarce and disperse". Cardoso (2010: 168). See also Franco (1983); Cavalcanti (1893); Franco (1948); Gambi (2010: 33–70).
68 Freycinet (1827: vol. 1, part 1, 297–313).
69 Alencastro (2000: 248–251); Martins (2007: 9–14).
70 Freycinet (1827: vol. 1, part 1, 297–300); BRASIL, Annaes do Parlamento Brazileiro, 24 de julho de 1828.
71 See Miranda (2009).
72 See Costa (1995).
73 Fragoso and Florentino in Cardoso and Vainfas (1997: 27–43).
74 See Motta (2009); Faleiros (2010).

References

Primary sources

Arquivo Histórico do Tribunal de Contas de Portugal. Erário Régio, Livros da receita e despesa do Tesoureiro-Mor do Erário Régio pelos rendimentos correntes, 1762-1833, livros 1–142.

Arquivo Histórico do Tribunal de Contas de Portugal. Cartórios Avulsos, caixa 77. "Mapas demonstrativos da receita e despesa que tiveram as capitanias do Rio de Janeiro, Bahia, Pernambuco, São Paulo, Maranhão, Pará, Minas Gerais. Goiás, Moçambique, Goa, Ilhas dos Açores, Ilha da Madeira".

Biblioteca Nacional do Rio de Janeiro/Divisão de Manuscritos. "Mapas da receita e despesa do Real Erário"; 1808 [II-30,27,028], 1816 [II-30,27,029], 1817 [II-30,27,030] and 1818 [II-30,27,031].
Coleção Casa dos Contos de Ouro Preto. Série permuta do ouro em pó de faisqueira:
Intendência da Vila do Príncipe
1810 Senhora do Porto 0608 044 0050
1810 Sucuriú 0609 044 0057
1810 Gouveia 0610 044 0063
1810 São Domingos 0611 044 0070
1810 Araçuaí 0614 044 0083
1810 Minas Novas 0617 044 0107
1810 Tijuco 0620 044 0125
1810 Tapera 0521 043 0320
1810 Conceição do Mato Dentro 0524 043 0344
1810 Gambá 0525 043 0352
1810 Arraial de Baixo 2949 164 0564
1810 Paraúna 0583 043 0874
1810 Santo Antônio Abaixo 0590 043 0926
1812 Rio Manso 0849 058 0521
1812 Rio do Peixe 0850 058 0526
1812 Paraúna 0851 058 0532
1812 Arraial de Baixo 0913 059 1074
1816 Tijuco 2795 158 0344
Intendência de Vila Rica
1809 Itabira do Campo 2603 147 0689
1809 Itabira do Campo 2604 147 0694

Secondary sources

Araújo, J. de S. A. P. e. (1820). *Memórias históricas do Rio de Janeiro*, 8 vols. Rio de Janeiro: Impressão Régia.
Balbi, A. (1822). *Essai statistique du Royaume de Portugal et d'Algarve, comparé aux autres états de l'Europe*, 2 vols. Paris: Chez Rey et Gravier libraries.
BRASIL. Annaes do Parlamento Brazileiro. Camara dos Srs. Deputados, 1826–1888. Rio de Janeiro: Tipografia Parlamentar, 1877, v. 3, 178–191 (sessão de 24 de julho de 1828) [Brazilian Parliament proceedings' records. Brazilian House of Representatives, 1826–1888].
Bulhões, M. E. L. de (1867). *A dívida portuguesa*. Lisbon: Tip. Portuguesa.
Carneiro, M. B. (1818). *Resumo chronologico das lei mais uteis no foro e uso da vida civil publicadas até o presente anno*. Lisbon: National Press, vol. 1.
Eschwege, W. V. (1922). *Pluto brasiliensis*. Belo Horizonte: Imprensa Oficial.
Falcão, L. de F. (org.) (1859). *Livro em que se contém toda a fazenda e Real patrimônio dos reinos de Portugal, India e Ilhas adjacentes*. Lisbon: National Press.
Freycinet, L. de. (1827). *Voyage autour du monde*, 9 vols. Paris: P. Aîné.
Oliveira, Fr. N. de (1804). *Livro das grandezas de Lisboa*. Lisbon: Royal Printing.
Silva, A. D. da (org.) (1828–1844). *Collecção da Legislação Portugueza desde a última compilação*. Lisbon: Typografia Maigrense.

Studies

Alden, D. (1968). *Royal government in colonial Brazil.* Berkeley, CA: University of California Press.

Alencastro, L. F. de (2000). *O Trato dos Viventes: formação do Brasil no Atlântico Sul, séculos XVI e XVII.* São Paulo: Companhia das Letras.

Almeida, M. S. de (1989–1990). Apólices do Real Erário mandadas emitir por D. João, príncipe regente; o problema das apólices falsas, *Nummus*, 2nd series, 12/13, Porto, 93–108.

Araújo, L. A. S. (2002). Contratos e tributos nas Minas Setecentistas: o estudo de um caso – João de Souza Lisboa (1745–1765). MA thesis. Niterói: Institute of Human Sciences and Philosophy (ICHF)–Federal Fluminense University.

Arruda, J. J. de A. (1980). *O Brasil no comércio colonial.* São Paulo: Ática.

Azevedo, J. L. de. (1922). *O Marquez de Pombal e a sua época.* Porto: Renascença Portuguesa.

Bethel, L. (1987). *Colonial Brazil.* Cambridge: Cambridge University Press.

Bethencourt, F., & Curto, D. R. (dir.). (2010). *A Expansão Marítima Portuguesa (1400–1800).* Lisbon: Ed. 70.

Bicalho, M. F. B. (2001). Monumenta Brasiliae: O Império Português no Atlântico Sul, in *Revista Tempo*, 6(11), Rio de Janeiro, UFF, 267–273.

Bordo, M. D., & Cortés-Conde, R. (2001). *Transferring wealth and power from the Old to the New World: Monetary and Fiscal Institutions in the 17th Through the 19th Centuries.* Cambridge: Cambridge University Press.

Cardoso, C. F. S. (1984). *Economia e sociedade em áreas coloniais periféricas: Guiana francesa e Pará (1750–1817).* Rio de Janeiro: Graal.

Cardoso, C. F. S. (1985). *O trabalho na América Latina colonial.* São Paulo: Ática.

Cardoso, C. F., & Vainfas, R. (orgs.) (1997). *Os domínios da História.* Rio de Janeiro: Campus.

Cardoso, J. L. (2010). Novos elementos para a história do Banco do Brasil (1808–1829): crónica de um fracasso anunciado, *Revista Brasileira de História*, 30(59), São Paulo, 167–192.

Cardoso, J. L. (2013). Lifting the continental blockade: Britain, Portugal and Brazilian trade in the global context of the Napoleonic Wars, in L. Coppolaro & F. McKenzie (eds.), *A global history of trade and conflict since 1500.* Basingstoke: Palgrave Macmillan, 87–104.

Cardoso, J. L., & Lains, P. (eds.) (2010). *Paying for the liberal state: the rise of public finance in nineteenth-century Europe.* New York: Cambridge University Press.

Cardoso, J. L., Monteiro, N. G., & Serrão, J. V. (eds.) (2010). *Portugal, Brasil e a Europa Napoleónica.* Lisbon: Imprensa de Ciências Sociais.

Carone, E. (1971). Roberto C. Simonsen e sua Obra, *Revista de Administração de Empresas*, 11(4), Rio de Janeiro, FGV, 23–28.

Carrara, A. A. (1997). Agricultura e Pecuária na Capitania de Minas Gerais (1674-1807). Ph.D. Thesis. Rio de Janeiro: IFCS/UFRJ.

Carrara, A. A. (2001). Espaços urbanos de uma sociedade rural: Minas Gerais, 1808–1835, in *Varia História*, 25, Belo Horizonte, FAFICH-UFMG, 144–164.

Carrara, A. A. (2005). *A Real Fazenda de Minas Gerais: guia de pesquisa da Coleção Casa dos Contos de Ouro Preto*, 3 vols. Ouro Preto: Editora da Universidade Federal de Ouro Preto.

Carrara, A. A. (2009a). *Receitas e despesas da Real Fazenda no Brasil; Minas Gerais, Bahia e Pernambuco, século XVIII*. Juiz de Fora: UFJF University Press.

Carrara, A. A. (2009b). *Receitas e despesas da Real Fazenda no Brasil, século XVII*. Juiz de Fora: UFJF University Press.

Carrara, A. A. (2010). *À vista ou a prazo: comércio e crédito nas Minas setecentistas*. Juiz de Fora: UFJF University Press.

Carrara, A. A., & Sánchez Santiró, E. (coords.) (2012). *Guerra e fiscalidade na Ibero-América colonial (séculos XVII–XIX)*. México-Juiz de Fora: UFJF University Press-Instituto Mora.

Cavalcanti, A. (1893). *O meio circulante nacional (1808–1835)*. Rio de Janeiro: Imprensa Nacional.

Costa, B. A. (2013). A vereda dos tratos: fiscalidade e poder regional na capitania de São Paulo, 1723–1808. Ph.D. thesis, São Paulo: Faculty of Philosophy, Arts and Human Sciences (FFLCH)/University of São Paulo.

Costa, I. d. da (1995). *Repensando o modelo interpretativo de Caio Prado Jr. (Cadernos NEHD, 3)*. São Paulo: Centre for studies of Demographic History – Faculty of Economics and Management (NEHD-FEA)/University of São Paulo.

Costa, L. F. (2002). *O Transporte no Atlântico e a Companhia Geral de Comércio do Brasil (1580–1663)*, 2 vols. Lisbon: CNCDP.

Costa, L. F., Sousa, R. M. de, & Rocha, M. M. (2013). *O ouro do Brasil*. Lisbon: Imprensa Nacional-Casa da Moeda.

Chaves, C. M. das G., & Silveira, M. A. (orgs.) (2007). *Território, conflito e identidade*. Belo Horizonte: Argumentum.

Elias, R., & Garcia, B. (2012). Contracorrente: an interview with Ciro Flamarion, in *Revista de História da Biblioteca Nacional*. Rio de Janeiro, 84 (September). Available at www.revistadehistoria.com.br/secao/entrevista/ciro-flamarion,

Erbereli Júnior, O. (2012). História Econômica no Brasil, c. 1951–1972: uma possibilidade de tratamento, in *Caderno de resumos& Anais do 6°. Seminário Brasileiro de História da Historiografia – O giro-linguístico e a historiografia: balanço e perspectivas*. Ouro Preto, EdUFOP, 1–25.

Falcon, F. J. C. (1982). *A Época Pombalina: Política Econômica e Monarquia Ilustrada*. São Paulo: Ática.

Faleiros, R. N. (2010). História Econômica, História em construção, in *Dimensões – Revista de História da UFES*. Vitória, PPG-HIS/UFES, 24, (Dossiê: Formas da História, Sentidos da Historiografia). Available at www.periodicos.ufes.br/dimensoes/article/view/2532/2028

Ferreira, D. (2011). Colonialismo e Fiscalidade na Capitania de Pernambuco (1770–1793). MA thesis, Recife: Centre of Philosophy and Human Sciences (CFCH-UFPE).

Figueiredo, L. R. de A. (1996). Revoltas, Fiscalidade e Identidade Colonial na América Portuguesa: Rio de Janeiro, Bahia e Minas Gerais (1640–1761). Ph.D. Thesis, São Paulo: Faculty of Philosophy, Arts and Human Sciences (FFLCH)/University of São Paulo.

Fragoso, J. (1990). Comerciantes, fazendeiros e formas de acumulação em uma economia escravista-exportadora no Rio de Janeiro: 1790–1888. Ph.D. thesis, Niterói: Federal Fluminense University.

Fragoso, J. (1992). *Homens de Grossa Aventura: Acumulação e Hierarquia Na Praça Mercantil do Rio de Janeiro (1790–1830)*. Rio de Janeiro: Arquivo Nacional.

Franco, A. A. de M. (1948). *História do Banco do Brasil.* São Paulo: Instituto de Economia da Associação Comercial.
Franco, B. de S. (1983). *Os bancos do Brasil.* 2nd ed., Brasília: Editora da UnB.
Furtado, C. (1972). *Formação Econômica do Brasil.* São Paulo: Companhia Editora Nacional.
Furtado, J. (1999). *Homens de negócio: a interiorização da metrópole e do comércio nas Minas setecentistas.* São Paulo: Ed. Hucitec.
Gambi, T. F. R. (2010). O banco da Ordem: política e finanças no império brasileiro (1853-1866). Ph.D. thesis, São Paulo, Faculty of Philosophy, Arts and Human Sciences(FFLCH)/University of São Paulo.
Garrido, A., Costa, L. F., & Duarte, L. M. (Orgs.). (2012). *Economia, Instituições e Império: estudos em homenagem a Joaquim Romero Magalhães.* Coimbra: Almedina.
Gil, T. L. (2009). Coisas do caminho: Tropeiros e seus negócios do Viamão à Sorocaba (1780–1810). Ph.D. thesis, Rio de Janeiro: Institute of Philosophy and Social Sciences (IFCS)/Federal University of Rio de Janeiro.
Godinho, V. M. (1955). *Prix et monnaies au Portugal, 1750–1850, avant-propos de Lucien Febvre.* Paris: Librarie Armand Colin.
Gonçalves, M. de A., & Gontijo, R. (2011). About history, historiography and historians: an interview with Francisco José Calazans Falcon, *Revista História da Historiografia*, 7 (November/December), 365–382. Ouro Preto. Available at www.historiadahistoriografia.com.br/revista/article/viewFile/319/224
Guimarães, C. G. (1997). Bancos, Economia e Poder no Segundo Reinado: O Caso da Sociedade Bancária Mauá, Macgregor & Companhia (1854–1866). PhD thesis, São Paulo, Faculty of Philosophy, Arts and Human Sciences (FFLCH)/University of São Paulo.
Junior, C. P. (1942). *Formação do Brasil Contemporâneo.* São Paulo: Livraria Martins Editora.
Junior, C. P. (1945). *História Econômica do Brasil.* São Paulo: Brasiliense.
Lapa, J. R. do A. (1968). *A Bahia e a Carreira da India.* São Paulo: Companhia Editora Nacional.
Lapa, J. R. do A. (1973). *Economia Colonial.* São Paulo: Editora Perspectiva.
Lapa, J. R. do A. (1982). Tendências atuais da Historiografia Brasileira, *Revista Brasileira de História*, São Paulo, 2(4), 153–172.
Lenk, W. (2013). *Guerra e pacto colonial: a Bahia contra o Brasil Holandês.* São Paulo: Alameda.
Lima, O. (2009). *D. João VI no Brasil.* Lisbon: ACD Editors.
Linhares, M. Y. (org.). (2000). *História Geral do Brasil*, 9th ed., Rio de Janeiro: Campus.
Lopes, G. A. (2008). *Negócio da Costa da Mina e Comércio Atlântico: Tabaco, Açúcar, Ouro e Tráfico de Escravos: Capitania de Pernambuco (1654–1760).* Ph.D. Thesis. São Paulo: Faculty of Philosophy, Arts and Human Sciences (FFLCH)/University of São Paulo.
Macedo, J. B. de. (1951). *A situação económica no tempo de Pombal: alguns aspectos.* Porto: Livraria Portugália.
Macedo, J. B. de. (1990). *O Bloqueio Continental: economia e guerra peninsular*, 2nd ed. Lisbon: Gradiva.
Mantega, G. (1989). Celso Furtado e o pensamento económico brasileiro, *Revista de Economia Política*, 9(4), São Paulo, 29–37.
Martins, A. C. D. (2007). *Governação e Arquivos: D. João VI no Brasil.* Lisbon: Torre do Tombo-Ministério da Cultura.

Martins, E. C. de R. (2011). Conhecimento histórico e historiografia brasileira contemporânea, *Revista Portuguesa de História*, 42, Coimbra, 197–219.

Menz, M. M. (2009). *Entre Impérios: formação do Rio Grande na crise do Sistema colonial português*. São Paulo: Alameda.

Miranda, M. E. (2009). *A estalagem e o Império: crise do Antigo Regime, fiscalidade e fronteira na província do Rio Grande de São Pedro (1808–1831)*. São Paulo: Hucitec.

Mont Serrath, P. O. (2013). O Império português no Atlântico: poderio, ajuste e exploração (1640–1808). Ph.D. thesis, São Paulo: Faculty of Philosophy, Arts and Human Sciences (FFLCH)/University of São Paulo.

Mota, C. G. (1972). *Nordeste 1817*. São Paulo: Editora Perspectiva.

Motta, J. F. (2009). Agonia ou Robustez? Reflexões acerca da historiografia econômica brasileira, *Anais da 25a RBA Saberes e práticas antropológicas desafios para o século XXI*, 1, 117–138. Available at http://brasilafrica.fflch.usp.br/sites/brasilafrica.fflch.usp.br/files/Motta%2C%20J%20F_Agonia%20ou%20Robustez..._Rev%20Econ%20PUC-SP%201%281%29_2009.pdf

North, D. C. (1990). *Institutions, institutional change and economic performance*. Cambridge: Cambridge University Press.

Novais, F. A. (1979). *Portugal e Brasil na Crise do Antigo Sistema Colonial*. São Paulo: Ed. Hucitec.

Novais, F. A., & Arruda, J. J. de A. (2003). Prometeus e Atlantes na forja da Nação, *Economia e Sociedade*, 12(2), Campinas, 225–243.

Oliveira, T. J. B. de. (1976). *Análise e organização do Erário Régio de Francisco Antônio Rebelo*. Brasília: ESAF.

Pedreira, J. M. (2000). From growth to collapse: Portugal, Brazil, and the breakdown of the Old Colonial System (1760–1830, *Hispanic American Historical Review*, 80(4), Durham, 839–864.

Pereira, A. M. (2014). Das Minas à Corte, de caixeiro a contratador: Jorge Pinto de Azeredo. Atividade mercantil e negócios na primeira metade do século XVIII. Ph.D. thesis, São Paulo: Faculty of Philosophy, Arts and Human Sciences(FFLCH)/ University of São Paulo.

Pinto, V. N. (1979). *O ouro brasileiro e o comércio anglo-português: uma contribuição aos estudos da economia atlântica*. São Paulo: Companhia Editora Nacional.

Puntoni, P. (1999). *A mísera sorte: a escravidão africana no Brasil holandês e as guerras do tráfico no Atlântico Sul, 1621–1648*. São Paulo: Ed. Hucitec.

Reis, J. C. (1999). *As Identidades do Brasil: de Varnhagen a FHC*, 2nd ed. Rio de Janeiro: FGV.

Resende, M. E. L. de (1999). A disputa pela história: traços inscritos na memorialística histórica mineira dos finais do setecentismo, *Revista Varia Historia*, Belo Horizonte, 20 (March), 60–77.

Salgado, Graça (coord.). (1985). *Fiscais e meirinhos: a administração no Brasil Colonial*. Rio de Janeiro: Ed. Nova Fronteira.

Sanches, M. G. (1997). Proveito e Negócio: regimes de propriedades e estrutura fundiária no Brasil: o caso do Rio de Janeiro entre os séculos XVIII e XIX. Ph.D. thesis, Rio de Janeiro: Institute of Philosophy and Social Sciences (IFCS)/Federal University of Rio de Janeiro.

Silva, M. B. N. da (1992). *Guia de História do Brasil Colonial*. Porto: Universidade Portucalense Infante D. Henrique.

Simonsen, R. C. (1969). *História econômica do Brasil*, 6th ed. São Paulo: Companhia Editora Nacional.

Souza, L. de M. e (2006). *O Sol e a Sombra: política e administração na América portuguesa do século XVIII*. São Paulo: Companhia das Letras.
Spix, J. B. V. (1981). *Viagem pelo Brasil: 1817–1820*. Belo Horizonte-São Paulo: Itatiaia-Editora da Universidade de São Paulo.
Tomaz, F. (1988). As finanças do Estado pombalino, 1762–1776, in *Estudos e Ensaios em homenagem a Vitorino Magalhães Godinho*. Lisbon: Sá da Costa, 355–388.
Vainfas, R. (dir.) (2000). *Dicionário do Brasil Colonial (1500–1808)*. Rio de Janeiro: Objetiva.
Varnhagen, F. A. de (1956). *História Geral do Brasil: antes de sua separação e Independência de Portugal*, 5 vols. Revisão e notas de Rodolfo Garcia. 5th ed. São Paulo: Melhoramentos.

6 Wartime trade and tariffs in Sweden from the Napoleonic Wars to World War I

Peter Hedberg and Henric Häggqvist

Introduction

Neutrality during periods of large-scale military (and political) conflicts has been a cornerstone of Swedish foreign policy since at least the 1780s.[1] A neutrality stance was in practice, in more or less full effect, since the end of the Napoleonic Wars.[2] Its origins were deeply connected to foreign trade, where neutrality was a tool to keep trade links open and to incite foreign merchants to direct shipping through safe Swedish ports. Since the Napoleonic Wars, Sweden's neutrality has mainly been based on security concerns, but foreign trade has always been an integral part of this policy stance. As the Swedish economy became increasingly reliant on foreign trade from the middle of the 19th century, safeguarding open and secure trade channels has been one of the main objectives of her foreign policy, and it has regularly gone hand in hand with a balancing strategy, ensuring a secure position between the major political powers of Europe.

In this chapter we examine the trade policy strategies and the development of Swedish foreign trade and shipping during three major armed conflicts: the Napoleonic Wars 1803–15, the Crimean War 1853–56, and World War I 1914–18. We assume that Sweden was able to take advantage of its neutral position during the three wars to increase her trade and shipping, but we also assume that trade policy was adjusted as a result of the circumstances of war and the encompassing neutrality. We will discuss short-term and long-term effects that the three wars may have had on Swedish trade and trade policy.

The chapter is organized as follows. In the following section Sweden's position during the wars is outlined and its neutrality policy is presented in more detail. Then we investigate the development of the shipping business and foreign trade by presenting a few key indicators. After that, we discuss changes made to trade policy by looking at the movement of tariffs and customs revenue before, during and after the three wars. We then conclude the chapter by assessing the impact on war on Swedish foreign trade and trade policy between 1800 and 1920.

Background: Sweden's position during the wars

This chapter covers a long and dynamic period of time, and the wars that are in our scope differ from one another as regards causes, impact, length, etc., and in certain important aspects they do not fully compare with one another. However, as regards the Scandinavian history of trade and foreign policy, the period as a whole has some important features in common.

The Napoleonic Wars

Some of the recurring features that lasted throughout the period were established during the Napoleonic Wars, when the power struggle between France and Britain resulted in naval and economic warfare that caused major implications for the development of European politics, economy – and trade.[3] This not only shifted the center of power to Great Britain and led to more than a century-long period of Pax Britannica, but also resulted in changes for the smaller states, such as Sweden. The Scandinavian nation attempted for the longest time to remain neutral between the two major blocks in the war and argued, together with Denmark, the rights of the Convention of Armed Neutrality from 1780, which stated that "free ships make free goods, and that provisions and ordinary naval stores could not be treated as contraband of war".[4] Safeguarding foreign trade was an integral part or even main feature of Sweden's foreign policy of the time. Merchants were a group who made a staunch stand against entry into the war, since they desired open trade links "in all directions", which could only be kept through uninterrupted neutrality.[5] Several works on Swedish trade history have emphasized the neutrality policy as a key explanation of its expansion. As a non-belligerent nation, Sweden could provide both neutral tonnage and neutral ports for international trade, which was otherwise blocked or ravaged by naval warfare.[6]

There is evidence which suggests that there was awareness among leading politicians and bureaucrats that the war would mean distinct advantages for Swedish shipping and foreign trade. In 1801, the National Board of Trade pointed out to the Swedish government that the competition between the European merchant fleets was "severely limited" in times of war, and that this was to be seen as a "preparedness point of view".[7] There was also a belief during the time that the country's merchant fleet, the fifth largest in Europe at the outbreak of the war, had expanded because ship-owners anticipated an increased demand for freight on Swedish vessels when the other great shipping nations were at war.[8] Sweden could not avoid being dragged into war,, however and fought against Russia from 1808 to 1809, which forced Sweden to give up Finland. Sweden was also forced by France to enter the Continental System against Britain, but according to Eli Heckscher this turn was a "mere confession of the lips" and in actual fact existed merely on paper.[9] Sweden eventually joined Britain in the anti-Napoleonic coalition toward the end of the war, effectively ending the previous neutral stance. Hence, Swedish neutrality can be said to have been conditional and practical during the Napoleonic Wars and heavily dependent on the actions and wills of the major political and military powers.

The Crimean War

Similarly, the preconditions for trade growth were good during the Crimean War and in some respect World War I (hereafter WWI) as well. Even though the Swedish king Oscar I plotted to draw Sweden into the Crimean War, in order to restore a new Great Swedish Empire by reconquering Finland (which was lost in 1809) from Russia, Sweden never entered the war.[10] This war distinguished itself by not being a "total war", as were the Napoleonic Wars and WWI. While international trade channels were largely destroyed during the Napoleonic Wars and WWI,[11] the Crimean War in some ways gave momentum to European industrialization:[12] armaments increased the demand for staple commodities, transportation developed as shipbuilding technology advanced, building of canals and railways increased, and the expanding financial market's ability to supply this process with capital increased, etc. Paradoxically nationalism and increasing needs to finance the state activities and the expanding public sector became a characteristic along with economic liberalism.[13] Thus, unlike the Napoleonic Wars and WWI, the Crimean War was not accompanied with economic de-globalization on the same scale or in the same sense.

In the literature it is stressed that the methods of economic warfare were different from other wars. For instance, according to Barbieri and Levy, neither systematic blockades, like during the Napoleonic Wars, nor rigid "trading with the enemy-acts", nor extensive contraband lists, were practiced during the Crimean war. Nonetheless, the warring sides soon developed strategies to deprive the enemy of resources. Instead temporary blockades and contraband captures became customary.[14] The rationale, accordingly, was to sustain British (and her allies') trade and at the same time acquire flexible tools to weaken Russia, which depended on trade for British growth and strength. The Royal Navy, which ruled the high seas and the allied French naval forces, proved far stronger than the Russian side.[15]

Another difference from the Napoleonic Wars was that during the Crimean War the major naval battles were mainly concentrated around the Black Sea and the Mediterranean Sea. But the impact of the naval activities in the Baltic Sea had great importance in depriving Russia from vital commercial exchange. This meant that Sweden as well as the Baltic countries and the trade routes in the Sound, in the Baltic Sea and in Skagerrak, were affected by the war events. Soon the superior British and French naval forces coerced the obsolete Russian Baltic Fleet to operate close to and with support from its coastal fortifications. While the first chose a careful strategy and blocked the Baltic transoceanic and coastal trade routes, and raided the Finnish coast, the latter was boxed in. In January 1856, when the Baltic Fleet surrendered, the

Russian economy was in ruin while her industries were left undeveloped.[16] Thus, for some years Sweden escaped competition from the Russians, which had had a strong position in the Baltic Sea. This partially explains why trade as well as shipping business expanded (see below) and, as a neutral country in the conflict, Sweden was (formally) safe from hostilities.[17]

World War I

World War I, the Great War, was fought on a different scale, and the costs, depth and length of the impact were greater than the Crimean War. Aside from the tragic loss of life, the costs of ruined material resources were enormous.[18] By the time the war started, the rights and obligations of neutral countries were more clearly defined than before, as set out by the Hague convention of 1907. There, for instance, it was stipulated that belligerents could not violate neutral territories and use them for acts of war or military operations, while neutral countries were also obligated to stand their neutral ground.[19] Sweden took a neutral stand again but this time the declaration (the definition) of neutrality was more specific. Neutrality was, for instance, instantly declared for the entire remainder of the conflict, regardless of how events would unfold. One of the main reasons for this was that the role of trade for the armament capacity had come to the fore, and the warring countries – Great Britain in particular – claimed that Sweden breached this declaration and that Swedish trade was conducted in avour of the Central Powers. In order to obtain trust and give credibility to her policy (and ensure that her trade was left undisturbed), Sweden was obligated to conduct her trade with the warring countries equally. Because of the increasing shortages of goods, in combination with the increasingly strict Allied blockade that was practiced as the war progressed (with the added negative impact of offensive German submarine warfare in 1917), Swedish trade conditions were seriously worsened.[20] As a result Sweden came out differently than during the Crimean War. The conditions also had a clear impact on domestic politics, as the sitting government led by a coalition of right-wing parties lost big in the parliamentary elections of 1917 –which was mainly blamed on the government's trade policy and close alignment with Germany.[21]

Shipping

As mentioned above, Sweden's shipping capacity increased during the French Revolutionary and the Napoleonic Wars. However, Swedish shipping activities increased during the Crimean War as well (Figure 6.1). During both the Napoleonic Wars and the Crimean War, cargo capacity increased by around 20 percent, while the number of vessels increased by 20 percent during the first war period. Considering the remarkable size and capacity of the merchant fleet before the Napoleonic Wars, this increase was notable. During the Crimean War and WWI, the number of vessels decreased; however, ships were built larger and had larger capacity during these periods. Thus, during

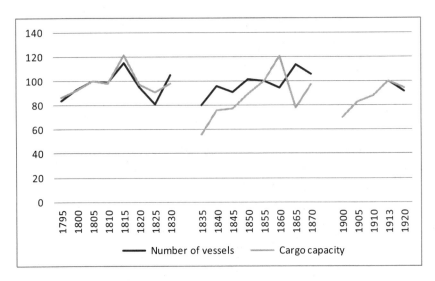

Figure 6.1 Indices of Swedish shipping capacity during the Napoleonic Wars (1805 =100), Crimean War (1855 = 100), and WWI (1913 = 100). Black graph represents number of vessels; grey graph represents cargo capacity (space).

Sources: Napoleonic: Underdåniga berättelser om Sveriges utrikes handel och sjöfart 1819–1857; Crimean: BiSOS F; WWI: SCB, Statistisk Årsbok, the merchant marine (1911–1938).

the first two periods, the war triggered a significant expansion of the Swedish shipping business. The capacity increase during the Napoleonic Wars was more short-lived, though, as both the number of vessels and cargo capacity decreased markedly soon after the end of the war up until the end of the 1820s.

During WWI, however, the shipping business declined. The reason for this was the efficiency of naval and economic warfare. Again, blockades became customary and even though the Royal Navy ruled the seas the improved capacity of, for instance, modern artillery forced the British to concentrate operations on safe seas instead of close to the ports. In addition, and perhaps more important, submarine warfare made counter-blockades far more efficient, whereas the blockade policies eventually (from 1917 onwards) prescribed targeting neutral merchants' vessels destined to enemy ports or carrying enemy goods. As a result, neutral shipping was more vulnerable to hostilities than before. Partly, this intention of the warring parties sought to hinder neutral shipping to support the enemy side. For instance, in 1917 about one-quarter of the ships sunk by the German submarines were neutral.[22] For this reason, this year marked the beginning of the war period called "the blockade years".[23] Yet another difference was that, during WWI, the control of trade was centralized to governments, in order to arrange and allocate trade and armaments. This meant that government intervention became far more extensive and coordinated than before.[24]

The development of foreign trade

Swedish foreign trade during the three wars roughly followed the development of shipping (Figure 6.2). The most dramatic changes during the Napoleonic Wars coincided with the Continental System and the systematic blockades between Britain and France. From 1807 to 1813 imports more than doubled, while domestic exports decreased by a little more than half. It should be noted that re-exports soared during the years when imports increased, particularly "colonial goods" such as coffee, sugar, tobacco, wine, but also textiles such as cotton.[25] The surprisingly large increase of imports is derived from large-scale purchases from Britain, which re-routed a lot of her colonial trade destined for continental Europe through the port of Gothenburg.[26] On the contrary, between 1801 and 1812, exports, particularly iron, decreased by about 70 percent. This decline coincided with Swedish partial participation in the war on the British side. The boom in imports may perhaps be interpreted as if Sweden took the place of the warring powers, which lost shares in the world trade during the period. When the war ended and trade was resumed, the country lost these shares. Thus, viewed in this rather short perspective, the expansion of Swedish imports and re-exports was related to the development of the war and the blockade in a major way. This mirrored the experience of the neutral American Republic during the same time.[27] In terms of bilateral flows during the war, Sweden's trade with France (and Holland) crashed, while the exchange with Britain and USA increased substantially, even though there were quite

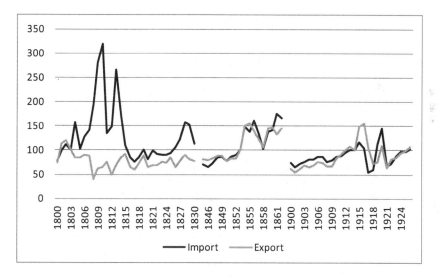

Figure 6.2 Swedish foreign trade during the Napoleonic Wars (1803 = 100), the Crimean War (1853 = 100) and WWI (1914 = 100). Black graph represents import; grey graph represents export.

Sources: Napoleonic: Häggqvist (2015); Crimea and WWI: BiSOS F, SOS.

heavy year-to-year fluctuations. This speaks even more of the impact of the blockades connected to the war.

During the following wars, both exports and imports increased, though at different rates, and during the Crimean War the trade increase lasted a bit longer. During this war, trade increased *pari passu* with a general growth cycle, while during WWI world trade was seriously disrupted. After the Crimean War, trade first declined, but as the industrialization process continued the commercial exchange increased again. The Swedish shipping companies were incited by the increasing demand from the armament industries abroad, which was already noticeable by 1853. As the competition from Russian iron, and products from her forestry as well as from the agricultural sector vanished after 1854, Swedish export industries expanded their activities. During the Crimean War both exports and imports increased (Figure 6.2), starting in 1851, though the increase was faster after 1852. Between 1853 and 1856 the exports and imports were doubled. Similar to developments during and after the Napoleonic Wars, wartime trade expansion during the Crimean War was followed by a short decline. Between 1856 and 1858, the import and the export dropped by about 50 percent. However, trade flows never fell below prewar levels, and when the war had ended, and the commercial exchange was resumed and normalized, trade flows began to grow again. Between 1858 and 1859, both exports and imports increased by about 40 percent. Re-exports, mainly of colonial goods such as coffee, sugar and tobacco, but also cotton and dyestuff, increased significantly compared to peacetime levels, but the upward trend was not as dramatic as during the Napoleonic Wars. Trade with France decreased notably once again during war years, but reached prewar levels once peace was restored. Trade with Spain also went down by about half from 1853 to 1857 compared to the decade preceding the war. As expected, trade with Finland and Russia decreased significantly, although it must be said that trade with the latter was quite small anyway and fluctuated heavily from year to year. Trade with neutrals such as Denmark and Holland increased shortly. Great Britain had become Sweden's single most important trade partner during the 1840s, and the Crimean War only strengthened that trend.

During WWI both exports and imports increased as well, but the growth trend was shorter. After the outbreak of the war, between 1914 and 1916 total trade increased by about 50 per cent.[28] The rapid decline during the ensuing years coincided with the escalated submarine warfare during the blockade years, from 1917 and the decline of the shipping business. It is worth noting that during WWI trade didn't drop as dramatically as during the Napoleonic Wars – especially as regards domestic exports. While both imports from and exports of particular goods, mainly of iron ore and forestry goods, to Germany continued bilateral trade worsened with Great Britain as a result of Swedish trade policy efforts.[29] Trade with France naturally also decreased significantly, particularly during the first half of the war. Bilateral trade with France and

Britain picked up again once peace was restored, while exports to Germany continued to decrease for a few years after 1918.[30]

For comparison, Swedish trade growth is related to British export (Sweden's export/Great Britain's export) in Figure 6.3.[31] Sweden gained trade shares from the "world market" during the Crimean War and WWI but not during the Napoleonic Wars (when domestic exports plummeted). Between 1853 and 1855, the increase exceeded more than 75 per cent but during WWI relative exports increased by close to 2.5 times. The increase during WWI didn't last, however, and the expansion was as temporary as was absolute trade growth. The market shares gained during the Crimean War, however, seem to have had more lasting positive impact on Swedish exports.[32] According to Hedberg and Karlsson, the Crimean War caused an annual increase of no less than 12.3 percent of the Swedish export volume (and annual growth of 22 percent of the import volume) over the whole war period. The trade growth, in combination with rapidly increasing terms of trade from the war-induced price shifts, gave momentum to Swedish GDP growth of around 1 percent per annum during the war. After hostilities had ceased trade and the terms of trade declined and the effects diminished, viewed over a longer period of time, during the immediate postwar period (1856–1869), the Swedish export increase during the war still contributed to around .2 percent of the annual GDP growth, which should be regarded as a sizeable contribution. The positive effect of the Crimean War on growth thus continued for at least 14 years after the war had ended.[33]

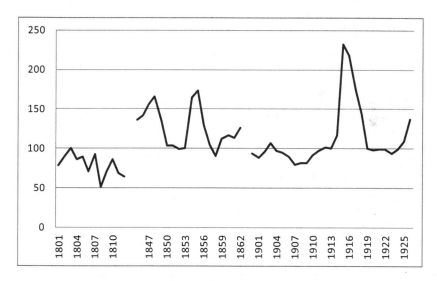

Figure 6.3 Swedish export relative to UK export during the Napoleonic Wars (1803 = 100), the Crimean War (1853 = 100), and WWI (1913 = 100).

Sources: Swedish exports: see Figure 6.2; UK exports: see Mitchell (1975).

Tariffs and trade policy

Eli Heckscher regarded that trade growth during the Napoleonic Wars was "obviously a course without any precedent in the past".[34] Considering that Swedish trade increased during all three wars in focus here, albeit in different ways, a relevant question is to ask whether trade increases were accompanied by domestic trade policy changes. We define trade policy by measuring tariff levels during the three war periods. We have calculated ad valorem tariffs by dividing the specific tariffs by the market price of the corresponding good, yielding each tariff as percent. As far as possible we have tried to use foreign (mainly British and German, but also Danish) prices to estimate the ad valorem tariffs, but we have occasionally been forced to use domestic prices. This is especially the case with the last period, even though we argue that it is less problematic there, since the prices used from the official Swedish foreign trade statistics closely followed international market prices.[35]

The tariffs have been selected on the basis that they targeted the most important commodities. This naturally yields a somewhat different selection and inclusion of goods over time. Machinery and a broader (and different) range of chemical goods and textiles/fabrics are, for instance, included in the two latter periods, compared to that for the Napoleonic Wars. We present both the average tariffs as well as tariff levels by a number of important commodity groups in order to gauge a possible change in tariff structure. All average tariffs are unweighted so as not to underestimate protected goods which might have had low or zero import levels.[36]

The Napoleonic Wars

The average import tariff (see Figure 6.4) decreased somewhat during the Napoleonic Wars, a result mainly of increasing import prices while specific tariffs were only partially changed during the war years. The Navigation Act, which had set different tariffs for domestic and foreign shipping, was suspended between 1807 and 1814, which brought down specific tariffs slightly, but it was most notable with the tariff on raw cotton. In the text accompanying the law lifting the Navigation Act, it was stressed that the circumstances of the warfare, making many foreign ports besieged by "hostile troops", had hindered Swedish shipping to those waters declared hostile, and hence the action of removing the toll differentiation was deemed necessary.[37] Decreasing import tariffs hence coincided with increasing import levels (and as a result increasing re-exports) during the Napoleonic Wars. When the war was over, tariffs were increased again, across most commodity categories (see Figure 6.5). This was especially so with tariffs that had decreased during the war, such as those on iron and metals, alcohol, and certain colonial imports, such as raw sugar and coffee. This is in line with Arthur Montgomery's view that the period of the Napoleonic Wars was more "liberal", while the prevailing system of mercantilism and protectionism was reinstated once the war was over.[38] The war hence had a brief downward impact on tariff rates, while it did not shake the protectionist base of Swedish tariff policy. Rather, the impact up until 1830 seems to

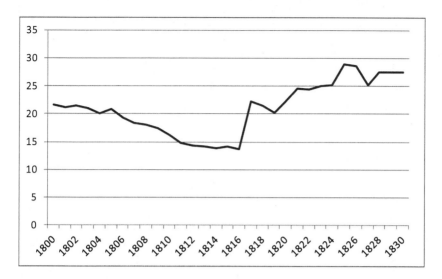

Figure 6.4 Average ad valorem import tariff 1800–1830.
Source: Häggqvist (2015: figure 5.4, p. 104).

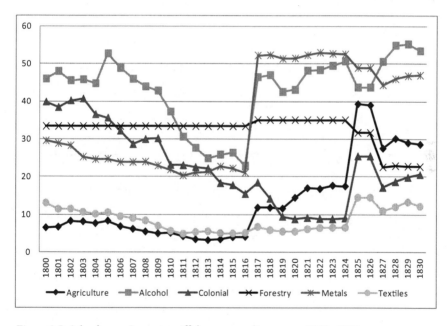

Figure 6.5 Ad valorem Import tariffs by commodity-group 1800–1830.
Source: Häggqvist (2015, figure 5.5, p. 105).

have been to drive tariff rates upwards. This is notable with agricultural tariffs, which increased markedly after 1816. This was a sector which had not benefited from the disruption of trade during the war, and so agricultural interests came to argue for increased protection from foreign competition after 1816.[39] High tariffs were in general maintained on iron and forestry (even though the latter were slightly relieved after 1826), the main export sectors during the period. Protectionism also extended to such sectors as beer, processed textiles and coal. Inflationary pressure was responsible for bringing down the level of the ad valorem tariffs, since these were not adjusted to compensate for increasing prices.[40] This is largely notable with the colonial products such as coffee, tea, sugar, and tobacco, whose prices increased tremendously during the war.

Export tariffs were generally quite high during this period of time, particularly on forestry goods such as battens and timber. They were also put on bar iron and as such brought in significant customs revenue. The fiscal argument was the main reason as to why the export tariff on bar iron remained until the 1850s. The suspension of the Navigation Act in 1807, when the difference in tariffs between Swedish and foreign ships was removed, brought down the average export tariff (see Figure 6.6). The decrease following from this became apparent as regards important export commodities such as bar iron and copper. However, the change was most substantial for products such as battens and timber, which in effect cut the tariff in half. From the view of Swedish forestry production, this was an important tariff reduction. Högberg, for instance, explained that this

Figure 6.6 Average ad valorem export tariff 1800–1830.
Source: Häggqvist (2015, figure 5.3, p. 103).

was why Swedish exports of battens to Britain continued to increase until 1810, when Canadian battens and timber took increasingly larger shares of the British market.[41] Export tariffs were then increased again once the war was over, but this policy had only a brief impact, as the tariff revision of 1818 brought down the tariff on all exports to a low general level. The cut was particularly noticeable on battens, timber and bar iron. Hence, it seems as if the experience of trade distortion and decreasing exports during the Napoleonic Wars brought about a decrease in the export tariff. Montgomery argued that this was a main cause for export interests, mainly in forestry, to petition the government for a cut in their tariff burden.[42] The decrease in export tariffs meant that customs revenue therefrom decreased, meaning that, in order not to suffer a large loss in total customs revenue, which was the single largest income for the government at the time, tariffs on fiscally important import commodities had to be increased. A decrease in export tariffs was therefore switched against increases in the duties on colonial and alcohol imports to keep a balanced central budget.[43]

The Crimean War

According to Jonsson and Montgomery, for instance, a deliberate liberal trade policy slowly but successively gained ground in Sweden after 1830. A large number of import bans were revoked in succession up until the 1850s but the ones that were still kept in effect targeted the most strategically important goods, such as pig iron, bar iron, iron ore, textiles like cloth, cotton and woolen textiles and foodstuffs. The import tariffs on manufactures on average came to about 25 percent, but the tariffs on some textiles, like cotton fabrics, were set at 100 percent ad valorem. Thus, a licensing system and prohibitive tariffs were still in full practice by the end of the 1840s.[44]

There were several factors that pushed trade policy towards a more liberal orientation. First of all, Swedish government representatives often ended up in difficulties when trying to offset high tariffs due to the highly variable tariff levels when Sweden was about to negotiate new trade agreements with foreign countries – especially with Great Britain. In addition, this stirred antagonism between traditional and emerging domestic industries as well as in parliament, which eventually led to changes in the parliamentary balance and the political alliances and alignments therein. During the beginning of the 1850s, prices of agricultural products increased, which was related to the armaments and the preparations for the war, and some staple commodities and foodstuffs were expected to be short in supply. Another factor was smuggling, which deprived the Swedish treasury of large sums. The strongest factor behind the liberalization, though, was that Swedish economic growth increased, partly driven by the Crimean War (see discussion in "The development of foreign trade").[45] Consequently, several export prohibitions were repealed but some remained – like that on iron ore.[46] As regards the import tariffs, important reductions were made, especially on foodstuffs and raw materials. The reductions also included some of the goods, like machines (e.g. steam engines) and finished goods, demanded by the advancing Swedish industries. By then, most export tariffs of significance were revoked. However, some were preserved, like the few export tariffs on products from forestry (battens).[47] The export of products from forestry became increasingly more important during the 1800s – especially after the British tariff reduction in 1851. In 1851–1855 this sector accounted for more than one-third of Swedish exports (while iron and steel and grain accounted for 31 and 20 percent respectively).[48] However, export tariffs have been left out of the analysis since they were virtually irrelevant during this time, even for customs revenue. Thus focus is placed solely on import tariffs.

Price levels continued to increase in general after 1853. From the view of Swedish consumers, the increases were burdensome, and shortly real wages followed commodity prices. For this reason, the tariffs on agricultural products were revoked for periods during 1854 and 1855, similar to during the Napoleonic Wars.[49] As is displayed in Figures 6.7 and 6.8, most tariffs were dramatically reduced shortly after the outbreak of the Crimean War. The commodities included here were typical for Swedish trade in different respects, either since they accounted for a large share of total trade (such as grains, iron and steel, textiles and products from the forestry) or were of strategic interest (such as steam engines, tools and devices). The decrease of the average tariff during the war was very large, going down from over 30 percent before the war down to 11 percent in 1857, when war was over.

As regards foodstuffs, two opposite trends were apparent: tariffs on foodstuffs of international character (e.g. sugar, coffee, tea, cocoa, peppers) were stable; while after the war they increased, whereas tariffs on bulk from adjacent

Figure 6.7 Average ad valorem import tariff, 1848–1861.

Sources: Tariffs: SFS, 1848, 1851, 1854, 1857, 1860. Prices: Adamson (1963); Clark (2004); Hansen (1974); Jacobs and Richter (1935); Jörberg (1972).

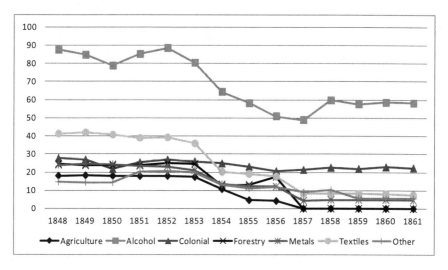

Figure 6.8 Ad valorem import tariffs by commodity group, 1848–1861.
Sources: See Figure 6.7.

markets, such as grain, meat, live cattle, butter, were dramatically reduced. This confirms the claims of Montgomery that the government wanted to reduce food prices. In 1857, tariff rates seemed to have dropped and this was partly a result of the fact that several tariffs on agricultural products were revoked (in such cases the tariff rate was set at 0). In 1860, though, some of them were reintroduced, which entailed a slight average tariff increase.

Tariffs on manufactures such as textile tariffs, metal tariffs (a rather heterogenous category, containing bar iron, as well as products consisting of copper, lead, tin, etc.) and tariffs on finished goods (like steam engines, tools and apparatus) were clearly reduced, as well. A 5 percent tariff was placed on steam engines and steam boilers in 1854, but then they became completely duty-free in 1857. Rates were also heavily cut on bar iron, sheet iron and steel. In fact, in 1857 the only tariffs within the category metals/machinery were placed on nails (around 10 percent) and unprocessed lead and tin. Most interesting, perhaps, are the tariffs on forestry products, which experienced the strongest tariff reduction when they became completely duty-free in 1854. The tariff differentiation between raw textiles and fabrics and cloth, clothing and processed textiles also largely disappeared, which brought down the average textile tariff markedly. To sum up, trend was one of decreasing tariff rates, followed by stagnating rates once the war was over. Alcohol was a category where this was apparent, with decreasing tariff levels during the war and a surge of imports, mainly of rum, but also of wine, genever and arrack. The tariffs which still remained high even after liberalization belonged to importables such as alcohol (beer, wine, foreign and domestic types of spirits) and exotic consumables such as coffee, tea, sugar, coffee, peppers and raisins. It seems, therefore, as if those tariffs which remained at high levels were there for fiscal reasons. Data seem to indicate that the import of particularly foreign alcohol, such as wine, rum, brandy and cognac (which increased significantly after 1830), made up an increasingly larger part of total customs revenue during the 1840s and 1850s, but also the shares of sugar and tobacco increased markedly.[50] Therefore, one big impact of the changes during the Crimean War was to "slim down" Swedish tariff structure, now to encompass a much larger and broader range of completely duty-free goods, while keeping tariffs on those goods which were deemed fiscally important. This seems to be very much in line with the British tariff structure that was in place during the same period.[51]

World War I

During WWI products from forestry still dominated, while iron and steel had lost export shares. In a way Sweden was far more dependent on continuous access to foreign markets, since she depended economically on her foreign trade more than during previous wars. In this respect the government had incentives to reduce trade barriers. First of all, it seems that the tariffs on commodities from adjacent markets (such as grains, meats and dairy) were set lower than on commodities from distant markets (coffee, tea, peppers, vanilla, sugar, etc.) (Figure 6.9). It is plausible to assume

Figure 6.9 Average ad valorem import tariffs, 1906–1920.

Sources: tariffs: BiSOS F 1906, 1908, 1910, Bidrag till Svensk Statistik; SOS 1914, 1916, 1917, 1918, 1919, 1920; prices: BiSOS F; SOS; Jacobs and Richter (1935).

that when the war broke out, expensive and luxurious commodities were undesired with regard to the capital reserves and the balance of payments, while commodities like regular foodstuffs and consumer goods (textiles) were high in priority – especially with regard to risk of inflation and risk of shortages. It could be mentioned that metals belonged to one of the traditional industrial sectors in Sweden, which previously had obtained a privileged and protected position, while fertilizers and chemicals to a large extent were imported from South America (guano) and Germany. Fertilizers and chemicals did not belong to the largest commodity categories, but they were of high strategic importance to (in particular) the agricultural and pharmaceutical sectors. The disrupted trade, the demand from the armament industries, in combination with the overall suspension of the gold standard in Europe, led to a strong inflationary pressure. According to Schön, prices increased by a total of 300 per cent between 1910 and 1918 – so, even before the blockade years.[52] This inflation, much like that during the Napoleonic Wars, brought down the average import tariff from about 20–25 percent before to below 10 percent between 1918 and 1920. A few key cuts in tariff rates furthered this trend, with significant decreases being made to alcohol tariffs and colonial imports such as sugar, tobacco, coffee and tea. Agricultural tariffs, which had been reinstated in force during the end of the 1880s, were also revoked during the war. Most grains, dairy and pork became completely duty-free imports during the end of the war. Low or non-existing tariffs were generally in place on metals, raw textiles and fabrics (while those on cloth and clothing were higher), and chemicals. Processed pasteboard and paper also saw significant tariff cuts from 1916 onwards (noticeable in the "forestry" category in Figure 6.10). It should be mentioned that certain tariffs during WWI were differentiated depending on the origin of imports; the largest of such goods probably being sugar.

Since some single commodities within these categories experienced strong price increases, this is in all probability reflected in the commodity categories in Figure 6.10. Such a measure was also in line with the increasing fiscal needs from skyrocketing government expenditures when the economy was centrally planned by an extensive administration.

Customs revenue

Customs revenue is presented in Figure 6.11, from which it appears that during the Napoleonic Wars and the Crimean War it generally fluctuated, as did trade. During WWI, customs revenue was rather stable, until 1916, when it decreased by some 60 percent in only two years, until the end of the war. In relation to imports, customs revenue already experienced a slump from the start of the war. This confirms that import levels decreased significantly and weren't furthered by tariff cuts on foodstuffs of international (sugar, coffee) or regional (grains, dairy, meats) character that were undertaken towards the end of the war. During the Napoleonic Wars, customs revenue

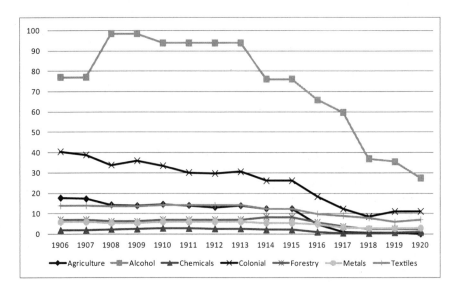

Figure 6.10 Ad valorem import tariffs by commodity group, 1906–1920.
Source: see Figure 6.9.

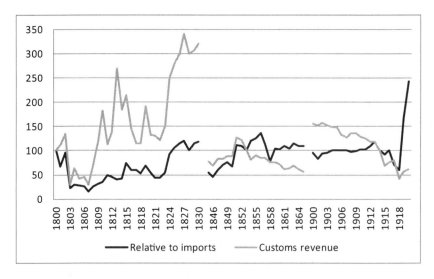

Figure 6.11 Indices of Swedish customs revenue during the Napoleonic Wars (1800 = 100), the Crimean War (1853 = 100), and WW I (1914 = 100). Black graph represents customs revenue relative to imports; grey graph represents customs revenue.

Sources: Napoleonic: Häggqvist (2015); Crimea and WWI: BiSOS F.

increased briefly when Swedish imports spiked to previously unpresented levels. During the Crimean War, customs revenue increased along with the increase in both imports and exports. It therefore seems as if the tariff cuts made during the 1850s did not decrease revenues from tariffs, at least not in the short term. During the Napoleonic and Crimean Wars, the tax collected from foreign trade was considerable, and in all probability became a welcome contribution to the treasury. Between 1800 and 1812, customs revenue increased by 50 percent, and between 1850 and 1855 by 68 percent. During the peak of the Napoleonic Wars, customs revenue made up about 25 percent of total government revenue, while it was around 40 percent during the Crimean War. It had then become less important on the eve of WWI, because of the introduction of income taxes a few years prior, but it still made up some 20 percent of total government revenues.[53] This figure then plummeted during the war, and during the blockade years of 1917 and 1918 customs revenue was at only 7 and 5 percent of total government revenue, respectively.

Conclusions

In this chapter we have showed that major armed conflicts between 1803 and 1918 all had a significant impact on the development of Swedish foreign trade and trade policy. All three wars brought with them an increase in total trade, albeit in quite different ways. Sweden was also able to gain shares in the world market for exports during the Crimean War and WWI. All three wars brought down tariff levels and hence liberalized Swedish trade policy, even though liberal tendencies were short-lived as a result of the Napoleonic Wars. Furthermore, the state was able to expand its fiscal capacity through an increase in customs revenue during the Napoleonic Wars and the Crimean War, but not during WWI. Neutrality in many ways therefore gave way for (1) trade expansion, (2) more liberal trade policy, and (3) increasing fiscal capacity at the government level.

However, and this is important to stress, neutrality had its clear limitations. During the Napoleonic Wars and World War I, the impact on trade was eventually largely negative. During the Napoleonic Wars domestic exports experienced a crisis when iron and forestry couldn't find an offset in foreign markets. The explosion in imports was short-lived and it is doubtful that it had any short-term or long-lasting positive effect on the Swedish economy.[54] During the blockade years in the final stages of WWI, both exports and imports plummeted (and as a result customs revenue as well), even though trade recovered quite quickly thereafter. Neutrality and trade policy decisions were hence not enough to counteract the totality of war which severely disrupted trade channels. Instead we find the largest positive events during the most minor of the wars in question here. During the Crimean War Sweden experienced a large increase in both exports and imports and the impact on the former was a long-lasting, positive one. In some aspects this episode launched Sweden into industrialization and decades of large and stable export-led economic growth.[55] It was also here that Sweden broke with mercantilism and protectionism, brought down tariff rates in a major way and liberalized trade policy. While inflation was partly responsible for the decrease in tariff rates during the Napoleonic Wars and WWI, the decrease was almost exclusively due to conscious policy decisions during the Crimean War.

Notes

1 Adhering to non-alignment (for instance, to military alliances) during peacetime is another issue. In this chapter we focus on Sweden's neutral status during times of war and military conflict. Sweden's non-alignment (an integral part of the neutrality policy of the country) has been a source of great debate and it has largely been questioned whether Sweden really was non-aligned and "neutral" during especially the Cold War. See for instance Dahl (1998); Agrell (2000).
2 Wahlbäck and Munch-Petersen (1986).
3 Preceded by the French Revolutionary Wars, 1793–1801. For a recent analysis of the impact of Swedish neutrality on shipping and trade during that war see Müller (2016).
4 Malmborg (2001, p. 63).
5 Malmborg (2001 p. 68); Ahnlund, Carlsson, and Höjer (1954, p. 107). See Müller (2004) for an analysis of the role of Swedish neutrality for trade and shipping.
6 Högberg (1969, p. 31).
7 Ibid., p. 220.
8 Ibid., p. 31.
9 Heckscher and Westergaard (1964).
10 Wahlbäck (2011, pp. 71–73).
11 Findlay and O'Rourke (2007, ch. 7 and 8).
12 Schön (2010, p. 112).
13 Magnusson (2009).
14 Barbieri and Levy (1999, p. 465).
15 O. Anderson (1961, pp. 38–39).
16 See Lambert (1990); Kirby (1996, pp. 118–119).
17 Davis and Engerman (2006, p. 8).
18 See Broadberry and Harrison (2009, pp. 26–28).
19 Bring (2008, pp. 155–159).
20 Fridlizius (1964, pp. 45–46).
21 Bring (2008, pp. 177–180).
22 Findlay and O'Rourke (2007, pp. 429–430). Most of these losses were accounted for in 1917, about 25 percent of total wartime losses. Davis and Engerman (2006, p. 180).
23 Fridlizius (1964, p. 45).
24 Findlay and O'Rourke (2007, pp. 429–430).
25 Meaning that net import (gross import-re-export) was lower. The trade balance still showed a clear import surplus during the war years. See Häggqvist (2015, ch. 4).
26 British exports to Sweden increased tenfold during the height of the Continental System, from 1808 to 1812, compared to previous years. See Crouzet (1958, p. 883, table 1).
27 Findlay and O'Rourke (2007, p. 367).

28 Exports increased faster than imports, and again the price levels began to increase. Between 1913 and 1916 both the export and the import price index increased by roughly 50 per cent. Fridlizius (1964, p. 44).
29 Bring (2008, pp. 177–178).
30 See Mitchell (1975), for figures on Swedish bilateral trade before, during and after the war.
31 It would be optimal to use annual trade data of Europe. Since Great Britain accounted for a relatively large share of the European trade, this might serve as a proxy for the European trade. It is worth noting that the Swedish followed the British trade relatively closely, which in all probability was a result from the close commercial exchange between the two countries (in 1850 Great Britain's share of Swedish trade came to 31.5 per cent). When the Crimean war broke out, it is clear that the Swedish and the British trade moved conversely; while the British exports declined by about 10 per cent the Swedish increased by more than 55 per cent. After that the Russian Baltic Fleet had capitulated, Swedish trade declined again. At the moment it is unclear whether this was due to the fact that armaments declined in Europe or if the competition from the Russian export industries increased. The decline was probably not related to Swedish tariff levels, which is discussed below.
32 Fridlizius (1960).
33 Hedberg and Karlsson (2015, pp. 69–70).
34 Heckscher (1949, p. 660).
35 This was however not the case during the Napoleonic Wars. See Vallerö (1969; Häggqvist (2015).
36 Anderson and Neary (2005).
37 Legislation: "Kongl. Maj:ts och Rikets Commerce-Collegii Kungörelse, Angående Det så kallade Product-Placatets whilande tils widare äfwen i anseende til de Farwatten och Orter, som äro inom Östersjön belägne. Gifwen Stockholm den 16 April 1807", National Archives.
38 Montgomery (1921, p. 5).
39 Ibid, p. 6.
40 This was a notable difference to war-time policy in Denmark, where tariffs were raised across the board two times during in order to adjust for inflation and to increase customs revenue to finance war-efforts.
41 Högberg (1969, pp. 141–142).
42 Montgomery (1921, p. 12).
43 Häggqvist (2015, pp. 118–125).
44 See in particular Jonsson (2005); Montgomery (1921, pp. 64–65).
45 Few direct references to the war were however made by members of parliament in discussions on trade policy changes.
46 Montgomery (1921, p. 68).
47 Ibid.
48 Fridlizius (1964, pp. 12–13).
49 Montgomery (1921, pp. 77–78).
50 Detailed data on customs revenue by commodity is available in Underdåniga berättelser om Sveriges utrikes handel och sjöfart 1819–1857; Kommerskollegium – Utrikes handel och sjöfart 1858–1910 (BiSOS F).
51 Irwin (1993).
52 Schön (2010, p. 235).
53 Gårestad (1985).

54 On the stagnating Swedish economy during the time see Schön and Krantz (2012).
55 Jörberg (1961).

References

Official publications and statistics

Bidrag till Sveriges officiella statistik (BISOS) F, Utrikes handel och sjöfart, 1858–1910 – various years
Generaltullstyrelsen, Underdåniga berättelser om Sveriges utrikes handel och sjöfart – 1819–1857
Statistisk årsbok, Statistiska Centralbyrån (SCB) – various years
Svensk författningssamling (SFS) – various years
Sveriges officiella statistik (SOS) – various years

Literature

Adamson, R. (1963). *De svenska järnbrukens storleksutveckling och avsättningsinriktning 1796–1860.* Göteborg: Göteborgs Universitet.
Agrell, W. (2000). *Fred och fruktan: Sveriges säkerhetspolitiska historia 1918–2000.* Lund: Historiska media.
Ahnlund, N., Carlsson, S., & Höjer, T. T. s. (1954). *Den svenska utrikespolitikens historia. 3.1/3.2, 1792–1844.* Stockholm: Norstedt.
Anderson, J. E., & Neary, J. P. (2005). *Measuring the Restrictiveness of International Trade Policy.* Cambridge, MA: MIT Press.
Anderson, O. (1961). Economic Warfare in the Crimean War. *Economic History Review*, 14(1), 34–47.
Barbieri, K., & Levy, J. S. (1999). Sleeping with the Enemy: The Impact of War on Trade. *Journal of Peace Research*, 36(4), 463–479.
Bring, O. (2008). *Neutralitetens uppgång och fall – eller den gemensamma säkerhetens historia.* Stockholm: Atlantis.
Broadberry, S., & Harrison, M. (2009). The Economics of World War I: An Overview. In *The Economics of World War I* (pp. 3–40). Cambridge: Cambridge University Press.
Clark, G. (2004). The Price History of English Agriculture, 1209–1914. In S. Wolcott & C. Hanes (Eds.), *Research in Economic History*. Bingley, UK: Emerald Group Publishing Limited.
Crouzet, F. (1958). *L'Economie britannique et le Blocus continental (1806–1813).* 2 vols. Paris: Presses universitaires de France.
Dahl, A.-S. (1998). The Myth of Swedish Neutrality. In C. Buffet & B. Heuser (Eds.), *Haunted by History: Myths in International Relations* (pp. 28–40). Providence, RI: Berghahn.
Davis, L., & Engerman, S. L. (2006). *Naval Blockades in Peace and War: An Economic history since 1750.* New York: Cambridge Unversity Press.
Findlay, R., & O'Rourke, K. H. (2007). *Power and Plenty: Trade, War, and the World Economy in the Second Millennium.* Princeton, NJ: Princeton University Press.

Fridlizius, G. (1960). The Crimean War and the Swedish Economy. *Economy and History*, 3(1), 56–103.
Fridlizius, G. (1964). Sweden's Exports 1850–1960. A Study in Perspective. In O. Bjurling, G. Fridlizius, I. Svensson, & L. Jörberg (Eds.), *Economy and History*, vol. 6. Lund: The Institute of Economic History.
Gårestad, P. (1985). *Industrialisering och beskattning i Sverige 1861–1914*. Uppsala: Academiae Ubsaliensis.
Häggqvist, H. (2015). *On the Ocean of Protectionism: The Structure of Swedish Tariffs and Trade 1780–1830*. Uppsala: Acta Universitatis Upsaliensis.
Hansen, S A. (1974). *Økonomisk vækst i Danmark. Bd 2, 1914–1970*. København: Akademisk førlag.
Heckscher, E. F. (1949). Sveriges ekonomiska historia från Gustav Vasa. D. 2, *Det moderna Sveriges grundläggning*, halvbd 2. Stockholm: Bonnier.
Heckscher, E. F., & Westergaard, H. (1964). *The Continental System: An Economic Interpretation*. Gloucester, MA: Peter Smith.
Hedberg, P., & Karlsson, L. (2015). Neutral Trade in Time of War: The Case of Sweden, 1838–1960. *International Journal of Maritime History*, 27(1), 61–78.
Högberg, S. (1969). Utrikeshandel och sjöfart på 1700-talet: Stapelvaror i svensk export och import 1738–1808. Stockholm: Bonnier.
Irwin, D. A. (1993). Free Trade and Protection in Nineteenth-Century Britain and France Revisited: A Comment on Nye. *Journal of Economic History*, 53(1), 146–152.
Jacobs, A., & Richter, H. (1935). *Die Großhandelspreise in Deutschland von 1792 bis 1934*. Sonderhefte des Instituts für Konjunkturforschung, 37. Berlin: Hanseatische Verlagsanstalt Hamburg.
Jonsson, P. (2005). *Handelsfrihetens vänner och förbuden: Identitet och politisk kommunikation i svensk tullpolitik 1823–1854*. Örebro: Örebro universitetsbibliotek.
Jörberg, L. (1961). *Growth and Fluctuations of Swedish Industry 1869–1912: Studies in the Process of Industrialisation*. Stockholm: Almqvist & Wiksell.
Jörberg, L. (1972). *A History of Prices in Sweden 1732–1914*, vol 1, *Sources*, Methods, Tables. Lund: Gleerup.
Kirby, D. (1996). *Östersjöländernas historia. 1772–1993*. Stockholm: Atlantis.
Lambert, A. (1990). *The Crimean War. British Grand Strategy against Russia, 1853–56*. Manchester, UK/New York: Manchester University Press.
Magnusson, L. (2009). *Nation, State and the Industrial Revolution*. London/New York: Routledge.
Malmborg, M. a. (2001). *Neutrality and State-Building in Sweden*. Basingstoke: Palgrave.
Mitchell, B. R. (1975). *European Historical Statistics 1750–1970*. London: Macmillan.
Montgomery, A. (1921). *Svensk tullpolitik 1816–1911*. Stockholm: Isaac Marcus boktryckeri AB.
Müller, L. (2004). *Consuls, Corsairs, and Commerce. The Swedish Consular Service and Long-distance Shipping, 1720–1815*. Uppsala: Acta Universitatis Upsaliensis.
Müller, L. (2016). Swedish Merchant Shipping in Troubled Times: The French Revolutionary Wars and Sweden's Neutrality 1793–1801. *International Journal of Maritime History*, 28(1), 147–164.

Schön, L. (2010). *Sweden's Road to Modernity. An Economic History*. Stockholm: SNS.

Schön, L., & Krantz, O. (2012). The Swedish Economy in the Early Modern Period: Constructing Historical National Accounts. *European Review of Economic History*, 16, 529–549.

Vallerö, R. (1969). *Svensk handels- och sjöfartsstatistik 1637–1813: En tillkomsthistorisk undersökning*. Stockholm: LiberFörlag.

Wahlbäck, K. (2011). *Jättens andedräkt. Finlandsfrågan i svensk politik 1809–2009*. Stockholm: Atlantis AB.

Wahlbäck, K., & Munch-Petersen, T. (1986). *The Roots of Swedish Neutrality*. Stockholm: Swedish Institute (Svenska institutet).

Part II
Trade and neutrality in conflicts

7 Small states in harm's way
Neutrality in war

Eric Golson

Introduction

On July 25, 1940, a month after the defeat of France, Swiss General Henri Guisan held a secret meeting with his unit commanders in the Rütli meadow on Lake Luzern, the birthplace of the Swiss Republic in 1291. Summoning the strength of the tiny mountainous nation, Guisan declared:

> We have reached a turning point in our history. Switzerland's existence is at stake. Here the soldiers of 1940 will gain strength from the lessons and spirit of the past in order to face the country's present and future with determination, and hear the secret spell that emanates from this meadow. If we look straight ahead we shall master the ever present difficulties which the Alliance of 1291 called the maliciousness of our times.[1]

Although he spoke for only thirty minutes, Guisan's words were echoed from the Rütli valley on wire services and through diplomatic channels all over the world.[2] Newspaper reports of the speech sent hope and nationalistic fervour amongst the Swiss, seeming to restore the principles of resistance which had sustained the Helvetic Confederation through dozens of conflicts.

In addition to reviving Swiss nationalism, Guisan reinvigorated the principle of neutrality. From the opening days of the war over ten months before, the legal principles of war had been eviscerated as one neutral after another succumbed to the aggressions of the German army. Recalling the strength of Switzerland's defences, Guisan's speech sought to disabuse anyone who expected that his country would discharge its troops and surrender in the face of aggression; instead, Guisan implied that he was ready to fight belligerents at any time.[3] By 1945, his Rütli speech had become mythic and Guisan a national hero.[4]

The aim of this chapter is to explore neutrality as a separate political economy concept, one which is dramatically affected by the changing character of warfare in the twentieth century. It provides a history of neutrality, particularly in the twentieth century, and outlines the shift from legally and military defence-based neutrality in the Great War to an economically based neutrality after June 1940. If only the reasons for a country's wartime survival could be reduced to a simple conflict of Swiss steadfastness and self-preservation before aggressive dictatorship. But neutrality, as this stance is called, is far more complicated, particularly for small states which are seen as remaining outside the conflict to exploit the situation for their own benefit. The popular media, politicians and lawyers have increasingly maligned the version of neutrality represented by the Swiss myth as merely a convenient figleaf for self-enrichment. The wartime histories of other neutrals, such as Argentina and Turkey, are sullied by this negative view of neutrality even though they were mostly in the Allied domain and therefore incapable of offering much to the enemy.

This chapter is related to a broader debate on neutrality and economic warfare. No central definition of neutrality has existed through time or has withstood the test of the changing character of war in the twentieth century. This chapter asserts that small countries have no simple formula for protecting themselves from the pressures and problems of the outside world. The independent survival of small neutrals in the world wars had many dimensions; the term 'neutrality' denotes a broad, ill-defined concept. This was good for neutral countries in some regards, as they were able to rely on their own vision of neutrality and use this to navigate through the war. On the other hand, this left them quite vulnerable to belligerent pressure. From the history delineated herein, it is clear military defence was important from at least 1914 to June 1940, but with the changing nature of war, it is now clear neutrals survived by economics from the Fall of France in June 1940 to the liberation of Europe in May 1945. From June 1940 onwards, neutrals benefited from what they sold, but they protected themselves and consistently prevented a *casus belli* by the rational economic framework for their transfers of labour, resources, trade in finished goods and capital; other specialized provision, including shipping capacity, was also made for belligerents by the Swedish and Portuguese.

The evolution of neutrality

The birth of a concept

Neutrality as a legal concept emerged in the early 1600s when the first vague definitions of non-participation in war occurred to Hugo Grotius, a philosopher of modern natural law. Grotius argued: "from those who are at peace nothing should be taken except in case of extreme necessity, and subject to the restoration of its value." Among the duties of those who remain at peace they should "show themselves impartial to either side in permitting transit, in furnishing supplies to his troops, and in not assisting those under siege."[5] Grotius' basic conception of neutrality as impartiality was cited by European countries which sought no conflict. Grotius' version of neutrality remains the most widely understood definition of the concept, even though it has become increasingly difficult for countries to be considered neutral.

Large-scale increases in trade and the birth of mercantilist empires from the mid-nineteenth to the early twentieth century initially re-created the idea of neutrality, focused on the realist principles of relative power. According to neutral law expert Nils Ørvik:

> The outcome of the struggle to establish [a system of neutral rights] has at all times been entirely dependent on the economic and military strength, the strategic position, and the perspicacity and persistence of the two sides. In short, the products of two forces pull in opposite directions, the final result being determined by the relative bargaining power of the parties.[6]

In Ørvik's view, neutrality evolved from strict impartiality into a realist system where the belligerents and neutrals continually re-evaluated their relations depending on their relative power.[7] This realist power balance had two critical components: the belligerent's strength and the neutral's deterrent against invasion. The belligerent's offensive strength over a neutral would have to be calculated with reference to the military, economic and political forces it could exert against the neutral and the credibility of its threats. Similarly, the neutral's defensive deterrent would involve some combination of the same forces, although the neutral must not only ensure the credibility of his deterrent, but also convince the belligerent of his willingness to defend himself.[8] In terms of game theory, a simple chicken game can be run repetitively to evaluate the outcomes of this scenario. Ørvik's theory can thus be put in the context of modern game theory.

The critical assumption behind this view is that in wartime states always try to secure the best possible economic, political and military outcomes for themselves, at the expense of other, rival states. A simplistic prisoner's dilemma framework can explain this: the belligerent–neutral relationship is a game of absolute gains where one party is always trying to get the better of the other.[9] The effect of military or economic power disparity on a country remaining neutral is noticeable; but when the two states are either equally strong or equally weak, the threat of force is academic; fighting is too risky and costly for both.

Historically, examples of equally matched neutrals and belligerents concern either great powers, which remain neutral when other great powers fight, or relationships between great powers and small states. The former include neutral France in the Austro-Prussian war of 1866, or Austria and Italy in the Franco-Prussian War.[10] The latter include the German threat to invade the Netherlands in the Great War, made to boost Germany's strategic position; however, the strengths on land of these two countries were equal, given the number of German troops tied down in the Eastern and Western campaigns.[11]

In this study, neutrality is important only when the belligerents are unevenly balanced against the neutral state. In the event there is a power disparity between the two parties, the stronger threaten the weaker. If the neutral is weaker than the belligerent, the latter gains at the neutral's expense (through either military conquest or economic domination) – which is best exemplified by Belgium in the two wars, when the country was invaded by far stronger German forces.[12] The rare converse example is a former neutral country, invaded and gaining at the belligerent's expense. Although the realist model from the eighteenth and nineteenth centuries still provides our theoretical basis for understanding neutrality, the growth of colonial empires and a number of smaller European wars led to the codification of neutrality in the 1900s to limit the spread of conflict, given the complexities of global empires. This was ultimately short-lived; realism quickly restored itself with the advent of total war.

Legal codification of neutrality

The Hague and Geneva Conventions, with other late nineteenth- and early twentieth- century treaties, reinforced and institutionalized the concept of neutrality to prevent small wars from growing. Each relies on the idea of neutrality as impartiality in war. They did not abandon the realist neutrality posited by Ørvik and others, but rather created rules to limit the spread of war and prevent uncertainty for all parties. They detail the rights and duties conceded to neutrals on land and at sea. Land rights include the inviolability of neutral territory, internment of combatants, ability to pursue trade and the traditional duties of protecting prisoners of war; whereas naval rights include the ability to pass freely through the lines of war and maintain their trading relationships.[13] Adopting these rules, the international community sought to lower the levels of uncertainty in wartime and prevent the spread of war to countries which wanted to remain outside it.

The clearly defined rules established by these treaties provided an institutional framework for neutrality, beyond the simple realist version. Although a realist power balance remained the ultimate neutral defence, these rules weakened the risk of neutrals being swept into wars by providing clear rules: for impartiality; for neutrals' functions in wartime; and for behaviour that would preserve their neutrality.[14] Codification also provided neutral states with methods of redress beyond simply entering the war if belligerents violated their neutrality. In such cases compensation was paid; for example, after the bombing of the Swiss city of Schaffhausen in 1944 by the US, which paid Switzerland $4 million.[15] Compensation was also payable when a neutral favoured one side: to avoid a diplomatic crisis, Great Britain paid the US $15.5 million after the American Civil War for granting "un-neutral privileges" in July 1863 to Confederate ships docking in British ports.

The collapse of the legal framework

The Great War and the interwar period proved critical for the concept of neutrality; with increasingly aggressive total war, the rules and institutions governing belligerent behaviour against neutrals were largely ignored, leaving neutral countries dependent again on realist defences. Aggression against belligerents and neutrals alike seemed preferable.[16] Realist principles became the best for neutrals resisting belligerent pressure; however, lacking naval forces, the neutrals confined their realism in resistance to land. Hence the rules laid down by the various treaties and conventions throughout the Great War were often violated. Despite the many treaties guaranteeing access, neutrals were denied international trading and other facilities, ports, and coaling stations and inevitably lost position.[17]

The blockade of the Netherlands and the Scandinavian countries as part of the larger encirclement of Germany is the most notable infringement of neutrality. Ships captured and later destroyed in violation of the rules include the Dutch *Elve* and *Bernisse*, which were forcibly rerouted by the British to French ports, despite carrying no contraband; being bound for France, the ships were sunk by a German submarine notwithstanding their neutral origins.[18] The European neutrals' situation was not helped by the US, which, as a semi-neutral, ignored many of the neutrality rules to serve its own desires.

Before joining the Allies in the Great War, the US, enabled by its economic size and status, ignored international law and unilaterally defined the concept of neutrality.[19] As a neutral, it was technically bound by Articles 7 and 9 of the Fifth Hague Convention, which state:

> Article 7: A neutral Power is not called upon to prevent the export or transport on behalf of one or other of the belligerents, of arms, of munitions of war, or in general, of anything which can be of use to an army or a fleet.

> Article 9: Every measure of restriction or prohibition taken by a neutral Power in regard to the matters referred to in Articles 7 and 9 must be impartially applied by it to both belligerents.[20]

However, despite the restrictions imposed by Article 9 regarding the trade in munitions allowed in Article 7, the US traded primarily with the Allies. As the trade statistics in Table 7.1 indicate, US exports to the Allies were respectively some 100 times and almost 940 times those to Germany in 1915 and 1916.[21] A significant amount of this trade was conducted on credit, New York bankers having implicit government backing.[22] Unlike previous wars when

Table 7.1 United States trade in World War I (millions of dollars)

	United States	1913	1914	1915	1916
Central Powers	Exports to	377	174	12	2
	Imports from	225	183	55	6
Allies	Exports to	1,320	1,254	2,539	4,251
	Imports from	737	736	681	908
European neutrals	Exports to	165	195	354	298
	Imports from	84	86	69	94
Other neutrals	Exports to	199	146	229	353
	Imports from	276	320	432	526

Source: Jefferson (1917: 477).

governments forbade the exporting of arms and ammunition to the belligerents, this war witnessed no such domestic American policy.[23] Consequently, by calling the US a neutral during the Great War, yet upholding none of the legal principles and frameworks agreed in treaties, President Wilson weakened the international definition of neutrality as it then stood. What saved most neutrals at the time was having relatively well-equipped and supplied military forces, at least to begin with. The Dutch mobilized nearly 300,000 troops in the first days of the Great War, the Swiss 220,000 infantry and 200,000 in support roles.[24] With Germany, France and Britain fairly well matched in terms of troop numbers on the Western Front, converting other neutrals into belligerents would serve only to sap the military strength of the aggressor. These shifts to realism became the neutrals' primary method of survival.

The rise of a new realism

Between the wars, the military deterrent which supported the neutrals in the realist power balance was upset in favour of the belligerents. In the era of collective security induced by the League of Nations, Europe's smaller states chose disarmament and a system of conflict prevention, which forced them to participate and conform to any international system. Prominent political philosopher Georg Cohn cites this shift as the death of neutrality as hitherto defined. In the new system, which Cohn calls neo-neutrality, the international laws supporting neutrality no longer applied and realism increasingly dominated:[25]

> not identical with traditional neutrality as established by former international law, but it does have in common with it (1) an unconditional demand for the privilege to remain outside the war, and (2) provision of the necessary means of measures for doing so, albeit in a somewhat modified form. Beyond this it recognizes no obligation of impartiality.[26]

However, neutral countries, lulled by collective security guarantees, did not recognize the need to shift their policies towards realism, even after European rearmament began in 1933. Most neutral countries believed the League of Nations removed the need for war, substituting a system of conflict prevention. This would settle all disputes by consensus, replacing the threat of war by the preferred method of economic sanctions.[27] The shift to using economic sanctions as punishment allowed the smaller European states to disarm and fall behind the technological curve. In 1914, when Europe's small states were most threatened, the gap in military power between them and the Great Powers concerned the quantity of personnel and weapons, not the quality and use of advanced equipment – for example, the 300,000 troops mobilized by the Netherlands in the first days of the Great War, against 200,000 in 1939–40.[28]

However, by 1939 significant technological capability differences also emerged between the two groups, which effectively devalued their infantry in favour of the mechanized and technologically superior forces of the belligerents. Nor had the neutrals developed new strategies against these new armies; instead, they chose on September 1, 1939 to re-employ strategies used in the Great War.[29] This combination of outdated military technology and techniques led to a rebalancing of the realist equation in clear favour of the more powerful belligerents and required those who survived the spring 1940 onslaught to develop new methods of deterrence to avoid being targets of aggression. Having been lulled between the wars into believing in collective defence, the neutrals provided no other means for maintaining neutrality.[30] This military disparity when the Second World War began left small states exposed to conquest.

Neutrality and economic realism

The degradation of the neutral legal framework in the Great War and the clear shift of the military power balance in favour of the belligerents allowed Germany to conquer and/or dominate many neutrals in the first eighteen months of the Second World War. It began with sixteen neutrals, but the defences of Belgium, Denmark, France, Luxembourg, the Netherlands and Norway were no match against the German army. Ultimately, only Ireland, Portugal, Spain, Sweden, Switzerland and Turkey remained independent or unaligned. Geography played an import role in preserving Ireland and Turkey, who were protected from direct attack by large bodies of water. Portugal, Spain, Sweden and Switzerland survived their encirclement and blockades through carefully conceived military and economic deterrents. From the military perspective, Sweden and Switzerland deployed a powerful navy and army, respectively. They would surely have put up a significant fight; however, the relative technical weakness of the Portuguese, Spanish, Swedish and Swiss militaries would have made it difficult, if not impossible, for them to resist German or even British aggression, but there was no way to build the machinery and train effective forces that could withstand such powerful armies.[31] Thus, in order to remain independent, a realist power balance along the lines described by Ørvik was maintained on an ad hoc basis, based primarily on economic concessions to the belligerents. The economic concessions given by these small states can be classified under three general headings: trade in goods and materials, labour, and capital. These concessions proved sufficiently valuable to let the countries continue to maintain their independence, despite continued threats of invasion.

Trade concessions

In neutral–belligerent merchandise trade, certain items were in particular demand; these goods gave Portugal, Spain, Sweden and Switzerland, the remaining European neutrals, some negotiating leverage and boosted their power. Mancur Olson has argued that material goods are substitutable in times of war and there is no such thing as strategic goods favoured by one party or another. In theory, the neutrals should have had no negotiating leverage, since the belligerents could have merely bought the goods elsewhere.

But in a modern war Olson's substitution idea is somewhat counterintuitive: the belligerents demand certain speciality manufactures which have few viable substitutes. These strategic goods make it possible to dismiss Olson's claim. The real price increases seen in neutral export goods such as Swedish ball bearings, Swiss watches and Spanish wolfram, show certain items particularly in demand by the belligerents.[32] Limited substitutes for these goods were sometimes possible, but were either prohibitively expensive or of inferior quality, as demonstrated by the ball bearings.[33] Substitute goods such as Olson suggests were therefore not altogether possible. This shifted the realist power balance in favour of the neutrals.

Each of the neutral countries that remained after June 1940 was able to assuage the belligerents' political intransigence and maintain friendly relations by exporting various material goods to each of the belligerent groups: for Sweden, iron ore and ball bearings; Switzerland, watches, metal goods and machinery; Spain, food, iron ore and wolfram; Portugal, leather hides and wolfram.[34] Swedish trade was particularly beneficial for the resource-strapped German Reich in military terms: iron ore, ball bearings and machine tools were used in the manufacture of German guns, tanks and aircraft.[35] These goods were also needed by the Allies, particularly Britain, for the continued manufacture of aero-engines. Despite its geographic location within the German sphere, the Swedish government allowed much-needed war materials to reach Britain illicitly. However, the trade relationships in all four cases also reflect a realist change in the balance of power: 1941 was the peak year for exports to Germany by Portugal, Sweden and Spain.[36] Switzerland, by virtue of being surrounded, was in a weaker position and its peak year of exports to Germany was 1943.[37] In this way, the neutrals quelled any German desire for invasion as well as ultimately serving Allied interests. The Allies were also successful in mandating the Swedish government to reduce exports to Germany, despite continued Swedish dependence on German fuel and food. Trade concessions by the Swedish government, in 1943 and 1944 in particular, enabled the Allies to recognize Sweden as a victim of the conditions of war,[38] but this was not true to the same extent for Spain or Switzerland.

Labour concessions

Maintaining a steady supply of available labour is an important part of any war economy; too few workers and soldiers foretell an eventual battlefront defeat. During the Second World War, imported labour became crucial to sustaining the economies of Germany and Great Britain. It can be argued that a lack of manpower prevented Germany from creating a sufficient military force to maintain its grip on much of Europe. Germany tried to use foreign voluntary and forced labour from Europe to replace German workers sent to the fronts, but these efforts ultimately proved insufficient.[39] Great Britain relied on help from its Commonwealth partners, the USSR and the US for additional manpower; the Allies ultimately won the Second World War through sheer mathematical advantage. A little-discussed contribution to both war efforts is neutral labour; Spanish and Swiss labour was initially viewed as a potentially critical contribution to the German war effort. Providing continued access to this labour in the first months of the war helped swing German realist views in favour of these countries.

A belligerent's ability to recruit foreign labour depended on its geographic access to neutrals and their ideological alignment. Geographical constraints twice limited Portuguese, Swedish, Swiss and Spanish labour participation in the war effort. Beyond the North Sea, no significant numbers of Swedes could work in Germany or Great Britain. The Portuguese were even further away from the Germans and, although some Portuguese worked in the British shipping industry, their numbers were quite small and the opportunities unorganized. Although they had access to both Germany and Britain, ideological alignment focused Spain on providing labour to Germany; they were frozen out of the closest British labour market, Gibraltar, owing to security concerns. Switzerland's close proximity to Germany allowed more substantive labour transfers; the Swiss could not work in Britain because of the blockade.[40]

Although originally predicted to be quite large, the Swiss and Spanish contributions were ultimately quite small in relation to the overall German war effort. The peak labour contribution of neutral Spain and Switzerland combined represented no more than 26,520 workers in Germany; with some 36,529,000 workers in Germany at the peak level of employment in May 1943, the penultimate Spanish and Swiss contribution represented less than 0.0723% of the German workforce.[41]

Nonetheless, the timeline for Spain and Switzerland allowing labour transfers was important with regard to resisting Germany's demands. The Spanish approach was direct government intervention in support of Germany during the war, in an attempt to curry diplomatic favour there. The Swiss approach involved less direct government intervention: individuals living in a certain area were allowed to work in Germany. The Swiss government ratified an agreement with Germany for a free trade and movement area in late August 1939; with Swiss–German relations frozen during the war, exchanges of workers continued at the workers' discretion insofar as the opportunities attracted them. In both cases, initial German pressure on these neutral countries to provide labour was satisfied with agreements that exceeded the German expectations for possible recruitment; but this did not materialize because of neutral government intervention. Shortly thereafter, the Swiss, in order to limit numbers, raised the cost of border permits and the Spanish imposed a temporary recruitment moratorium.[42]

By providing a net contribution to the German war effort, both Spain and Switzerland demonstrate their versions of neutrality as sufficiently flexible to allow transfers of economically important workers to belligerents, but they went on to limit them as the German position weakened. Thus, using labour concessions, they provided enough to satisfy the military and other demands made on the neutrals by the belligerents.

Capital concessions

Realist concessions on the part of neutral countries also mean engaging with belligerents in capital transactions. Despite the different political situations and two unique payment systems, actual neutral–belligerent payments were substantially similar across all four main cases. In their relations with the belligerents, the European neutrals provided a variety of needed services: Portugal provided the British with shipping services; Sweden provided the Allies and Axis powers with diplomatic, shipping and insurance services; the Swiss provided diplomatic, protecting power, banking and insurance services; and, although Spain was generally less service-oriented, it was still paid for providing shipping to the Allies and diplomatic representation to the Germans.[43] The belligerents were ultimately net payers to the neutrals in most of these relationships.

Despite considerable transfer restrictions during the war, the neutrals also accepted net positive private transfers. All belligerents severely restricted the transfer of funds to neutral countries, to prevent hot money flows and destabilization. In most of the neutral–belligerent relationships, these transfers in favour of neutrals amounted to between 0.1% and 0.5% of GDP, the exceptions being Sweden–UK at 0.8% and Portugal–UK at 1.1%. Significant increases in transfers from Germany occurred in the last years of the war, as German defeat became more likely.[44]

The neutrals also allowed large loan balances to accumulate in order to conciliate the Germans and the British on whom they depended. Some smaller loans were settled with capital transfers. Portugal allowed Britain to run a clearing deficit, later converted into a loan, which at the end of the war amounted to nearly 28.6% of Portuguese GDP.[45] Generally Switzerland and Sweden allowed Germany to run net clearing deficits, and, although the Swedish one was largely paid off by the end of the war, the Swiss one amounted to nearly 10.7% of Swiss GDP in 1945.[46] despite the fact that Spain also provided clearing loans, overall it owed Germany money to cover civil war debts, but precise figures are not available. Various loans and short-term clearing agreements were provided, but ultimately many capital account balances were settled in gold, particularly when the war was not going well for that particular side (Britain before 1941 and Germany after 1942). Both the Allied and Axis powers transferred gold to the neutrals to pay deficits, despite significant shortages of monetary gold.[47] The acceptance of this gold has become a point of controversy, given its origins from plundered central banks and murdered Jews.

Conclusions

This chapter has argued that neutrality is a separate political economy concept, one which is dramatically affected by the changing character of warfare in the twentieth century. Initially seen as impartiality in war and codified as such in the Hague and Geneva Conventions, with the heavy military fighting in the Second

World War, neutrality took its place in a new realist framework which included economic warfare. No simple formula enables a country to protect itself from the pressures and problems of the outside world. In the opening to this chapter, it was suggested that Switzerland had resisted honourably through its military power. In order to maintain their independence, neutrals had to offer economic concessions to the belligerents to make up for their relative military weakness. Despite their different starting points, the concessions by Portugal, Spain, Sweden and Switzerland were largely similar; they comprised labour transfers, trade in resources and materials, together with capital transfers from neutrals to belligerents. The popular media, politicians and lawyers have increasingly maligned the version of neutrality represented by the myth of steadfastness as no more than a convenient excuse for self-enrichment. For small states, neutrality in conflict is a complex issue and from World War II required an increasing use of realist economic tools to avoid conflict. For these countries, survival was everything.

Notes

1 Barbey (1948: 31).
2 Bonjour (1973: vol. 7, 185–186); Ciano (1947: 263).
3 Gauye (1984: 11).
4 Butler, Pender, and Charnley (2000: 47–71).
5 Grotius (1925: 783).
6 Ørvik (1971: 13).
7 Ørvik (1971: 13–16).
8 Achen and Snidal (1989: 143–169); Lebow (1989: 208–224); Levy (1988: 485–512); Mearsheimer (1983); Waltz (1979).
9 Relative gains and the related concept of absolute gains are discussed in the realist literature. The concept of relative gains emphasizes the struggle between states amidst a tendency toward conflict. For more information, see Powell (1991: 1303–1320); Snidal (1991: 701–726).
10 Pottinger (1966).
11 Smit (1972: 23–34).
12 Hyde (1937: 81–85).
13 The Fifth Hague Convention of 1907 in *Treaties and Other International Agreements of the United States of America 1776 to 1917* (1968: vol. 1).
14 North (1990).
15 Helmreich (1977; 2000: 45–55).
16 Snyder (1984: 108–146).
17 Ørvik (1971: 50–61).
18 van Eysinga (1932: 71–72).
19 Mearsheimer (2001: 238–256).
20 The Fifth Hague Convention of 1907, Articles VII and IX, in *Treaties and Other International Agreements of the United States of America 1776 to 1917* (1968: vol. 1); Deák and Jessup (1939).
21 Jefferson (1917: 479).
22 Clements (1999: 153).
23 During wars in 1905 and 1912, the United States banned the exportation of arms and munitions, whereas in the Great War it specifically allowed such sales.

See "Proclamation Prohibiting the Exportation of Arms and Munitions of War to the Dominican Republic, October 14, 1905" and "Proclamation Prohibiting the Exportation of Arms and Ammunition to Mexico, March 14, 1912" in Deák and Jessup (eds.), *A Collection of Neutrality Laws*, pp. 1214–1215, contrasting with the Great War declaration: "Public Circular issued by the Department of State regarding Neutrality, Contraband, and the Seizure of Ships and Cargo, August 15, 1914" in the same edition, pp. 1250–1252, which specifically states "Commerce between this country and countries at war is not suspended" (p. 1250).
24 *Historisches Lexikon der Schweiz* (Unknown, 2002); Smit (1972: 22).
25 Cohn (1939: 251–259).
26 Ibid.: 282.
27 Ibid.: 251–259.
28 Smit (1972: 22ff.); for statistics on other European armies, see Golson (2016: 269–270).
29 Sweden relied on a 1925 strategy almost identical to their Great War neutral strategy; see Ulf Olsson, "The State and Industry in Swedish Rearmament" in Fritz (1982: 60. Switzerland relied on General Guisan's defence in depth scheme which was employed in September 1939, but later proved inadequate and was replaced by the réduit; see Guisan (1946: 91–126). Franco apparently lacked a grand military strategy for Spain.
30 Graham (1927: 371–372).
31 It took Germany three and a half years (1935 to 1938) to build an air force with 50,000 men and train them in the various new aircraft types; *Le Réarmament Clandestin du Reich 1930–1935* (Castellan, 1954: 139–154). Switzerland tried to defend itself but in vain against a superior German military at the time. Swiss General Guisan built a national réduit in July 1940, a series of linked defensive fortifications in the Alps based on the chance that highly skilled Swiss troops would defeat German mechanization. Gautschi (2003: 240–273). After fifteen years of spending under $50 million per annum, Swedish military spending in 1939 was increased to $322 million. It peaked in 1942 at $527 million. Little data exist on Spanish military forces during this time.
32 Golson (2011).
33 Golson (2012: 165–182).
34 Golson (2011).
35 Golson (2016).
36 Golson (2011).
37 Golson (2014b: 71–97).
38 Golson (2016).
39 Tooze (2006).
40 Golson (2011).
41 Golson (2013: 145–170; 2014a: 16–44).
42 Ibid.
43 Golson (2011).
44 Ibid.
45 National Archives and Records Administration, College Park, Maryland (hereafter NARA), RG234/16/19, report on preclusive operations, NARA RG84/UD2162/34, chart dated 30 March 1044; National Archives, Kew Gardens (hereafter NA) T160/1273, memos dated 19 April 1943, June 1943, 19 November 1943 and 10 May 1944. Ministry of Foreign Affairs, memos dated 3 January 1941, XIV: 384–386; Bank of England (hereafter BoE) OV213, memo dated 12 May 1942; BoE OV6/214, minute dated 8 June 1942.

46 NARA RG107/160/929, folder marked "Swiss Credit to Germans" report dated 22 February 1945.
47 Bower (1997).

References

Achen, C., & Snidal, D. (1989). Rational Deterrence Theory and Comparative Case Studies. *World Politics*, 41(2, January), 143–169.
Barbey, B. (1948). *Fünf Jahre auf dem Kommandoposten des Generals: Tagebuch des Chefs des Persönlichen Stabes General Guisan 1940–1945*. Bern: H. Lang & Cie.
Brown, P. M. (1939). Neutrality. *American Journal of International Law*, 33(4, October), 726–727.
Bonjour, E. (1973). *Neutralität*, vol. 7. Zurich: Heibing & Lichtenstein.
Bower, T. (1997). *Blood Money: The Swiss, the Nazis and the Looted Billions*. London: Pan Books.
Butler, M., Pender, M., & Charney, J. (2000). *The Making of Modern Switzerland, 1848–1998: Between Community and Change*. Basingstoke: Macmillan.
Castellan, G. (1954). *Le Réarmament Clandestin du Reich 1930–1935*. Paris.
Ciano, G. (1947). *Tagebücher 1939–1943: Übertragung aus dem Italienischen*. Bern: A. Schers.
Clements, K. A. (1999). *Woodrow Wilson: World Statesman*. London: Ivan R. Dee.
Cohn, G. (1939). *Neo-Neutrality*. New York: Columbia University Press.
Deák, F., & Jessup, P. C. (1939). *A Collection of Neutrality Laws, Regulations and Treaties of Various Countries*, vol. 2, Washington, DC: Carnegie Endowmenr for International Peace.
van Eysinga, W. J. M. (1932). The Netherlands and the Law of Neutrality during the Great War. *Transactions of the Grotius Society*, vol. 18, *Problems of Peace and War, Papers Read before the Society in the War* (pp. 71–72). Cambridge: Cambridge University Press.
Fritz, M. (1982). *The Adaptable Nation: Essays in Swedish Economy during the Second World War*. Stockholm: Almqvist & Wiksell International.
Gautschi, W. (2003). *General Guisan: Commander in Chief of the Swiss Army in World War II*. London: Front Street Press.
Gauye, O. (1984). Au Rütli, 25 juillet 1940, Le discours du Général Guisan: nouveaux aspects. *Studien und Quellen*, 10, Bern: Swiss Federal Archives.
Golson, E. (2011). The Economics of Neutrality: Spain, Sweden and Switzerland in the Second World War. D.Phil. dissertation, London School of Economics.
Golson, E. (2012). Did Swedish Ball Bearings Keep the Second World War Going? Re-evaluating Neutral Sweden's Role. *Scandinavian Economic History Review*, 60(2, June), 165–182.
Golson, E. (2013). Spanish Civilian Labour for Germany? Re-evaluating Neutral Spain's Role. *Revista de Historia Económica: Journal of Iberian and Latin American Economic History*, 31(1, March), 145–170.
Golson, E. (2014a). Swiss High Skilled Labour for Germany during the Second World War. *Schweizerische Zeitschrift für Geschichte*, 64(1, March), 16–44.
Golson, E. (2014b). Swiss Trade with the Allied and Axis Powers during the Second World War. *Jahrbuch Für Wirtschaftsgeschichte*, 55(2, November), 71–97.
Golson, E. (2016). Sweden as an Occupied Country? Swedish-Belligerent Trade in the Second World War. In Jonas Scherner & Eugene N. White (eds.), *Hitler's War and Nazi Economic Hegemony in Occupied Europe*. Cambridge: Cambridge University Press.

Graham, M. W., Jr. (1927). The Effect of the League of Nations Covenant on the Theory and Practice of Neutrality. *California Law Review*, 15(5, July), 357–377.

Grotius, H. (1925). *De jure belli ac pacis*. London.

Guisan, H. (1946). *Bericht an die Bundesversammlung über den Aktivdienst 1939–1945*. Lausanne: Verkehrsverlag.

Helmreich, J. E. (1977). The Diplomacy of Apology: U.S. Bombings of Switzerland during World War II. *Air University Review* (May–June).

Helmreich, J. E. (2000). The Bombing of Zurich. *Aerospace Power Journal* (Summer), 92–108.

Hyde, C. C. (1937). Belgium and Neutrality. *American Journal of International Law*, 31(1, January), 81–85.

Jefferson, M. (1917). Our Trade in the Great War. *Geographical Review*, 6(3, June), 477ff.

Lebow, R. N. (1989). Rational Deterrence Theory: I Think, Therefore I Deter. *World Politics*, 41(2, January), 208–224.

Levy, J. S. (1988). When Do Deterrent Threats Work? *British Journal of Political Science*, 18(4, October), 485–512.

Mearsheimer, J. J. (1983). *Conventional Deterrence*. Ithaca, NY: Cornell University Press.

Mearsheimer, J. J. (2001). *The Tragedy of Great Power Politics*. New York: W. W. Norton.

Merli, F. J. (2004). *The Alabama, British Neutrality, and the American Civil War*. Bloomington: Indiana University Press.

North, D. (1990). *Institutions, Institutional Change and Economic Performance*. Cambridge, UK: Cambridge University Press.

Ørvik, N. (1971). *The Decline of Neutrality, 1914–1941*. London: F. Cass.

Pottinger, E. (1966), *Napoleon III and the German Crisis*. Cambridge, MA: Harvard University Press.

Powell, R. (1991). Absolute and Relative Gains in International Relations Theory. *American Political Science Review*, 85(4, December), 1303–1320.

Smit, C. (1972). *Nederland in de Eerste Wereldoorlog (1899–1919)*, vol. 2: *1914–1917*. Groningen: Wolters-Noordhoff.

Snidal, D. (1991). Relative Gains and the Pattern of International Cooperation. *American Political Science Review* 85(3, September), 701–726.

Snyder, J. (1984). Civil-Military Relations and the Cult of the Offensive, 1914 and 1984. *International Security*, 9(1, Summer), 108–146.

Tooze, A. (2006) *The Wages of Destruction: The Making and Breaking of the Nazi Economy*. London: Allen Lane.

Treaties and Other International Agreements of the United States of America 1776 to 1917 (1968), vol. 1, *Multilateral 1776–1917*, Washington, DC: US State Department.

Unknown (2002). *Historisches Lexikon der Schweiz (HLS)*. Available at www.hls-dhs-dss.ch

Waltz, K. (1979). *Theory of International Politics*. Reading, MA: Addison-Wesley.

8 The Atlantic orientation
Norway and the western blockade of Germany, 1914–1918

Knut Ola Naastad Strøm

Introduction

During the Great War, Norway and the Norwegian economy were caught between the devil and the deep blue sea, as global conflict disrupted traditional trade flows and supply routes. This chapter examines the chronological development of Western economic warfare policy between 1914 and 1919 in the context of Norwegian economic and foreign policy, analysing how public policy facilitated dramatic economic growth during the first half of the conflict, while failing to prevent equally rapid contraction during the latter half. In order to do this, the chapter combines a study of diplomatic correspondence with the findings of earlier works on Western and Norwegian wartime policy, arguing that the relative reluctance of the Norwegian government to engage diplomatically with the warring parties during the first two years of the war left it increasingly incapable of resisting Western economic warfare efforts from 1916 onwards.

Over the course of the first two years of the Great War, German demand for imports of all kinds boosted domestic Norwegian production, and saw Scandinavia become a hub for the transhipment of overseas goods to the Central Powers. Countering Germany's ability to engage in international trade by way of Norwegian markets became a key objective of the Western powers' economic warfare efforts from the autumn of 1914 onwards. Recent research by Dehne, Lambert and Morgan-Owen into the early blockade has helped shed light on how the British government nevertheless struggled to effectively pursue economic warfare during the first year and a half of conflict. This complements earlier research on Norwegian wartime trade by Riste and Berg, emphasizing the increasing ability of the Western allies to gain control over Norwegian trade during the latter half of the conflict. Together these strains of literature show how economic policy and foreign policy became two sides of the same coin, as the Norwegian government sought to tightrope the demands of maintaining both neutrality and economic prosperity, building on prewar priorities and interpreting neutrality in the vein of economic liberalism. British inability to impose effective blockade measures allowed the Norwegian government to adopt a hands-off approach to trade policy between 1914 and 1916, allowing the domestic economy to grow rapidly as it responded to overseas demand. This relative failure to regulate overseas trade increased the already high reliance on Western imports, making the Norwegian economy increasingly vulnerable to Western economic pressure. Attempts to avoid direct engagement with the blockade could thus only be successful as long as the Western allies allowed them to be. Once Western pressure did begin to materialize in earnest from late 1915 onwards, the Norwegian government was forced into increasingly desperate diplomatic rearguard actions in order to preserve domestic economic prosperity and a veneer of political neutrality, eventually culminating in a wide-reaching Norwegian–American trade agreement in April 1918.

The first part of the chapter contextualizes the Norwegian economic and foreign policy concerns as they stood at the outbreak of war. Thereafter follows a section combining and evaluating the findings of previous studies on Norwegian, British and American wartime trade and economic warfare policy. The final part of the text utilizes archival material to provide an account of allied efforts to force the Norwegian government into restricting trade with the Central Powers during the final years of the war.

Economic expansion and neutrality

When war broke out in 1914, the Norwegian government asserted political neutrality, announcing its desire not to involve the country in the conflict engulfing Europe. This decision was founded on a sober assessment of the country's long-term economic and security interests. The Norwegian economy was highly dependent on international trade, exports of goods and services alone accounting for almost two-fifths of GDP on the outbreak of war. Britain was the most important market for Norwegian exports, taking almost 25 per cent of the total in 1913, with Germany coming in second at 17 per cent. The United States took 7.6 per cent, while neighbouring Sweden and Denmark took only 6.6 and 2.3 per cent respectively. In return, Germany provided almost 32 per cent of Norwegian imports by value, against Britain at 26 per cent. Other countries were all in single digits, with Sweden providing 8.3 per cent, the US 7.1 per cent and Denmark 5.1 per cent.[1]

Yet the seemingly balanced division of trade between Norway and both belligerent blocks obscures the inherent vulnerability of the Norwegian economy to economic pressure from the Entente. Norwegian industries relied on imports of coal and raw materials, most of which came from Britain and the West. Even more important was the maintenance of large-scale imports of foodstuffs. Between 1905 and 1914, grain imports, mainly of Russian rye and American wheat, peaked at 64–67 per cent of total domestic consumption. The export of services from the important shipping sector was also heavily geared towards the West, as the merchant fleet depended on access to Britain's global network of ports and bunker stations. In 1913, Norwegian vessels made over 7,000 calls at UK ports, against only 4,000 calls in Norway. This dependence on British infrastructure was further exacerbated in the decades leading up to 1914 as international transactions were increasingly routed through the City of London financial services industry. In 1914, the Norwegian merchant marine stood at almost two million gross tons, second only to the British and German merchant navies, and roughly similar to the French and American fleets. In 1905, shipping services accounted for no less than 32.5 per cent of Norwegian exports by value, rising to almost 40 per cent by the outbreak of war.[2]

The importance of the merchant fleet and the dependence on Western trade were powerful influences on Norwegian foreign policy. Through the 1890s and early 1900s the pursuit of trade and economic prosperity also went hand in hand with a commitment to neutrality. There was broad political agreement in Norway to avoid foreign military or diplomatic entanglements. No alliances or foreign security commitments would be contemplated in the years leading up to 1914. Yet there also existed a tacit understanding among Norwegian politicians that national security and economic prosperity was reliant upon maintaining good relations with Britain. Norwegian foreign policy must thus be understood in light of the high reliance on overseas trade. Favourable conditions for the merchant fleet and access to foreign markets had to be maintained. Neutrality in wartime was likewise important in safeguarding domestic prosperity, but international isolation would be disastrous for the economy as a whole. This realization permeated across the Norwegian political spectrum in 1914.[3]

Britain and the failure of economic warfare

Both the commitment to neutrality and the Atlantic orientation of Norwegian foreign policy before 1914 would be sorely tested during the Great War, when the Northern European neutrals were the Central Powers' only entry points for trade with the rest of the world. From the very first weeks of the conflict the British cabinet worried that transatlantic imports were reaching Germany via neutral North Sea ports. Yet the British Admiralty nevertheless believed that direct interference with neutral shipping could be kept at a minimum. As long as British shipping was prevented from being used to increase the total quantity of neutral imports, any such increase would be limited to what could be carried on neutral ships alone. The effective use of such neutral shipping could be further reduced through Britain's control of financial services and global trade infrastructure, as well as the more underhand means of harassment by the Royal Navy. The inability of neutrals to substantially increase their imports from overseas should in turn reduce the ability of these economies to respond to increased German demand for goods.[4]

Although plans for economic warfare along such lines had been in existence at the Admiralty for several years before the outbreak of the war, effort towards having them adopted as official government policy had met with little success. Moreover, in the late summer and autumn of 1914, cabinet compromise on blockade policy would not be easy to reach. When the war began in the late summer of 1914, it was presaged by a financial crisis of its own. Fear of a great power conflict breaking out grew over the course of July, rattling market confidence in London and elsewhere. International liquidity rapidly dried up as investors across Europe and the US began repatriating their holdings. On 31 July, both the New York and London stock exchanges were forced to close their doors. Within the space of a few short days international trade ground almost to a halt, bringing the City of London financial system close to collapse.[5]

In Britain government officials were taken aback by the suddenness and severity of the crisis. Having spent the first week of August working to avert the immediate threat of complete financial meltdown, the Treasury was very reluctant to accede to any Admiralty requests that might exacerbate the problems facing the British economy. The Board of Trade (BoT) was likewise seized with the need to get international trade going again, lest British exporters and shippers face economic ruin. The Foreign Office (FO), in turn, was worried about the need to maintain good relations with neutrals, believing that avoiding their enmity – especially that of the US – would be vital to the British war effort. The proponents of economic warfare within the British cabinet thus faced an uphill struggle to implement any of the Admiralty's plans to restrict trade in the North Sea. Nor did it help that the cabinet was deeply divided on the question of joining the war in the first place. Only Germany's violation of Belgian neutrality allowed Prime Minister Asquith to avoid a major cabinet split. Ostensibly, Britain would go to war in order to contain illegitimate German aggression against a minor neutral. Yet this moral argument also precluded the rapid adoption of policies that would directly impinge on neutral trading rights.[6]

Improvising a blockade

By late 1914 the British government had come to abandon most vestiges of the Admiralty's prewar economic warfare policy, replacing it with a more traditional blockade at the northern and western entrances to the North Sea. Under the new system, gradually implemented from October 1914 onwards, the effort to prevent the rerouting of German trade through the northern neutrals relied on the promulgation of lists of commodities which the Central Powers would not be allowed to import. To these contraband lists would be applied the doctrine of continuous voyage – a legal concept whereby goods bound for a neutral port could be treated as contraband if ultimate enemy destination could be proved. Finally, a British order-in-council of 29 October also adopted new FO proposals that Britain should encourage the northern neutrals to voluntarily restrict their re-export of goods to Germany. The new British strategy thus involved two distinct means by which German trade should be restricted: reducing the supply of goods from overseas through traditional blockade and reducing European demand through voluntary neutral rationing of imports.[7]

The return to a traditional blockade involved establishing the ownership and ultimate destination of individual cargoes. The Foreign Office assumed that the number of shipments which would need to be tracked was relatively low. This in turn was based on the belief that only Dutch ports had the infrastructure and spare capacity to respond to German demand. Shipments of non-contraband goods, as well as shipments to other northern neutrals, were thought safe to ignore. It therefore came as a very unpleasant surprise to the British government when news began reaching London in September 1914 that the quantity of goods being transhipped to Germany through Norway and the rest of Scandinavia was increasing dramatically.[8]

The first serious move to tighten British control over this trade came on 2 November 1914, when the cabinet officially declared the entire North Sea to be an "area of war". Shortly thereafter, merchant shipping bound to or from the Atlantic was advised by London to abandon any northern route around the British Isles, and instead use the English Channel in order to be guided across the North Sea by the Royal Navy. Any civilian vessel – regardless of flag – crossing the Atlantic to and from Norway would now have to pass through extensive stretches of British home waters, thus subjecting themselves to British inspection and sailing instructions.[9]

Information flow problems were nevertheless hampering British efforts. Blockade authorities quickly found themselves struggling to cope with the wealth of data required to decide whether a cargo was ultimately destined for the Central Powers. Nor were neutral governments on either side of the Atlantic keen to comply with the blockade. In October, the US State Department ordered that the manifests of all ships sailing from American ports be kept confidential for thirty days after departure. In the same month, the Danish, Swedish and Norwegian governments announced that their public trade figures would not be published for the duration of the conflict. These problems were also exacerbated by the rivalries and conflicting priorities which continued to plague British government departments. The end result was that, well into 1915, the majority of suspect vessels stopped by the Royal Navy and taken to British port for inspection were released again without charge.[10]

By early 1915 it was becoming increasingly obvious to British policymakers that their blockade efforts were not producing the desired results. Scandinavian imports stood at levels well above the prewar average, in turn ensuring a steady flow of goods to Germany. Even more embarrassingly, much of the trade across the North Sea basin was still being carried by British shipping. In an effort to tackle this last issue, the Cabinet decided to greatly expand the list of commodities for which licence would be required for export from Britain. The new lists were promulgated in March 1915. To consider applications for export licenses, the cabinet also authorized the creation of a new War Trade Department (WTD). Yet this new body quickly ran into difficulties. Because the surge in licence applications proved greater than anticipated, the fledgling department was quickly swamped. In order to cope with the rapidly growing backlog, the WTD made the decision to rubber-stamp all new applications, in turn leading to a substantial increase in exports to Scandinavia – the exact opposite of what the new system was intended to ensure. Overall, UK exports to Norway increased by around 40 per cent between 1914 and 1915.[11] American exports to Norway more than doubled over the same period. Figures 8.1 and 8.2 show how overall exchange of goods between Norway and its main trading partners changed over the course of the war.[12]

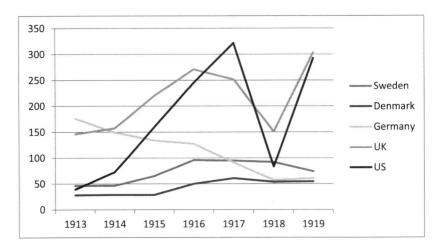

Figure 8.1 Norwegian goods imports, 1913–19, million Norwegian Krone, 1913 prices.

Source: Mitchell (2003, table E2).

Note: CPI deflator, Bank of Norway (2015).

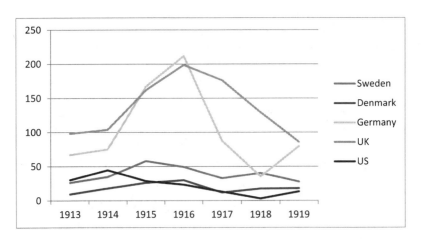

Figure 8.2 Norwegian goods exports, 1913–19, million Norwegian Krone, 1913 prices.

Source: Mitchell (2003, table E2).

Note: CPI deflator, Bank of Norway (2015).

Norwegian branch agreements

Aside from classifying Norwegian trade data, Prime Minister Gunnar Knudsen's government restricted itself to a measured response to Britain's early blockade efforts. British interference with Norwegian trade remained largely ineffective, and once the initial war scare and the worst effects of the July financial crisis had subsided, imports from overseas quickly picked up again. The conduct of foreign policy along these lines in 1914 and 1915 was made all the easier by the British failure to flex economic and military muscle in the North Sea. Price rises notwithstanding, Norway suffered few serious supply shortages during the first years of conflict. As long as the domestic economic situation did not deteriorate, the Knudsen government could therefore limit itself to avoiding outright conflict with any of the warring parties. Germany remained a major trading partner, and any foreign policy entanglements that could be construed as unneutral might well invite some form of retaliation from German authorities. Neither Knudsen nor Foreign Minister Nils Ihlen were therefore keen on compromising Norwegian neutrality by overt cooperation with British blockade authorities.[13]

The continuing policy chaos reigning in London through the spring and summer of 1915 would preclude more forceful economic warfare efforts. Cabinet reform, the continuing debacle of the military offensives in France and the Mediterranean, various financial and economic issues and American protests against British policies all combined to divert the government's attention away from tackling the blockade issue head on. A number of government departments, including the Board of Trade, also remained deeply opposed to any tightening of British export regulations or increased restrictions on British merchants sailing on neutrals.[14]

As an alternative to engaging further with the Norwegian government, the Foreign Office, from early 1915 onwards, instead led efforts to negotiate directly with private Norwegian enterprise. These efforts were more wide-ranging than simple prohibition on the re-export of imports. British authorities would also seek to prevent Norwegian exports to Germany of domestic produce – especially of such goods as were important to the German war industry. These arrangements also suited the Knudsen government. If Norway could accommodate British blockade efforts without compromising overt political neutrality or the domestic economy, then so much the better.[15]

British dealings with Norwegian private firms over the course of the spring and summer of 1915 were not without difficulties, but by autumn the Entente had gained control over the output of a number of important Norwegian companies and industries through various supply and compensation schemes. British blockade authorities also succeeded in reaching a number of agreements with Norwegian business associations. Under these so-called "branch agreements" association members undertook to guarantee that British imports would not be re-exported to the Central Powers, and instead used only to meet domestic demand. The first of these was signed in late August, with more following over the course of late 1915 and early 1916.

Reforming the system

Towards the end of 1915 the pressure from Parliament and within the Cabinet itself for a more forceful conduct of the blockade finally began to produce results. In December 1915, Lord Robert Cecil, under-secretary of state at the FO, pushed through a proposal that the British government adopt an improved blacklist system for international trade. Any company or individual, regardless of nationality, found or suspected to be involved in trading with the Central Powers would now be placed on what became known as the Statutory Lists, and blocked from all access to British-controlled infrastructure. This allowed the British government much greater scope for enforcing agreements with neutrals. After well over a year of war, the British were finally making serious progress towards translating their control over international trade into a viable weapon.[16]

The end of 1915 and beginning of 1916 also saw a range of efforts towards improving coordination between the various bodies engaged in blockade work. In February 1916, this work culminated in the creation of a Ministry of Blockade (MoB), which for the first time would have the authority to compel intra-governmental cooperation on economic warfare. The new ministry was led by Cecil as Minister of Blockade and retained close ties with the FO. Shortly after its creation, the Ministry collated and published the first edition of the new Statutory Lists. In March this was followed by the creation of a new type of navigation certificate. Such "Navicerts" could be obtained by merchant shippers agreeing to have their cargoes screened by Entente inspectors overseas before shipment to Europe and would guarantee ships unhindered passage through the British blockade belt. This in turn reduced the risk of delays, further incentivizing neutral shippers to cooperate with the British authorities.[17]

Following the centralizing of policymaking and commercial intelligence gathering under the aegis of a dedicated ministry, the British authorities were finally both willing and increasingly able to challenge the Norwegian government's policy of non-involvement in blockade affairs. The first issue that would be the focus of British pressure was the Norwegian fisheries. Over the course of late 1914 and 1915, German buyers had cornered the Norwegian market in fish products. The MoB threatened retaliation by restricting Norwegian imports, should the Norwegian government refuse to limit fish exports to Germany. Desirous to avoid full-scale confrontation, the Norwegian government was forced to commit to a permanent settlement. An Anglo-Norwegian fisheries agreement was signed on 5 August 1916, stipulating that sales to Germany would be limited to 15 per cent of total fish exports. The fisheries agreement marked the beginning of the end for the Knudsen government's policy of non-involvement with blockade affairs. Agreements with the Entente could be negotiated, but they could no longer be avoided.[18]

That the MoB was prepared to place severe economic pressure on Norway would become clear later the same year. Negotiations for an agreement restricting the exports of Norwegian copper ore and copper pyrites to Germany had been taking place parallel to those on fisheries. Not only was copper an important component in armaments production in its own right, but much of the Norwegian pyrite also contained sulphur. Sulphur was a key ingredient in explosives, and by 1916 Norway was Germany's sole remaining foreign supplier. Resolving the issue therefore had a high priority at the MoB. In return for a Norwegian prohibition on exports of copper ore and pyrites to the Central Powers, the British government would be prepared to guarantee Norwegian imports of 8,000 tons of refined copper per annum.[19]

The carrot was sizeable. There was limited capacity in Norway for refining copper ore into useful product, and since overseas imports had been blocked by the British since the beginning of the negotiations there was a severe shortage of the metal in the country. A further British promise to allow the immediate one-time import of 3,000 tons of copper to relieve the domestic shortage sealed the deal. The Norwegian government therefore agreed to limit copper exports from September 1916.

The MoB was initially very pleased with the outcome of the negotiations. Yet serious disagreements soon arose over the interpretation of the agreement. Some of the Norwegian sulphuric pyrite had such a low copper content that it was not commercially regarded as cuprous. The Norwegian government did not believe these covered by the agreed export prohibition, and the sale of such pyrites to Germany continued unabated over the course of the autumn. For their part, the British were very clear that, in their view, pyrites containing even trace amounts of copper were covered by the agreement. The cessation of exports of such sulphuric pyrites to Germany had been a key British objective in negotiating the accord, and any attempt by the Norwegian government to continue these was seen by the MoB as outright fraud. Following repeated Norwegian failures to put an end to exports in October and November, the MoB finally responded by instigating a complete coal embargo on Norway from 23 December onwards.[20]

Ihlen did not immediately offer any substantial concessions on the pyrite issue. The fear of German retaliation, as well as resentment over what was seen as British attempts to interfere with Norwegian neutral rights, remained extant. Yet Cecil and the MoB refused to budge. By the second week of February Ihlen had been forced into a complete climbdown. Norway would ban the export of all pyrites to Germany. On 17 February, the British government lifted the coal embargo.[21]

At the height of the pyrite controversy, Germany announced the return of unrestricted U-boat warfare from 1 February 1917. Aside from a brief interruption as shippers and insurance organizations adapted to the new situation, the direct short-term impact of renewed U-boat campaign on Norwegian trade was limited. The German policy nevertheless set the stage for one final Anglo-Norwegian blockade agreement. Neutral losses in the North Sea had long caused the British to fear the withdrawal of neutral tonnage from Entente shipping routes. Germany's announcement provided a pretext by which this could be prevented. Within a few days of unrestricted submarine warfare being introduced, the MoB announced that no neutral merchant ship present in a British port would be allowed to leave unless replaced by an equal amount of incoming tonnage. At the same time, mounting losses of lives and ships to U-boats – in March 1917 some 20 per cent of all merchant vessels lost worldwide were Norwegian – prompted the Knudsen government to look into ways through which the safety of ships could be better ensured. A British proposal to reflag Norwegian ships to the Entente, which would have allowed the vessels to be armed, providing a measure of defence against submarines, was rejected. Instead, Norwegian and British representatives came up with a scheme by which tonnage would be exchanged. British merchant ships would take over the North Sea traffic almost in its entirety, in return for unarmed Norwegian ships being requisitioned to run in less dangerous waters. Britain would maintain the export of coal to Norway for the duration against a guarantee that Norwegian tonnage would continue to sail in Entente service. This arrangement proved acceptable both to the Knudsen government and to the MoB. A confidential Anglo-Norwegian tonnage agreement to this effect was signed in April 1917 and gradually implemented over the course of the summer.[22]

The American embargo

The tonnage agreement and the introduction of the Navicert system brought a significant part of the Norwegian merchant fleet under British control. Together with the Statutory Lists and the branch agreements these measures went a long way towards reducing the number of German imports transhipped through Norway, as well as limiting Norwegian capacity to export domestic produce to the Central Powers. By early 1917, the British government had thus managed to increase its degree of control over transatlantic trade substantially. America's entry into the war in April 1917 would make this control more or less complete, although it would take time to turn this potential into practical policy. Yet the tonnage agreement was also in many ways a double-edged sword for the British government. It guaranteed Entente access to Norwegian shipping, but in return it also secured Norway's ability to import coal and export shipping services. As long as the arrangement remained in operation it would substantially improve the capacity of the Norwegian government to resist further allied economic pressure.

American readiness for war in April 1917 was woeful. No steps of any consequence had been taken to limit US–Scandinavian trade by the time a British blockade delegation arrived in Washington DC on 22 April 1917. In a series of meeting over the following weeks the State Department warned the British delegates that it would be impossible for the US to accede to every British suggestion. The American government would not be party to an outright blockade of Norway and the northern neutrals. Nor could the US government adopt the Statutory Lists, which were far too controversial with the American public. New US export permits would also have to replace the Navicert system in allowing merchantmen through the British blockade cordon. Furthermore, the US would agree to appoint representatives to the various British and Allied blockade committees, against assurances that no agreements with neutrals would be made without approval from Washington, essentially giving the American representatives a veto on blockade measures.[23]

The MoB representatives found the American reservations to be more theoretical than practical. As long as US policy on exports and bunker control was strict – and the American negotiators gave every impression that this would be so – the British had no serious objections to the US replacing the British machinery. What was needed was for the American authorities to have the knowledge and time necessary to set up its own system. When the British blockade delegation left the US on 25 May, the future of Norwegian transatlantic trade therefore rested to a large extent in US hands.[24]

The American government took the first major step towards setting up its own blockade apparatus on 12 June, when Congress passed the Espionage Act, empowering the President to control the flow of US exports. On 9 July, Wilson proclaimed an American export embargo. The list of embargoed goods was limited, prohibiting only the free export of armaments, fuel, fertilizers, iron, steel and certain foodstuffs. It had also been a long time coming. Some of the delay no doubt stemmed from the slow passage through Congress of the necessary legislation. Yet it was also characteristic of the way in which the Wilson administration continued to handle American preparation for war. It was a lack of urgency which would come to exasperate the British blockade authorities through to the end of 1917. In late June, both the British and French ambassadors in Washington delivered notes to the State Department underlining the urgent need to put an end to all further exports to Norway and the other northern neutrals. The embargo proclamation of 9 July drew some of the sting from the complaints, but by no means all. On 12 July, the MoB let the American ambassador in London know that they considered the US embargo list too narrow.[25]

On the 24th, the Wilson administration delivered a memorandum to the Norwegian Legation in Washington, setting out the basis for American blockade policy. It bluntly stated that "the American people cannot be expected to part with food supplies other than in such minimum amount as will make up the deficiency in the food values arising after the most intensive endeavours [by Norway]".[26] Norway would only be allowed to import such goods as were required for domestic consumption, and should not expect the US to alleviate any shortages created by exports of domestic produce to Germany. Despite its reluctance to adopt Navicerts, blacklists and other Entente blockade tools outright, the Wilson administration had thus, for all practical intents and purposes, bought into the British policy of neutral rationing.[27]

The prospect of reduced access to American goods caused a great deal of anxiety within the Knudsen government. A Norwegian government trade delegation headed by polar explorer Fridtjof Nansen arrived in New York on 25 July. Months would nevertheless pass before any serious negotiations for a Norwegian–American trade agreement began. Nansen was initially unable to respond to US demands for detailed Norwegian trade statistics. Nor was Ihlen forthcoming in forwarding the required information to Washington, preferring instead to delay in the hope of securing concessions. The continuing operation of the Anglo-Norwegian tonnage agreement meant that Norwegian coal supplies and foreign earnings from the fleet remained secure for the time being. The stoppage of grain imports was more worrying, but stocks in Norway remained sufficient to avoid severe shortages in the immediate future. Ihlen and the permanent Norwegian Minister in Washington also persisted in their belief that US blockade policy would turn out more lenient than what proved to be the case.[28]

For its part, the US administration was minded to do little beyond letting the effects of the embargo take hold. Ostensibly the US was happy to supply Norway's "fair requirements", provided Norway made an effort to prove what those requirements might be. The British government was also eager to help push the US towards establishing an effective American blockade operation. On 11 August the British ambassador in Washington made it clear to the Americans that that the UK government was prepared to break its current agreements with the northern neutrals in the pursuit of an acceptable Anglo-American blockade policy. This left the Wilson administration with virtually a free hand to negotiate on behalf of the Entente.[29]

On 21 August, Wilson established a new Exports Administrative Board (EAB), tasking it with administering and carrying out US blockade policy. The new head of the EAB, Vance McCormick, quickly reaffirmed the United States' intention to withhold export licences for goods to Norway until such a time as a general trade agreement had been negotiated. On the 27th, the Wilson administration upped the ante yet further by issuing a second embargo proclamation. This expanded the list of embargoed goods to cover more or less all US exports to the northern neutrals, creating an almost complete American blockade of Norway. On 12 October, Wilson once again reformed the fledgling US blockade administration. The EAB was expanded and renamed the War Trade Board (WTB). Under McCormick's leadership the economic power and administrative clout of the American blockade administration was thus growing rapidly.[30]

The Washington negotiations

By November 1917, the combined Anglo-American embargo was causing significant shortages in Norway. Although outright hunger was still some ways off, growing public dissatisfaction with the deteriorating economic situation was piling pressure on the Knudsen government. On 14 November, Ihlen finally instructed Nansen to propose that the US government renew the issuing of export licences for Norway. In return, the Knudsen government would ban all exports to Germany, with the exception of 48,000 tons of fish per annum and significant quantities of minerals, including renewed copper and pyrite exports.[31]

Parallel to Ihlen formulating the Norwegian proposals, both the MoB and the WTB were becoming increasingly worried about the lack of progress in the Norwegian negotiations. At a conference in London in early November, representatives of the allied governments established that the goal of the forthcoming negotiations should be to limit Norwegian exports to Germany to a maximum of 40,000 tons of fish per annum.[32] All other exports to the Central Powers would have to be prevented. The MoB was especially vehement that copper and pyrite exports must remain banned. On 27 November the WTB responded to the Norwegian proposals along those lines. The US would accept Ihlen's fish quota, but no other goods or mineral export would be allowed.[33]

This initial exchange began a protracted tug of war between the Norwegian and American negotiators. In a counterproposal on 7 December, Ihlen reiterated the need to maintain limited exports of certain minerals to Germany. Norway would also reserve the right to maintain exports of any class of goods not specifically covered by the agreement. This last was a major break with US and British thinking of limiting Norwegian exports to established quotas. Ihlen's proposals were therefore rejected out of hand by the WTB on 20 December. The uncompromising US stance was also supported by the American Minister in Norway, Albert Schmedeman. He argued that public opinion in Kristiania was turning increasingly in favour of the Western allies, and that the deteriorating supply situation would make eventual Norwegian acceptance of American demands inevitable.[34]

By early 1918, the lack of overseas imports was causing serious shortages of industrial raw materials in Norway. Rationing of foodstuffs was finally introduced on 1 January. On the 17th, Knudsen met with Schmedeman and intimated that continued refusal on the part of the US to allow even limited exports to Germany of minerals would cause the government great embarrassment. In accordance with his instructions from the WTB, Schmedeman rebuffed the prime minister. The American minister instead telegraphed home that the supply situation in Norway was becoming increasingly critical and reiterated that concessions from the WTD would only prolong negotiations further.[35]

On 2 February, Nansen forwarded Ihlen's latest set of counterproposals to the WTB. In addition to fish products, substantial mineral exports to Germany remained extant. Ihlen argued that retaining exports at this level was the absolute minimum compatible with the maintenance of Norwegian neutrality. A week later, the WTB let Nansen know that some concessions to the prohibition on mineral exports might be allowed, but that the quantities stipulated in the 2 February proposal were far too high. Furthermore, neither pyrites nor any non-mineral exports except fish could be contemplated. Nansen was also informed that if the American proposals were not accepted in full, negotiations would be broken off.[36]

Despite the ultimatum, discussion continued over the precise quantities Norway should be allowed to export. Ihlen took up a compromise solution suggested by the French Minister in Kristiania and, on 14 February, instructed

Nansen to propose that the WTB allow some increase in mineral quotas. Despite British misgivings, the WTB eventually authorized that a revised draft proposal encompassing these changes – with the further provision that Norway would be allowed to continue exports to Germany of a range of less important goods in quantities not exceeding those exported in 1917 – should be delivered to the Norwegian government on 15 March. Negotiations nevertheless dragged out for another month on a number of issues raised by Ihlen. In the last week of April, the WTB finally informed Nansen that if the present round of negotiations failed, the US government would not consider itself bound by any concessions made up to that point. Feeling he could delay the matter no longer, Nansen on 30 April signed an agreement along the lines proposed by the WTB. Ihlen retroactively endorsed Nansen's decision the following day.[37]

In short order the American–Norwegian trade agreement was endorsed by the British and other allied governments. An Inter-Allied Trade Commission would be created in Kristiania to provide oversight and guarantee compliance with the agreement. These steps completed, the WTB began releasing goods for shipment to Norway from the second week of May 1918. Some of the restrictions on Norwegian trade were eased following the Armistice in November 1918, but the agreement itself remained in operation until after the signing of the Treaty of Versailles in the summer of 1919.[38]

The devil and the deep blue sea

The signing of the Norwegian–American trade agreement in April 1918 brought a degree of respite to the domestic Norwegian economy. It also represented the culmination of a process of increasing regulation of trade and private enterprise, bringing the Norwegian economy fully into the allied blockade of the Central Powers. Yet it took the Western Allies until the spring of 1918 to achieve this, and for much of that time British blockade efforts were spectacularly ineffective. Between 1914 and 1916, the Norwegian economy enjoyed a period of rapid and sustained growth, fuelled largely by booming foreign trade as private enterprise responded to the opportunities created by the disruption of traditional patterns of European trade. Norwegian companies were operating in a wartime economic environment while attempting to play by peacetime rules. That they were able to do so was not so much a result of skilful political manoeuvring by Norwegian politicians; rather, it was the inevitable consequence of the British government's failure to enforce any other regulations due to conflicting interdepartmental priorities.

The policies adopted by the Knudsen government between 1914 and 1917 were largely in line with those pursued in peacetime, promoting domestic economic growth while avoiding foreign policy entanglements. Norwegian reliance on transatlantic trade links meant that options for resisting allied pressure were limited. As long as that pressure was ineffectual, the highly lucrative trade with Germany could be allowed to flourish. Only after the British blockade apparatus began to overcome its inability to impose policies on the Norwegian government were the Western allies able to reverse the expansion of Norwegian trade. From early 1916 onwards, the Norwegian government increasingly found itself unable to avoid making concessions curtailing Norwegian exports to the Central Powers. The economic–diplomatic brinkmanship pursued by the Knudsen government in resisting US demands over the course of late 1917 and early 1918 must be understood in light of its reluctance to compromise political neutrality and accompanying economic liberalism beyond what had already been done. The option of forgoing a general agreement remained open throughout, but although outright starvation would probably have been avoided, failure to reopen trade with the West would mean that the throttling of the domestic economy would continue. The WTB's threat in the spring of 1918 to rescind the few concessions already granted to Nansen unless an agreement was signed immediately finally broke the last vestiges of reluctance on the part of the Norwegian government, presaging the conclusion of an accord on 30 April. From May 1918, Norwegian trade operated fully under the umbrella of allied blockade agreements. Western economic warfare policies as pursued between 1914 and 1919 were thus not altogether unfavourable for the Norwegian economy. As long as those policies failed to accurately target neutral economic activity, Norwegian traders were able to respond to the increased demand caused by Germany being partially cut off from international markets. Only after almost two years of war had worn down British inhibitions were the allies gradually able to curtail and roll back Norwegian economic expansion.

Notes

1 Salmon 2004, table 2.
2 Berg 1995, pp. 16–17; Berglund 1920, table 1.
3 Berg 1995, pp. 101–104, 122; Riste 1965, pp. 42–43, 51–52; Bjørgo, Rian and Kaartvedt 1995, pp. 312–314, 342–347; Salmon 2004, pp. 71–75.
4 On the Admiralty's planning for economic warfare, and the failure to implement these plans following the outbreak of war in 1914, see Goldrick 2015; Lambert 2012. UKNA (UK National Archives), CAB 24\8: "Statement with regard to the blockade", Imperial Conference 1917; Strachan 2001, pp. 394–395, 397, 401.
5 Lambert 2012, pp. 186–189; Roberts 2013, pp. 48–54, 172–174, 208–209; Strachan 2001, pp. 820–822.
6 Goldrick 2015, pp. 61–62; Kramer 2014, pp. 466–467; Lambert 2012, pp. 195–200, 236; Morgan-Owen 2017, pp. 311–321; Strachan 2001, pp. 1006, 1012.
7 Lambert 2012, pp. 270–274.
8 Kramer 2014, pp. 467, 469.
9 Berg 1995, pp. 189–190; Salmon 2004, p. 132.
10 Goldrick 2015, p. 181; Lambert 2012, pp. 278, 376–377, 393; Riste 1965, p. 49.
11 See Figure 8.1.
12 Lambert 2012, pp. 275–278, 384–385.
13 Berg 1995, pp. 185–186.
14 Dehne 2016, pp. 333–334; Lambert 2012, pp. 304, 366, 416.
15 Berg 1995, pp. 194–197.

16 Dehne 2016, pp. 337–340.
17 On the creation of the Ministry of Blockade, see Dehne 2016.
18 Berg 1995, pp. 199–201.
19 Ibid, pp. 202–204.
20 Ibid, pp. 204–207.
21 Ibid, pp. 223–226; Riste 1965, pp. 162–166.
22 UKNA, FO 382/1755: No. 226214, *The Norwegian Tonnage and Coal Agreement*; 30 November 1917; Riste 1965, pp. 174–176; Salmon 2004, pp. 143–144.
23 Burk 1985, pp. 100–110; Lambert 2012, p. 421.
24 USNA, RG 182-11-38, Norway Memos Jan 16 to July 17: Percy to Polk; 17th July, 1917.
25 Bailey 1942, pp. 69–70, 71–73, 79–81; FRUS: 1917, Supp. 2, Part II; Executive order 2645; 22nd June, 1917; Ibid; Page to Secretary of State; 12th July, 1917; USNA, RG 182-11-38, Spring Rice to Lansing; 27th July, 1917; Ibid, Memorandum on Norway; 17th July, 1917.
26 USNA, RG 182-11-38, ANAI: Memorandum on US blockade policy; 24th July, 1917.
27 Ibid: Memorandum on US blockade policy; 24th July, 1917.
28 Bailey 1942, pp. 108–115; Berg 1995, pp. 230–232, 234; USNA, RG 182-11-38, Norway Memos Jan 16 to July 17: *Aide-Memoire* from Norwegian Legation to Lansing; 28th June, 1917; Ibid: Percy to Polk; 17th July, 1917.
29 Bailey 1942, pp. 87–88.
30 Bailey 1942, pp. 88–93; FRUS: 1917, Supp. 2, Part II; *The Secretary of State to the Diplomatic Representatives in Certain Countries*; 27th August, 1917.
31 Bailey 1942, pp. 119; Berg 1995, pp. 234–235, 243; USNA, RG 182-11-38, ANAI: Nansen to Jones; 16th November, 1917.
32 Norwegian fish exports to Germany for 1916 totalled 181.000 tons. USNA, RG 182-11-38, Norway Memos Jan 16 to July 17: No. 435, Schmedeman to Secretary of State; 23rd July, 1917.
33 USNA, RG 182-11-38, ANAI: No. 590, *Note on the proceedings at the first meeting at the Foreign Office with the United States Blockade Representatives* . . . ; 9th November, 1917; Ibid: Percy to Jones; 17th November, 1917; Ibid: No. 10, WTB to McCormick; 17th November, 1917; Ibid: No. 7768, McCormick to WTB; 22nd November, 1917; Ibid: Jones to Nansen; 27th November, 1917.
34 Berg 1995, pp. 237–238; USNA, RG 182-11-38, ANAI: Nansen to Jones; 7th December, 1917; Ibid: Percy to Jones; 11th December, 1917; Ibid: WTB to Nansen; 19th December, 1917; Ibid: No. 440, Schmedeman to WTB; 30th December, 1917; Ibid: No. 202, WTB to Schmedeman; 5th January, 1918; Ibid: No. 446, Schmedeman to WTB; 12th January, 1918; Ibid: No. 6319, WTB to Sheldon; 22nd January, 1918
35 USNA, RG 182-11-38, ANAI: No. 478, Schmedeman to WTB; 18th January, 1918; Ibid: No. 480, Schmedeman to WTB; 18th January, 1918; USNA, RG 182-11-40, ANAII: Nansen to McCormick; 7th February, 1918.
36 Ibid: Nansen to McCormick; 2nd February, 1918; Ibid: WTB to Nansen; 9th February, 1918; Ibid: WTB to Sheldon; 9th February, 1918.
37 Ibid: Nansen to Chadbourne; 14th February, 1918; Ibid: No. 12672, Tardieu to McCormick; 18th February, 1918; Ibid: No. 212, McCormick to Schmedeman; 15th March, 1918; Ibid: No. 407, WTB to Sheldon; 27th April, 1918; Ibid: No. 790, Schmedeman to WTB; 30th April, 1918; USNA, RG 182-11-40, NNB3: No. 693, Schmedeman to WTB; 1st May, 1918; USNA, RG 182-11-40, ANAIII: Lansing to Lord Reading; 3rd May, 1918.

38 USNA, RG 182-11-40, NNB3: *AGREEMENT executed April 30, 1918 between WAR TRADE BOARD and NORWEGIAN GOVERNMENT*; 30th April, 1918; Ibid: No. 706, Dye to WTB, 6th May, 1918; Ibid: No. 455, WTB to Sheldon; 10th May, 1918; USNA, RG 182-11-40, ANAIII: Balfour to Lord Reading; 14th May, 1918.

Bibliography

Archival sources

UK National Archives (UKNA)

CAB (Records of the Cabinet Office)
24 (War Cabinet and Cabinet: Memoranda)
FO (Records created or inherited by the Foreign Office)
382 (Contraband Department and Ministry of Blockade: General Correspondence)

US National Archives (USNA)

RG 182 (Records of the War Trade Board)
11 (Records of the Executive Office, Executive Country File)

References

Ahlund, C. (ed.) 2012. *Scandinavia in the First World War: Studies in the War Experience of the Northern Neutrals*. Lund: Nordic Academic Press.

Bailey, T. A. 1942. *The Policy of the United States Toward the Neutrals, 1917–1918*. Baltimore: Johns Hopkins University Press.

Bank of Norway. *Consumer Price Indices 1516–2015* [online] Available at www.norges-bank.no/en/Statistics/Historical-monetary-statistics/Consumer-price-indices/ [accessed 12th July, 2017]

Berg, R. 1995. *Norsk utenrikspolitikks historie 2: Norge på egen hånd: 1905–1920*. Oslo: Universitetsforlaget.

Berglund, A. 1920. The War and the World's Mercantile Marine. *American Economic Review*, 10(2, June), 227–258.

Bjørgo, N., Rian, Ø. & Kaartvedt, A. 1995. *Norsk utenrikspolitikks historie 1: Selvstendighet og union: Fra middelalderen til 1905*. Oslo: Universitetsforlaget.

Broadberry, S. & Harrison, M. (eds.) 2005. *The Economics of World War I*. Cambridge: Cambridge University Press.

Burk, K. 1985. *Britain, America and the Sinews of War 1914–1918*. Boston, MA: George Allen & Unwin.

Coogan, J. W. 1981. *The End of Neutrality: The United States, Britain and Maritime Rights 1899–1915*. Ithaca, NY: Cornell University Press.

Dehne, P. 2016. The Ministry of Blockade during the First World War and the Demise of Free Trade. *Twentieth Century British History*, 27(3), 333–365.

Goldrick, J. V. P. 2015. *Before Jutland: The Naval War in Northern European Waters, August 1914–February 1915*. Annapolis: Naval Institute Press.

Haug, K. E. 1994. "Falls Norwegen auf die seite unserer feinde tritt" – Det tysk-norske forhold fra sommeren 1916 til utgangen av 1917. Licentiate (Hovedfag) thesis, University of Trondheim (UNIT).

Haug, K. E. 2012. Folkeforbundet og krigens bekjempelse: Norsk utenrikspolitikk mellom realisme og idealisme. Ph.D. thesis, Norwegian University of Science and Technology (NTNU).

Hodne, F. & Grytten, O. H. 1992. *Norsk økonomi 1900–1990.* Oslo: Tano.

Hull, I. V. 2014. *A Scrap of Paper: Breaking and Making International Law during the Great War.* Ithaca, NY: Cornell University Press.

Klovland, J. T. 2013. *Contributions to a History of Prices in Norway: Monthly Price Indices, 1777–1920.* Bank of Norway Working Paper 2013/23. Oslo.

Kramer, A. 2014. Blockade and economic warfare. In J. Winter (ed.), *The Cambridge History of the First World War,* vol. 2, *The State.* Cambridge: Cambridge University Press, pp. 460–490.

Lambert, N. A. 2012. *Planning Armageddon: British Economic Warfare and the First World War.* Cambridge, MA: Harvard University Press.

Mitchell, B. R. 2003. *International Historical Statistics 1750–2000: Europe,* 5th ed. Houndsmills: Palgrave Macmillan.

Morgan-Owen, D. G. 2017. Britain, Europe, and the War at Sea, 1900–1918. *European History Quarterly,* 47(2), 311–321.

Riste, O. 1965. *The Neutral Ally: Norway's Relations with Belligerent ower in the first World War.* Oslo: Universitetsforlaget.

Roberts, R. 2013. *Saving the City: The Great Financial Crisis of 1914.* Oxford: Oxford University Press.

Salmon, P. 2004. *Scandinavia and the Freat Powers 1890–1940.* Cambridge: Cambridge University Press.

Strachan, H. 2001. *The First World War: To Arms.* Oxford: Oxford University Press.

United States Department of State. *Papers Relating to the Foreign Relations of the United States (FRUS), 1917, Supplement 2, Part II.* Washington, DC: United States Government Printing Office.

9 What was the impact of World War I on Swedish economic and business performance?

A case study of the ball bearings manufacturer SKF

Eric Golson and Jason Lennard

Introduction

Understanding economic and business development during a war is not as simple as it might seem. In peacetime, clear long-term patterns and trends emerge over time which allow social scientists to run regressions and determine long-run patterns. Where such changes might have taken place over decades, the sharp shock of a war will often see the wholesale adoption of new technology, logistics and production patterns within a short period of time. Building on other chapters in this volume that have been focused on macroeconomic topics, this chapter asks a simple question which relates the macroeconomic to firm-level microeconomics. What was the impact of World War I on the neutral Swedish economy and Swedish business? It reviews the Swedish economy during the war and examines the industrial evolution of the ball bearings manufacturer SKF as an example of wider Swedish industrial development in this period. SKF has been chosen because its ball bearings are in heavy export demand, and therefore it is one of the Swedish companies most exposed to external trends.

Many economic historians have examined the general macroeconomic trends during wartime, in particular Broadberry and Harrison, who looked generally at several countries in World War I.[1] Unlike the countries covered in Broadberry and Harrison's study, Sweden is a neutral. We are not studying the economic factors which contribute to victory or defeat in World War I, but rather are focused on the effect of the war on the broader Swedish economy and specifically on Swedish business. Specific studies examining the Swedish economy, including Schön, Glete and Lindgren, suggest nominally low indebted firms which could attract savings through new mechanisms and reap profits from the war would survive the downturn of the 1920s.[2] They make only limited comments on productivity. This new study applies their theory, with updated statistics, to the SKF case study. Other studies have examined companies in critical industries such as the aluminium industry, ball bearings, machine parts businesses, many specifically during the more recent World War II, given the heightened levels of business participation in politics and the conduct of the war.[3] Although the tools of business strategic analysis can be applied from these works, the SKF case in World War I is unique because of the competitive forces which rose against SKF and the extensive nature of the firm's growth, two things rarely seen in other wartime business cases, as demonstrated in the Rauh and Wipf works, where both neutral companies studied faced increasing government intervention and drive towards efficiency.[4]

Instead of addressing either economic performance or business performance, this chapter is an extension of both branches of this work, combining business and economic history to demonstrate how the development of the Swedish economy during the First World War was dependent on and interlinked with the progress of Swedish business in the war. Just as with any war, the process of business and economic development was accelerated by the belligerents' demand for specific industrial goods, in which Sweden was a leader. The war did not interrupt general microeconomic trends of economic and business development in the long term but accelerated conditions for structural and business change in the short term, particularly in the areas of domestic savings and investment. The effects of this surplus and the overinvestment changed Swedish business through the early 1920s. Although the war planted the seeds for an eventual industrial revolution based around Fordist principles, economic growth during the war was largely still based on extensive principles.

World War I consolidated the importance of Swedish industry in international markets and set the stage for long-term growth in the 1920s period and beyond. Sweden was a late industrializer and, despite German dominance in metal-mining and heavy industry, the period from 1890 marked substantial industrial growth in Sweden. Companies like the ball bearings manufacturer SKF rose during this period thanks to strong industrial growth and favourable resource endowments. Hand in hand with this business development, the Great War had the effect of pushing Swedish industrial development by two approaches: first, by selling heavy industrial goods and metals to both belligerents it became a natural source of additional heavy war material; and second, by increasing its capital investment and production capability, it gained increased monopoly power over some strategic goods, such as ball bearings. The country benefited substantially from this achievement – by the end of the war, it was not only more industrialized, but also richer, with a significantly higher capital stock, even though its GDP had stagnated by 1918.

Sweden's neutrality in the Great War

There can be no question that politically Sweden was in a tight position between the two belligerents throughout the First World War. Lured by the prospect of cooperating with the Germans and making territorial gains in Finland against the Russians, the Swedes initially gave guarantees to the Germans in the July crisis; but the Swedish government stepped back from this position when war broke out, declaring its neutrality. Economically, Sweden found itself in an excellent position throughout the war. When international conflict cascaded through Europe in 1914, the Swedish economy was still undergoing the "Second Industrial Revolution", which began around 1890 and ultimately lasted some 40 years.[5] However, the country's geographic location – in the middle, but just to the north, of the theatres of war – had the potential to jeopardize its ongoing industrialization. However, Swedish neutrality ensured this was not the case: an external focus allowed the continual sale of additional goods to all parties. Its excellent position and proximity to both warring factions hastened the process of economic expansion and growth. Specialized Swedish metals and industrial goods were in particularly heavy demand.

SKF, as it is now known, originally Svenska Kullagerfabriken, is Sweden's premier manufacturer of ball bearings. It rose to particular prominence in the Great War given the increased mechanization of warfare and the need for high-quality steel and speciality products. Founded in 1907, the company produces ball and roller bearings, which are speciality engineering products using balls to reduce rotational friction and support loads by separating moving axles. Found widely today in most mechanical devices with axles, they were a relatively new invention at the turn of the century. Swedish ball bearings manufacturing was generally of the highest possible quality, with SKF purchasing or controlling the highest-strength materials and machine tools during the war. SKF also established or purchased 185 subsidiaries and sales organizations in countries around the world to augment exports from Sweden by their own domestic production. These included the Skefko Ball Bearing Company Ltd in Luton, England, as well as smaller German operations in a purchased subsidiary, Norma, which would later join the amalgamated concern Vereignte Kullagerfabriken. Some of these subsidiaries represented other major Swedish business, including electrical, motor and machine tool companies such as Atlas-Diesel and ASEA. Members of the SKF board of directors were found running other major Swedish companies throughout the two world wars.[6] Because of the importance of its products to the mechanization of the belligerents' war effort and the interlinking of SKF with so many other major Swedish businesses, it provides one of the best case studies of Swedish industrial development during the Great War.

The economics of Sweden's neutrality

Sweden's economic position during the war reflected the general trends of European economies in World War I. The first years witnessed a surge in the belligerents' demand for goods as the latter shifted resources towards the raising of an army. As Figure 9.1 shows, the first half of the war (1914–16) was associated with strong growth in Swedish exports. This is a direct consequence of the war, for over half of the increase went to the belligerent economies of Britain, France, Germany and Russia.[7] The articles driving the growth were largely industrial, namely metals (both worked and unworked), ships, vehicles, machines, instruments, and wood products.[8] The second half of the war (1917–18) brought retrenchment as naval blockades and trade embargoes prevented the flow of goods to and from the neutral. The gains of the first half were exhausted by 1917, and by the Armistice the value of real exports was one third below pre-war levels. As with the boom, the bust can also be linked to developments on the

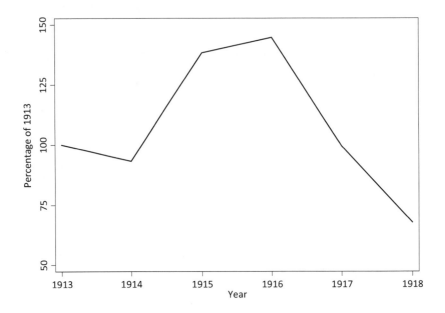

Figure 9.1 Swedish exports, 1913–18 (1913 constant prices).

Source: Statistiska centralbyrån, Historisk statistic för Sverige: Del 3. Utrikeshandel, 1732–1970: 300; Edvinsson and Söderberg (2010).

Note
Real exports calculated by deflating nominal exports by consumer price index.

battlefield, since the biggest reductions came from the big belligerent economies. The products in greatest decline were mostly agricultural, which in the case of Britain may reflect the new domestic policy geared toward increasing the "home supply of calories",[9] but there was also a general shift in British trade towards the United States during this period. Though not entirely separate from this, the more general source was the unrestricted submarine warfare that raged in the Baltic and North seas from February 1917.[10] In that year alone, German U-boats sank 2,639 civilian ships (74 per cent Allied, 26 per cent neutral), bringing down 6.1 million gross tons with them.[11] To be sure, both directly and indirectly, this development discouraged imports of Swedish goods.

Swedish ball bearing exports

Ball and roller bearings were essential components in many wartime products. They are used in airplane motors, tanks, automobiles, guns, submarine engines and similar war material.[12] As such, one would expect a rise in overseas demand for Sweden's bearings during World War I. To test this expectation, a panel data set of total exports of bearings by destination has been gathered from Sveriges Officiella Statistik. It is worth noting that the figures presented hereafter represent SKF alone until 1916. After this date, NKA is also included.[13]

Exports of bearings in Sweden exhibited marked growth (Table 9.1), which continued in value terms after the 1916 decline seen in the overall export statistics. The value of bearings exported increased on average by 47.49 per cent annually. However, given the mounting inflation in this period, the more informative metric is the *quantity* exported, which grew by 23.41 per cent annually. In the year after the onset of the war, the quantity exported more than doubled. Thereafter, the rate of increase slowed, before turning negative in 1918. Though the chronology is not perfect, this inverted quantity-based "U-shape" mirrors the course of Swedish exports in general.

The aggregated export figures tell us that foreign demand for Swedish bearings was high during World War I but they do not make clear whether this was a consequence of the war or of overseas industrialization. One way in which we may approach this issue is to look at the growth rates of exports to belligerent and neutral countries. Doing so throws up some methodological issues surrounding classification of belligerents. Perhaps the most natural method, prima facie, would be to categorize each country as "neutral" until it entered the war, if at all, and as "belligerent" thereafter, but to do so severely overstates the growth rate of exports to the increasing number of combatants. An alternative may be to categorize a late entrant, such as Brazil, as a belligerent for the entire period. This assumption, however, is also difficult to justify. This chapter limits its focus to the Triple Entente (Britain and its colonies, France and Russia) and the Central Powers (Germany and Austria-Hungary), which yields a time-invariant definition of belligerency.[14]

Consistent with the general trends in the Swedish economy, Table 9.2 shows exports rose substantially to belligerents and neutrals alike. From this it is possible to infer that the war *and* industrialization were the sources of the booming foreign demand for Swedish bearings. That the growth rate of exports to the belligerents was lower than that to the neutrals during World War I may at first appear surprising. However, the greater part of the growth came from three economies caught in the crossfire of the war: Denmark, the Netherlands and Norway. It may be that wartime economic conditions affected the demand for Swedish bearings in these countries. In the Netherlands, for example, de Jong notes that high profits led to rising investment in machinery and equipment, of which ball bearings would have been a necessary component.[15]

Table 9.1 Value and quantity of Swedish exported ball and roller bearings, 1913–18 (crowns and current prices)

	Value	Quantity
1913	3,641,741	764,323
1914	4,022,516	579,062
1915	11,005,610	1,464,152
1916	14,189,832	1,782,961
1917	17,825,495	1,898,543
1918	21,509,876	1,570,807
Average annual growth rate (%)	47.49	23.41

Sources: Golson and Lennard (2016).

Table 9.2 Quantity of bearings exported from Sweden to belligerents, neutrals and others, 1913–18 (kilograms)

	Quantity exported to		
	Belligerents	Neutrals	Others
1913	471,499	63,691	229,133
1914	265,918	70,240	242,904
1915	665,430	164,120	634,602
1916	854,688	278,416	649,857
1917	934,322	305,946	658,275
1918	856,605	384,103	330,099
Average annual growth rate (%)	22.16	48.87	14.83

Sources: see Table 9.1.

An alternative explanation lies with the possibility of trade diversion. The British placed increasing pressure on Denmark and the Netherlands throughout the war, amid suspicions that the two were re-exporting contraband goods to the Central Powers. However, we have no evidence to support this position.[16]

Balance of payments and surplus funds increase investment

The effect of changing trade patterns in the conflict at sea is also evident in the new estimate of the balance of payments figures presented in Table 9.3. The visible balance, the net trade of physical objects – those which require transportation – declined markedly after 1917, while the invisible balance, the net trade of services – including transportation services – remained strong. Nevertheless, the current account shows the sum of the sub-accounts remained in surplus throughout the war.

This had two implications for the Swedish economy. First, if a current account surplus is not fully invested overseas then the economy's central bank, the Riksbank in this case, will begin to accumulate reserves. The official settlements balance shows that reserves increased by 216 million crowns between 1914 and 1918. In theory, unless the increased reserve is sterilized, the consequence would probably be an expansion of the domestic money supply. Indeed, Figure 9.2 shows a sharp increase in narrow money (M0) – of which Riksbank notes constituted about 90 per cent. The upshot of this, and of other war-related developments, was, of course, inflation. Increases in the general price level were sheer and persistent throughout the war years. If a basket of everyday items cost 100 crowns in 1913, the same basket would have cost 244 crowns in 1918.[17] Unfortunately, incomes did not keep pace. By the Armistice, real wages in industry were in fact 12 per cent below prewar standards.[18] The differential that emerged between nominal wages and prices contributed to rising profit rates in manufacturing, which, in 1916, climbed to what would become the highest of the century.[19] The peak in the profit rate was associated with a glut of new firms, in industry in particular, where the number of new establishments increased by a factor of 5.[20]

Table 9.3 New estimate of Swedish balance of payments, 1913–18 (million crowns and current prices)

	1913	1914	1915	1916	1917	1918
Current account balance	33	110	290	618	666	333
Visible	−50	46	144	338	471	−13
Invisible	83	64	146	280	195	346
Capital and financial account balance including error term	−3	−157	−175	−525	−666	−278
Official settlements balance	−30	47	−115	−93	0	−55

Sources: Mitchell (1975: 438); Sveriges Riksbank, 1668–1924, Bankens tillkomst och verksamhet: 68; Lindahl, Dahlgren and Kock (1937: 613).

Notes
The capital and financial account balance has been calculated as: 0 − (Current account balance + Official settlements balance). Thus, statistical error and the imperfections of the current account balance calculation, which are discussed in Lindahl et al. (1937) are carried through into the capital and financial account balance. The official settlements balance is equal to the rise (−) or fall (+) in the Riksbank's reserves of gold and foreign exchange between two consecutive periods.

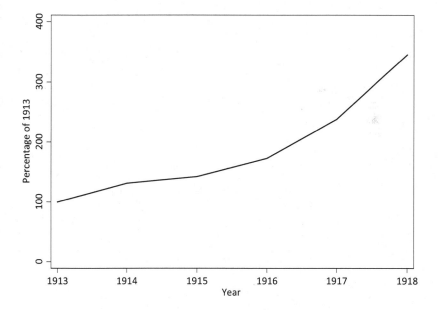

Figure 9.2 M0, 1913–18 (current prices).
Source: Edvinsson (2007).

The second implication of a current account surplus is a proportionate build-up of domestic saving over domestic investment. The favourable external imbalances that developed over the course of the war would therefore have yielded a sufficient pool of savings to channel into worthwhile investments.[21] The opportunities within Sweden were rich, particularly when it came to the electrification of industry.[22] We see that total average real investment across the war years was 11 per cent above the previous five. A particularly important channel was in machinery, where real investment increased by one-third. Here SKF provides the perfect example, with machinery and factory investment increasing by at least two-fold during the period.[23] By 1918, real gross fixed capital formation was 15 per cent higher than peacetime levels.[24] However, we do not see increased TFP (total factor productivity) growth so much as we see amplified extensive industrial output growth, as becomes apparent when we look at the SKF case study.

On the surface, these developments had no impact on the aggregate economic performance of Sweden. In 1913 real GDP stood at 3.77 billion crowns, as it did in 1918 (Figure 9.3). However, the continuity found at these intervals masks the volatility in between. Like exports and profits in industry, GDP peaked in 1916, having expanded by 4 per cent on average since the onset of the conflict.[25] In the second half of the war, the gains slipped away. The reversal was led at first by falling consumption, and then, in 1917, by a weakening

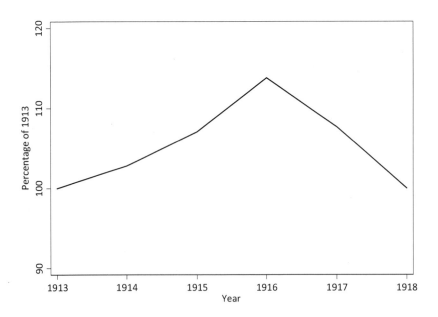

Figure 9.3 Swedish GDP, 1913–18 (1910/12 constant prices).
Source: Krantz and Schön (2012).

of net exports on account of the unrestricted submarine warfare. Another item of interest which lies beneath the surface of Table 9.3 is the continuation of the structural change that was in motion before the war. Between 1913 and 1918 the share of the labour force engaged in agriculture fell 4 per cent and industry pulled away from agriculture as the biggest sector contributing to GDP at factor prices.[26] Thus, though national income had not improved, the Swedish economy was more industrial and had a greater stock of capital at the end of the war than it had had before 1914.

The war would continue to exert its influence upon the Swedish economy long after the Treaty of Versailles. Granted, normality returned to Sweden in 1919, but it was not long before the economy sank into "one of the deepest crises that Sweden and the Western world have experienced in modern times".[27] Schön considers the origins of the 1920–21 crisis in the following areas: in the deflation that necessarily followed the normalization of wartime conditions, in the crippling of Germany as a major trading partner and in the austere economic policies that were designed to restore the government debt and exchange rate to peacetime levels.[28] Many of the firms (including many SKF competitors) formed in the first half of the war, when profits were high, were unable to weather the crisis.[29] The downturn, however, did not persist for very long, and by 1922 the economy had more than recovered its losses in real terms. Businesses like SKF started to re-expand production from late 1922 onwards, with bearings production in Sweden more than tripling and overall worldwide production increasing over 50 per cent.[30] It also started to invest in subsidiary businesses, including the automobile maker which would eventually become Volvo.

The eight years that followed are one of several golden ages in the modern economic history of Sweden. As Table 9.4 confirms, it posted average annual real GDP growth (Y) of more than 4 per cent. Using a simple growth accounting framework, we can estimate the sources of this growth on the basis of changes in capital (K) and labour (L). From these observables, we can also gauge total factor productivity (TFP), a measure of long-run technological change. The figures show that growth during the war and in the troublesome years that followed was largely extensive. We see, for example, that between 1914 and 1918 changes in the capital stock contributed 1.39 per cent to GDP growth and helped offset regressions in TFP. Again, between 1919 and 1921 it was capital that drove growth and companies like SKF finally mechanized production at the expense of labour. It was not until the postwar boom that technological change took hold. We may in part consider this as the fruits of the investments in electrification and mechanization that were made during World War I. Rationalization of firms might also play a role. But it was not only the wartime investments at home that drove the growth of the 1920s; it was also investments abroad. Income (dividends, interest and profits) from Swedish capital invested abroad increased monotonically from 15 million crowns in 1922 to 110 million in 1929.[31] Given that Sweden had been a large capital importer from around 1870 until the outbreak of the war, this may be seen as

Table 9.4 New growth accounts for Sweden, 1914–29 (per cent per year)

	Due to capital	Due to labour	TFP growth	GDP growth
World War I, 1914–18	1.39	0.25	−1.07	0.57
Intermediate years, 1919–21	1.10	−0.75	0.94	1.29
Postwar boom, 1922–9	0.99	0.93	2.47	4.40

Source: Krantz and Schön (2012).

Notes
Based on the neoclassical growth accounting equation where: $\Delta Y/Y = 0.48 \Delta K/K + 0.52 \Delta L/L + \Delta TFP/TFP$. Values for the coefficients represent factor income shares and are calculated from Edvinsson (2005: 314, 386). Note that reasonable deviations from these figures do not change the sign or general magnitude of the results. The series for capital is the present authors' estimate of real gross fixed capital formation. The series for labour represents the total labour force. Where columns 2 to 4 do not sum perfectly to column 5, rounding error is responsible.

a consequence of the large capital exports that accumulated between 1914 and 1918.[32] The mounting profits are correlated with the rising prosperity of the global economy in the 1920s.

The Swedish ball bearing industry, 1907–18

Though the four years of the Great War seemingly left the Swedish economy as it had been at the start, it was a period of great volatility, and inevitably among both industries and firms there were winners and losers. The ball bearings industry was particularly susceptible to the needs of the war because of the high demand for its product. In tracing it, we explain: (1) the firm-level strategies which were deployed as a consequence of the war, together with their outcomes; and (2) the impact of the war on the business more generally.

SKF's pre-Great War expansion into Germany, the United Kingdom and other markets took different strategic routes. Given its focus on iron and steel, Germany developed a competing ball bearing industry in 1907. Patents registered in Germany locked SKF out of the international market. To overcome this problem in 1912, SKF Sweden purchased a 50 per cent interest in the Norma company, a ball bearings cartel member operating in Cannstadt, for 2 million Marks. The principal reason for the purchase was to gain access to patents (the first internationally recognized ball bearing patent) as part of the German ball bearings cartel and to sell Swedish bearings in the international market, from which SKF had previously been barred.[33] This strategy of purchasing competitors to gain new markets and for the sake of horizontal expansion would be furthered during the Great War when SKF undertook vertical integration by buying out the steel mining firm Hofors Bruk, as discussed below.

Both domestic and international competition arose during the war. Six new domestic competitors were formed by 1917, but five soon faded out. The surplus funds available in the economy because of the expansion of the money supply, mentioned previously, and the relatively high demand for ball bearings made investment in ball bearings companies look particularly attractive. Five of the six firms never made any money. Only one survived the war – Nordiska Kullageraktiebolaget (NKA), also known as Northball. NKA had the advantage of deep pockets of funding, notably from one of its directors, Melcher Lyckholm, a beer magnate. The company expanded in terms of capital and sales as quickly as SKF. It expanded vertically and horizontally, acquiring a major German manufacturer of bearings as well as the engineering firm necessary for building the machines and a metals mining company, but never acquired enough machinery to actually produce the steel balls itself. It demonstrates the bubble mentality of investing when ball bearings prices were high and not anticipating the collapse of prices that would come with the end of the war.[34]

The Great War would help SKF cement this strategy of industry control, eventually allowing it to acquire the full rights to the Conrad patent from Deutsche Waffen & Munition-Fabriken for $600,000 just before the entry of the US into the war. With this patent, SKF gained royalty payments from both its American and international competitors, which were estimated by the Americans to have exceeded the cost of the patent.[35] This allowed SKF to consolidate its control over its competitors, taking a proportion of their revenues and putting them at a pricing disadvantage, in particular during the later stages of the war.

SKF also retained tight control over this network of subsidiary firms and as a result controlled ball bearings production overall. The most important ball bearing machinery, and in many cases the high-quality steel, had to be imported from Sweden. This allowed the parent company to control the market for ball bearing production in foreign countries.[36] For example, in the United States, SKF Philadelphia, as the US subsidiary was ultimately called, was constrained from expanding manufacturing capacity despite significant government requests to do so. While each of the competing domestic producers was a substantial manufacturer of ball bearings, American reports indicate that none was able to acquire the raw material and requisite intellectual knowledge to produce bearings as robust and durable as those of SKF, leaving the market undersupplied in relation to government demands. This left the market dependent on exports from Sweden to meet the excess demand in the run-up to war.[37]

Supply-side effects

In addition to its influence on overseas demand, the war also affected supply-side conditions. As briefly discussed above, the nominal rigidity of industrial wages in the face of mounting inflation led to great additional profits for industry. These forces worked favourably for bearings producers as well. Table 9.5 displays an index of bearings prices, constructed by dividing the total sales of mid-weight bearings by the total exported in each year, against nominal wages in industry. In the first year of the war we see that the price of bearings outpaced wages. Thereafter, absolute wage growth kept up with bearings prices but the initial differential persisted. The net result of the trends discussed in the present and previous sections – rising international demand and a positive spread between prices and wages – was large profits. At SKF net profits increased, on average, by 30 per cent per annum between 1915 and 1918 (Table 9.6). The

Table 9.5 Index of bearings prices and industrial wages, 1913–18 (current prices)

	Percentage of 1913		
	Bearings prices	Industrial wages	Surplus
	I	II	III = I – II
1913	100	100	0
1914	119	102	17
1915	129	110	19
1916	137	121	16
1917	161	148	13
1918	235	214	21

Sources: Same as Table 9.1; Mitchell (1975: 74).

Table 9.6 SKF balance sheets, 1915–18 (thousand crowns and current prices)

	1915	Percentage of 1915			
		1915	1916	1917	1918
Assets	32,398	100	180	299	416
Receivables	10,079	100	148	169	235
Machinery and tools	6,873	100	137	192	188
Shares	6,317	100	319	650	958
Stock	4,934	100	179	305	500
Factory buildings	2,979	100	120	196	244
Land	925	100	100	100	160
Patents and trademarks	134	100	72	63	108
Furniture	74	100	158	126	295
Other assets	83	100	194	4,246	4,699
Liabilities	32,398	100	180	299	416
Share capital	12,000	100	175	467	700
New issues	6,331	100	22	0	0
Statutory reserve	2,500	100	140	280	392
Renewal fund	2,108	100	142	177	277
Bank debt and loans	1,059	100	735	356	813
Contingency fund	781	100	320	928	1,054
Pension fund	200	100	250	250	250
Other liabilities	1,724	100	375	315	275
Profit	5,695	100	211	230	232

Sources: Steckzén (1957: 236); SKF annual report 1918; National Archives and Records Administration, RG169/211/1, Report of SKF: 21.

impressive returns of 1916, in particular, had the adverse implication of enticing new competition. However, founded upon unrealistic projections of future trade, the new entrants would not see out the war, whereas SKF would weather the downturn and invest in mechanization in the 1920s.

Production at SKF's factory in Gothenburg ramped up from 1.1 million bearings in 1914 to 2.8 million in 1918. Achieving this feat required improvements in the firm's productive capacity. With the aid of the firm's balance sheets (Table 9.7) for the years 1915 to 1918, the earliest available, we can identify the stock and flow of the firm's investments. We see that factory buildings were an important channel. In 1918, "large expansions at the Gothenburg factory were completed . . . [and] factory capacity thus caught up with demand."[38] Perhaps a good proxy for the scale of the expansion is the increase in employment there. Already the largest employer in the city, SKF's labour force in Gothenburg rose from 1,900 in 1914 to 4,500 in 1918.[39]

It is also clear that the firm's stock of machinery and tools increased sharply during the period, rising 88 percentage points in nominal terms. As in the wider economy, it seems that growth was largely extensive, coming from additions to the labour force and capital. Columns IV and V show that despite increases in machinery and tools per head, bearings per head initially increased only moderately and then fell after 1915/1916, which indicates either declining labour productivity. Capital used per bearing (Column VI) increased 15% over the use of the war, but when combined with the declining bearings per worker, it is evident costs were merely increasing. This confirms the extensive nature of the output growth, consistent with the general Swedish economy in this period.

Table 9.7 SKF sources of growth, 1915 and 1918 (current prices)

	Bearings manufactured	Machinery and tools (crowns)	Employees	Bearings per head	Machinery and tools per head	Machinery and tools per bearing
	I	II	III	IV = I ÷ III	V = II ÷ III	VI = II ÷ I
1914	1,100,000		1,900	579		
1915	1,700,000	6,873,000	2,500	680	2,749	4.04
1916	2,400,000	9,416,000				3.92
1917	2,800,000	13,196,000	4,300	651	3,068	4.71
1918	2,800,000	12,932,000	4,500	622	2,874	4.62
1922	200,000		820	244		
1923	700,000		566*	1,236		
1939	16,300,000		3,840*	4,245		

Sources: Fritz and Karlsson (2012: 33–35, 50–51, 61–62); Svenska Kullagerfabriken, *SKF 1907–57*; Steckzén (1957: 236).

Note
Asterisks (*) indicate employees imputed from available production and bearing-per-head values.

A further point that is apparent from the asset side of the balance sheets is the increase in share ownership. For SKF, World War I was a time of great domestic vertical integration and overseas horizontal expansion. At home, the firm's growing demand for a consistent supply of steel saw it acquire Hofors Bruk in 1916, a large mill north of Stockholm. The purchase "gave SKF control over the entire manufacturing process, from the mining of the iron ore to final honing, which became a strong marketing argument for the quality of SKF ball bearings".[40] According to a report of the US Foreign Economic Administration, this acquisition was funded "with the profits derived from its tremendous sales to all belligerents".[41] While this may have been true, much of the investment in the period was financed by the issuance of share capital. In this regard also, the war fostered favourable conditions. Schön notes that wartime trends in capital and profits helped buoy the Stockholm Stock Exchange, as it did the shares of SKF (Figure 9.4).[42] The firm's shares traded some 25 per cent above the level of 1915 before a (now familiar) tapering off set in. The significance of rising share prices for an expanding company should not be underestimated. The implication is that the firm was able to raise the necessary funds for investment in exchange for

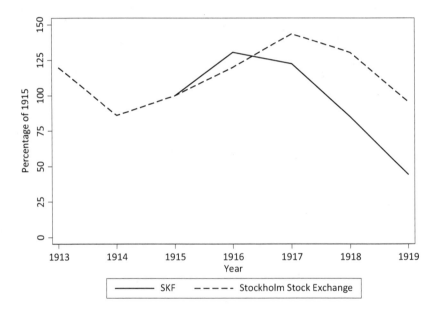

Figure 9.4 SKF share price and index of Stockholm Stock Exchange, 1913–19 (current prices).

Sources: Affärsvärlden: 1917:2:1903; Affärsvärlden: 1918:1:69; Affärsvärlden: 1920:1:49; Waldenström (2007).

Note
SKF share price calculated as the midpoint between its annual high and low.

a lower proportion of equity, and indeed lower future profits, than might otherwise have been possible.

Aside from profits and share capital issues, the remaining investment was funded with bank debt and loans. Here, too, the wartime inflation had positive consequences. The real value of SKF's liabilities diminished in the wake of climbing prices. Take, for example, the purchase of Hofors Bruk in 1916. To fund this acquisition and other expenditures, the firm borrowed 7.7 million crowns from domestic banks. By 1918, though the nominal value had risen to 8.8 million crowns, on account of interest charges, the real value of this debt had fallen to 3.7 million.[43] Even after the deflation and the tight monetary policy of the postwar crisis, the real value of the debt stood at just 6.17 million crowns.

To expand the point made in passing above, the war also influenced the course of SKF's overseas horizontal expansion. In 1913 the firm was largely an export-led enterprise with 85 per cent of its bearings manufactured in Sweden.[44] The remaining supply was produced by the firm's British subsidiary. But by the end of the war only 47 per cent of the group's bearings were being produced domestically. The biggest advances were made in the US, where, in 1915, a factory in Connecticut was built. The US Foreign Economic Administration described the venture in the following way:

> At the outbreak of World War I SKF saw an opportunity for development in the US. Before that time it was customary for Germany to export ball bearings to the US. Realising, however, that the British blockade would affect Germany's exports to the US, SKF centred its attention on the US market.[45]

The conventional wisdom would have it that the above statement implies an unrealistic degree of foresight on behalf of SKF, but new evidence presented by Harrison finds that all but "ordinary uniformed citizens" expected a long war.[46] It follows that SKF's expansion to the US may very well have been a calculated means through which it could enjoy the advantages, but circumvent the disadvantages, of the war. In these terms, the venture in the US was by no means unique. In France, too, a new factory was built.

In Britain it was not SKF that led the expansion but the government. The procurement of bearings was considered a business of the utmost importance to the war effort. In fact, the Ministry of Munitions established an exclusive ball bearings supply branch in 1916. The statistics presented in Table 9.8 show that the output at Skefko, SKF's British factory, increased incrementally from 20,000 units in the last quarter of 1916, equivalent to capacity at the time, to over 31,000 units in the corresponding quarter of 1917. The necessary expansion was centrally planned at the Ball Bearings Conference of July 1916 which considered "the immediate extension of the Skefko Plant at Luton . . . so important that authorisation should be given to them to proceed at once, with an assurance that an equitable arrangement will be arrived at with the finance department".[47]

Table 9.8 Sources of Britain's supply of ball bearings, 1916:Q4–1918:Q4 (physical units and monthly averages)

	Home supply		Overseas supply		Total	SKF share
	Skefko	Other	SKF	SRO		
	I	II	III	IV	V	VI = (I + III) ÷ V
1916:Q4	20,000	107,676	36,923	11,707	176,305	32.29
1917:Q1	22,000	111,286	62,991	15,729	212,007	40.09
1917:Q2	24,000	123,308	42,791	18,476	208,576	32.02
1917:Q3	26,000	129,393	75,061	19,490	249,944	40.43
1917:Q4	31,246	142,971	69,271	12,217	255,705	39.31
1918:Q1	26,299	156,028	150,826	19,192	352,345	50.27
1918:Q2	30,895	151,874	102,449	16,589	301,806	44.18
1918:Q3	26,741	148,575	93,608	16,295	285,219	42.20
1918:Q4	27,652	185,232	116,030	7,660	336,574	42.69

Source: National Archives (Kew Gardens), *Work of the ball-bearings supply branch (2nd draft)*: 73–75.

Note
SRO was a Swiss supplier. Supplies from the US are not included, due to imperfect underlying sources.

While production increased at the new factories in the US, France and Britain, SKF entered into a venture in Russia which was arguably less successful. As with the US, the war displaced Germany as Russia's main supplier of bearings.[48] Sensing an opportunity, the firm started work on a plant in Moscow in 1916. However, the revolutionary developments there saw the factory nationalized before a bearing had been produced. But, when contrasted with the great gains made elsewhere, this was a minor cost in what was otherwise a highly profitable war.

SKF as a neutral company?

Given the firm's expansion and the benefits it incurred because of the war, we have to ask the question of SKF's neutrality during the war. The Allies during World War I suspected SKF was directly serving the interests of the Central Powers. Britain went so far as to place SKF on its "'Black List' because of its extensive trade with Germany".[49] Records of the US Foreign Economic Administration note that, in addition to extensive trade, SKF granted the German government and Krupp Munitions Works a 40 per cent discount on its bearings.[50] Contrasting suspicions of favouritism towards one particular belligerent is also important to understanding SKF's position. New volume and price data for trade with the Triple Entente and Central Powers has been collected from Swedish government sources (*Sveriges Officiella Statistik*) and is reported below. Total exported bearings is reported in three weight-based categories. We use only one, the largest by quantity exported, to minimize the issues associated with the heterogeneity of bearings and their prices. It is also important to mention that values are reported as free on board and are therefore not influenced by the transport costs incurred between Sweden and the importing country.[51] Ultimately, the series is calculated by dividing the value of exports by the quantity of exports to both the Triple Entente and the Central Powers.

The fears of the Allies are not realized in the data presented in Table 9.9. The Triple Entente, in fact, received a much larger volume of bearings than did the Central Powers. For every kilogram of bearings received by the latter in 1914, the former got two. In the next three years, this disparity rose to 9:1, before falling to 6:1 in 1918. That the climax of exports to the Triple Entente came in 1917 can be mainly explained by external developments. In France, where the largest absolute decline occurred, there was a conscious effort to improve the trade deficit, which had deteriorated, in real terms, by over 400 per cent in relation to peacetime levels.[52] In 1917, a policy was introduced whereby imports required government authorization, which was ultimately successful in reducing France's reliance on overseas goods, including Swedish bearings.[53] In Russia the Bolshevik Party's seizure of power in October 1917 brought the country's participation in World War I to an end, along with a substantial demand for bearings.[54] The decline in exports to these two countries accounts for most of the aggregate decline between 1917 and 1918. A further factor, which explains a certain amount of the decline in France and Russia and of the decline elsewhere, is, of course, the unrestricted submarine warfare, which, as noted above, plagued Swedish exports from 1917.

In addition to a greater supply of Swedish bearings, the Triple Entente secured a lower average price per kilo than did the Central Powers in every

Table 9.9 Quantity and average price of bearings weighing between 1 and 15 kilograms exported from Sweden to the Triple Entente and Central Powers, 1913–18

	Quantity exported to (kilograms)			Average price per kilo (crowns and current prices)		
	Triple Entente	Central Powers	Ratio	Triple Entente	Central Powers	Triple Entente's surplus
	I	II	III = I ÷ II	IV	V	VI = V − IV
1913	226,881	81,145	2.80	5.15	6.22	1.07
1914	171,291	78,630	2.18	6.93	7.31	0.39
1915	556,183	76,665	7.25	7.43	7.36	−0.07
1916	677,460	100,922	6.71	7.86	7.99	0.13
1917	790,049	86,601	9.12	9.37	9.64	0.27
1918	472,688	76,719	6.16	13.49	15.74	2.26

Sources: Same as Table 9.1.

year but 1915. This small concession may reflect a degree of "pragmatic neutrality".[55] Fritz and Karlsson note that "there was a tightrope to be balanced, with requests and demands from both alliances, and the necessity of maintaining an international market even once the war was over also always had to be borne in mind".[56] Nevertheless, taking the war years together, the Triple Entente enjoyed, on average, a discount of over 6 per cent relative to the opposing forces. It would therefore appear, contrary to the suspicions of the Allies, that SKF's bias favoured not the Central Powers but the Triple Entente. Additionally, if we view World War I as a war of attrition, the rising inequality in the supply of bearings strengthened the military capabilities of the Triple Entente in relation to the Central Powers. What is more, for the same quantity of bearings, the latter had to exhaust a larger sum of its foreign exchange. In this regard, SKF positively influenced the war effort of the Triple Entente while undermining that of the Central Powers.

In summary, the bearings industry, and SKF in particular, was one of the great winners in the Swedish experience of World War I. The firm adapted its strategy for the war, giving divisions more autonomy and favouring those countries with which it had a more developed economic position. As in the wider economy, external trade swelled with the onset of the war before the misery that must necessarily accompany a conflict of this scale set in. However, unlike those in the wider economy, the gains in international trade were only partially offset by the developments in the seas and the trenches.

Long-term growth: the 1920s and beyond

SKF set up a long-term dominating position owing to the World War I and survived the initial cyclical downturn quite well. SKF, as Marcus Wallenberg put it, had "management and organization [as] . . . the main strengths of the company, and they are far more difficult to imitate than the product."[57] Oversupply in the initial period after the war gave SKF the advantage because of its existing large operations, vertical supply chain integration and control of the relevant patents. With a lower cost base than its competitors, it could more easily adapt to purchasers' requirements given existing factory capacity. In the period immediately after the Great War, the German ball bearings market was not in a position to compete with Sweden's, given both its supply problems with basic materials and the lack of demand in Europe generally. SKF domination of the industry hit a peak in the 1920s, when it bought out European competitors, established control over the German, French and British markets, as well as increasing its presence internationally, including the United States. This helped cushion the postwar demand decline in the European market. In the meantime, many of the competitors were going out of business. Domestic competitor NKA, which had grown to 4,500 employees, did not survive the postwar period. NKA was deeply in debt and, after filing for bankruptcy in the summer of 1921, production was kept at a low level until 1925. It had been a victim of falling prices amid too much debt.[58]

The establishment of overseas subsidiaries during the Great War rewarded SKF with a further advantage. Protectionism was on the rise in Europe and elsewhere throughout the 1920s, particularly in the case of manufactured goods, like ball bearings.[59] The League of Nations put the ad valorem equivalent tariff at 5 per cent in Britain in 1925, compared with perfect free trade in 1913; at 20 per cent in Germany, against 13 per cent before the war; and at 37 per cent in the United States, compared with 25 per cent in 1914.[60] The tariffs essentially raised the price of, and thus depressed the demand for, imported goods. SKF's expansion into these key markets allowed them to circumvent the tariffs by supplying the demand directly, which constituted an effective discount against overseas competitors. Commercial policy was more favourable in Sweden, where general tariffs actually decreased by 3 percentage points in 1925, from 16 per cent in 1913.[61] Thus, importing energy and raw materials for production in Sweden eased with the passing of the war.

Industry consolidation would ultimately place SKF in a position to provide nearly 80 per cent of all ball bearings and sizeable percentages of ball bearings to the Germans and British during World War II.[62] Local German and British manufacturing owned by SKF was controlled by the Swedish firm through the provision of manufacturing equipment and raw materials. Additional supplies were provided through exports from Sweden. As suggested by Golson, the SKF firm controlled most of the European ball bearings market, directly providing 58 per cent of German supplies and 31 per cent of British.[63] Just as was seen in the Great War there were pricing differences, with favouritism shown first towards the Germans and then, as the fortunes of war shifted, towards the Allies.[64]

The presence of SKF in Sweden also provided several other industrial enterprises with agglomeration benefits. For its size and economic strength, Sweden proved to be a major industrial leader in engines, cars and trucks. Although SKF focused strictly on the bearings business, the agglomeration benefits can be separated into two major points: first, increased technological development; and second, the increased presence of skilled engineers who could then transfer to other parts of industry with training from SKF. SKF has nearly 11,000 engineers and technical personnel in 1910; this figure increased to 30,000 by the beginning of World War II.[65] As ball bearings production reduced in the early 1920s, the company expanded into other areas, shifting labour and investing capital in businesses including car production at subsidiary Volvo, expansion of toolmaking operations and investing in new steel mill capacity.[66] The reduction in ball bearings production during the early 1920s also left spare capacity in the local Gothenburg economy for industrial development, including electrical power from a newly established large-scale power plant built for purpose in 1917.[67] The manufacturing cluster which results increases Gothenburg's share of Swedish GDP from 7 per cent in 1910, to 9.19 per cent by 1920, and 9.78 per cent by 1930.[68]

SKF's success applied the benefits of ball bearings throughout Swedish industry. We do not see productivity improvements during or after the Great War; however, we do see an investment in new businesses and industrial deepening/

broadening. Then production improvements were implemented as part of the industrial recovery from the Great Depression. This placed Sweden in a favourable position heading into World War II and after – both from a productivity perspective and in terms of diversified industries. Swedish TFP growth remained higher than that of the world economy, and competitive with Japan and the United States from 1900 to 1990. Particularly notable is TFP, which outpaced capital and labour growth contributions from 1950 to 1975.[69] The benefits of SKF and its relatively early industrial development were used by other firms, placing them ahead of their competitors and enabling their international expansion.

Conclusions

SKF's experience is merely one example of Swedish industrial development during the war, but its pattern follows the general trends in Swedish economic performance in this period. This chapter has demonstrated that the period from 1890 marked substantial industrial growth in Sweden: by selling heavy industrial goods and metals to both belligerents it became a natural source of additional heavy war material; and by increasing its capital investment and production capability, it gained increased monopoly power over some strategic goods, such as ball bearings. The Great War encouraged this economic development, with Sweden exporting most of its manufactured goods to the belligerents; however, during the war most of the growth was extensive. Efforts were made to increase manufacturing using existing methods and resources rather than retool industries. Swedish GDP initially rose, but given the pressures of the war this rise was unsustainable. Capital investment and production capability rose and in some strategic goods (including ball bearings) Sweden gained significant market control and pricing power. The country benefited substantially from this achievement – by the end of the war, it was not only more industrialized, but also richer, with a significantly higher capital stock, even though its GDP had stagnated by 1918. Companies which had made gains during the war, such as SKF, used the 1920s to improve their production techniques, overtaking their competition and improving total factor productivity. So, as a result of the war, Swedish long-term economic growth and performance were ultimately enhanced well into the 1920s and beyond.

Notes

1 Broadberry and Harrison, 2005.
2 Schön, 2000, 2012; Glete, 1994; Lindgren, 1994.
3 Rauh, 2009; Fritz and Karlsson, 2005.
4 Wipf, 2011.
5 Schön, 2010: 178.
6 National Archives and Records Administration, College Park, Maryland (NARA), RG169/211/Box 1: 4–6.
7 Statistiska centralbyrån, 1972, *Historisk statistik för Sverige: Del 3. Utrikeshandel, 1732–1970*, Stockholm: 300.
8 Ibid.: 261.

9 Broadberry and Howlett, 2005: 211.
10 War Office, 1922, *Statistics of the Military Effort of the British Empire during the Great War*: 831.
11 Findlay and O'Rourke, 2007: 430.
12 Golson, 2012.
13 Fritz and Karlsson, 2006: 37.
14 Finland is categorized as "other" in order to maintain a consistent definition of belligerency. In reality, it was part of the Russian Empire until December 1917 and a neutral thereafter. Moreover, exports to other Central Powers, such as Bulgaria and the Ottoman Empire, are not covered in our dataset. The probable explanation for this is the lack of trade in bearings with these countries.
15 de Jong, 2005: 163.
16 Findlay and O'Rourke, 2007: 430.
17 Edvinsson and Söderberg, 2010.
18 Mitchell, 1975: 74.
19 Edvinsson, 2005: 398.
20 Sveriges Officiella Statistik, 1915, *Industri, 1914*: 41; Sveriges Officiella Statistik, 1916, *Industri, 1915*: 55; Sveriges Officiella Statistik, 1917 *Industri, 1916*: 52.
21 Schön, 2010: 245.
22 Ibid.: 236.
23 NARA, RG169/211/1, *Report of SKF*: 21; SKF, 1919, Annual Report 1918.
24 Calculated from Krantz and Schön, 2012. Real gross fixed capital formation is equal to the sum of current and past buildings investment and machinery investment. The former is assumed to have a service life of 50 years and the latter 15 years.
25 Average annual growth rates are calculated econometrically.
26 Krantz and Schön, 2012.
27 Schön, 2010: 246–267.
28 Ibid.: 246–251.
29 Sveriges Officiella Statistik, 1923, *Industri, 1922*: 42.
30 Fritz and Karlsson, 2006: 33, 68–69.
31 Lindahl et al., 1937: 596.
32 Schön, 2010: 245.
33 NARA, RG169/211/1, *Report of SKF*: 4.
34 Fritz and Karlsson, 2012: 36–40.
35 NARA, RG169/211/1: 5.
36 Ibid.: 9.
37 NARA RG107/160/925, file marked "General Ball Bearings SKF": report entitled "The Swedish Ball Bearing Business", draft May 1944: 9.
38 Steckzén, 1957.
39 Fritz and Karlsson, 2012: 34–35.
40 Ibid.: 37.
41 NARA, RG169/211/1, *Report of SKF*: 21.
42 Schön, 2010: 237.
43 Deflated using Edvinsson and Söderberg, 2010. For the interest rate we use the Riksbank discount rate from Sveriges Riksbank (1931), *1668–1924, Bankens tillkomst och verksamhet*: 138. If the rate was changed in a given year, we use the maximum.
44 Fritz and Karlsson, 2006: 33.
45 NARA, RG169/211/1, *Report of SKF*: 17.
46 Harrison, 2014.
47 National Archives (Kew Gardens, London), 1919, *Work of Ball-Bearings Supply Branch (2nd Draft)*.

48 Fritz and Karlsson, 2006: 44–45.
49 Aalders and Wiebes, 1996: 71.
50 NARA, RG169/211/1, *Report of SKF*: 4.
51 Statistiska centralbyrån, 1972: 80.
52 Hautcoeur, "Was the Great War a Watershed?": 182.
53 Ibid.: 193.
54 Gatrell, 2005: 235.
55 Golson, 2012: 204.
56 Fritz and Karlsson, 2006: 32.
57 Ibid.: 41.
58 Fritz and Karlsson, 2006: 41.
59 Findlay and O'Rourke, 2007: 445.
60 Ibid.: 444.
61 Findlay and O'Rourke, 2007: 444.
62 NARA, RG169/211/1, *Report of SKF*: 20.
63 Golson, 2012.
64 Ibid.
65 Fritz and Karlsson, 2006: 59.
66 Ibid.: 68.
67 SKF, 1919, Annual Report 1918.
68 Enflo, Henning and Schön et al., 2014.
69 Schön, 2004.

References

Aalders, G. and Wiebes, C. (1996), *The Art of Cloaking Ownership: The Case of Sweden*, Amsterdam: Amsterdam University Press.
Broadberry, S. and Harrison, M. (eds.) (2005), *The Economics of World War I*, Cambridge: Cambridge University Press.
Broadberry, S. and Howlett, P. (2005), "The United Kingdom During World War I: Business as Usual?", in S. Broadberry and M. Harrison (eds.), *The Economics of World War I*, Cambridge: Cambridge University Press.
de Jong, H. (2005), "Between the Devil and the Deep Blue Sea: The Dutch Economy During World War I", in S. Broadberry and M. Harrison (eds.), *The Economics of World War I*, Cambridge: Cambridge University Press.
Edvinsson, R. (2005), "Growth, Accumulation, Crisis: With New Macroeconomic Data for Sweden 1800–2000", Ph.D. thesis, Stockholm University, Department of Economic History.
Edvinsson, R. (2007), *Money Supply 1871–2006*, Stockholm: Sveriges Riksbank.
Edvinsson, R. and Söderberg, J. (2010), "The Evolution of Swedish Consumer Prices 1290–2008", in R. Edvinsson, T. Jacobson and D. Waldenström (eds.), *Exchange Rates, Prices, and Wages, 1277–2008*, Halmstad: Ekerlids Förlag.
Enflo, K., Henning, M. and Schön, L. (2014), "Swedish Regional GDP 1855–2000: Estimations and General Trends in the Swedish Regional System", *Research in Economic History*, 30, 47–89.
Findlay, R. and O'Rourke, K. H. (2007), *Power and Plenty: Trade, War, and the World Economy in the Second Millenium*, Princeton, NJ: Princeton University Press.
Fritz, M. and Karlsson, B. (2006), *SKF – A Global Story*, Stockholm: Informationsförlaget.
Gatrell, P. (2005), "Poor Russia, Poor Show: Mobilising a Backward Economy for War, 1914-1917", in S. Broadberry and M. Harrison (eds.), *The Economics of World War I*, Cambridge: Cambridge University Press.

Glete, Jan. (1994), *Nätverk i näringslivet: Ägande och industriell omvandling i det mogna industri-samhället 1920–1990 [Corporate networks: Ownership and industrial restructuring in the mature industrial society]*, Stockholm: SNS Förlag.

Golson, E. B. (2012), "Did Swedish Ball Bearings Keep the Second World War Going? Re-Evaluating Neutral Sweden's Role", *Scandinavian Economic History Review*, 60(2), 165–182.

Golson, E. and Lennard, J. (2016), "Swedish Business in the First World War: A Case Study of Ball Bearings Manufacturer SKF", in A. Smith, K. Tennant and S. Mollan (eds.), *The Impact of the First World War on International Business*, London: Routledge.

Harrison, M. (2014), "Myths of the Great War", *CAGE Working Paper No. 188*, University of Warwick, 1–38, available at http://warwick.ac.uk/cage/manage/publications/188-2014_harrison.pdf

Krantz, O. and Schön, L. (2012), "Swedish Historical National Accounts 1560–2010", *Lund Papers in Economic History*, 123, 1–34.

Lindahl, E., Dahlgren, E. and Kock, K. (1937), *National Income of Sweden, 1861–1930*, Stockholm: Norstedt, Institute of Sociology.

Lindgren, Håkan. (1994), *Aktivt ägande: Investor under växlande konjunkturer [Active ownership: Investor in variegating business cycles since 1916]*, Stockholm: Stockholm School of Economics, Institute for Research in Economic History.

Mitchell, B. R. (1975), *European Historical Statistics 1750–1970*, London: Palgrave Macmillan.

Rauh, C. (2009), *Schweizer Aluminium für Hitlers Krieg? Zur Geschichte der "Alusuisse" 1918–1950*, Munich: C. H. Beck.

Schön, L. (2004), "Total Factor Productivity in Swedish Manufacturing in the Period 1870–2000", in S. Heikkinen and J. L. van Zanden (eds.), *Exploring Economic Growth: Essays in Measurement and Analysis*, Amsterdam: International Institute of Social History.

Schön, L. (2010), *Sweden's Road to Modernity: An Economic History*, Stockholm: SNS Förlag.

Schön, L. (2012), *An Economic History of Modern Sweden*, London: Routledge.

Steckzén, B. (1957), *Svenska Kullagerfabriken: En Svensk Exportindustris Historia, 1907–1957*, Gothenburg: Svenska Kullagerfabriken.

Waldenström, D. (2007), *Stock Prices, Returns and Bonds 1856–2006*, Stockholm: Sveriges Riksbank.

Wipf, H. U. (2011), *Georg Fischer AG, 1930–1945: Ein Schweizer Industrieunternehmen im Spannungsfeld Europas*, Zurich: Chronos Verlag.

10 The macroeconomic effects of neutrality

Evidence from the Nordic countries during the wars

Jason Lennard and Eric Golson

Introduction

During the course of the twentieth century, Europe experienced two deadly world wars, unprecedented in expense and destruction. While the macroeconomics of belligerency during World War II has been well studied, less is known about that of neutrality. In order to address this issue, this chapter asks a simple question. How did the two world wars affect the Nordic economies? These countries are an interesting case study due to their differing political histories, involvement in the wars and economic conditions.

Scandinavia, with only limited economic involvement and shipping blockades, managed to avoid the intense economic and physical destruction found on the western battlefields of World War I (WWI). From some perspectives, WWI may even be seen as beneficial for the Nordic countries, for investment and employment rose and factories increased capacity using old-style pre-Fordist production methods. Companies such as the ball bearings manufacturer SKF rose during this period thanks to strong industrial growth and favourable resource endowments.[1] Hand in hand with this business development, WWI had the effect of pushing Scandinavian industrial development by two lines of conduct: first, by selling heavy industrial goods and metals to both belligerents, these countries became a natural source of additional heavy war material; and, second, by increasing their capital investment and production capability, they increased their monopoly power over certain strategic goods, as the Swedish ball bearings industry did. The Nordic countries generally benefited from these achievements, with current account surpluses and higher capital stock, even though by 1918 GDP had stagnated.

But the character of war changed. With the advent of total economic war in World War II (WWII), the Nordic countries were not able to avoid conflict. Norway and Denmark were invaded and occupied by the Germans; Finland was involved in the war, invaded by the Soviet Union, temporarily allying itself with different groups to win back territory; only Sweden was able to maintain its neutrality. Even so, it suffered from a strict blockade, worsening economic conditions, and the same reduced standards of living in the latter part of the war as many of the non-neutrals were facing. In all of these countries, externally, negative current account positions were driven by their failure to be economically self-sustaining; internally, the emphasis on wartime production also caused significant economic dislocation. The trend of moving firms towards Fordist methods of production and maximizing output which had started in the 1920s was accelerated during the war; potential productivity rose, although actual output was frequently hampered by wartime events.[2] As a collective unit, the economies of the Nordic countries which had suffered only mildly in World War I shrank almost twice as much in World War II as they had done in the Great Depression.

Several lessons emerge from this comparative study. Although Scandinavia was far from the epicentre of both wars, the countries were still significantly affected by the fighting, both positively and negatively. Initially, the outbreak of WWI served to stimulate the Nordic economies, since their exports were demanded by the belligerents. The Nordic countries came to be significant suppliers of various critical materials. However, by 1917, with the evolution of total economic warfare that put submarines in the North Sea and the Baltic, the exposure of the Nordic countries (Finland – as described later, a part of Russia – in particular) to war led to accumulated losses by 1922. Finland lost 33% of a year's output, while Sweden, at the opposite extreme, lost 5%. Second, WWII losses were higher than those of WWI in three of the four Nordic countries; Finland at 12% is the exception, but it took longer to recover. Recovery for the group generally took longer after 1918 than after 1945. Three of the Nordic countries were occupied or directly involved in fighting. Their economic losses in WWII were about twice as great as their losses in the Great Depression. Most of the wartime gains and losses can be seen as closely related to their current account. All the Nordic countries' current accounts were strongly positive until 1916, as was growth, then strongly negative until 1918, as was growth. In WWII, however, the current account surplus dwindled, as did growth. This chapter next reviews the existing literature on Nordic countries during the wars, before discussing the methodology and results.

Previous research

The existing literature on the effects of warfare and neutrality on Nordic states over this long period can be divided into three types: long-term histories in which the wartime position is merely a footnote in a country's overall development; political economy-based histories, generally lacking in specific economic evidence, but providing significant historical context; and economic histories which have generally looked at specific wartime events, but not as a rule at long-term cycles of economic development and warfare.

Wylie approaches the survival of the Scandinavian neutral countries from a political economy perspective. With this approach, losses for a Nordic country should look relatively limited so long as it was able to stay out of the war. Of course, this is not what happened in practice. Wylie's conception of small state neutrality is closely related to non-belligerency.[3] It harks back to an eighteenth-century version of neutrality which allows countries to do as they please and discriminates against belligerents who were judged to be in the wrong. In practice,

Wylie's book demonstrates that the idea of neutrality was completely inadequate at providing the basic needs for these states throughout the WWI period. Self-restraint was removed once the violation of Belgium and Luxembourg demonstrated that strategic gains could be made; neutrals were increasingly seen as expendable if gains against the enemy were at stake. Looking at the evolution of neutrality into WWII, small states suffered under increasing pressure from economic and irregular warfare. The distinction between neutral and belligerent faded further and economic pressure increased significantly. The concept of neutrality as non-participation in the war effort increasingly applied to military participation alone. In all other areas, neutral countries faced consistent pressure from the belligerents to participate actively in their war efforts.[4]

Staying in the area of political economy, Salmon examines general Nordic relations with the great powers over the first half of the twentieth century. With respect to Norway, he points out that the natural economic and political links which developed between Britain and Norway between 1905 and 1940 meant that Britain was the ultimate defender of Norway's territory. But this also gave Britain tremendous power, for in the winter of 1916–17 the coal embargo imposed by the British on Scandinavia caused considerable hardship in Norway and other Scandinavian countries. Although the embargo was notionally to enforce Norwegian compliance with Allied demands, it had the natural effect of temporarily driving Norway and the other Scandinavian countries closer to Germany in pursuit of energy and trade goods. It also caused severe economic damage at a time when many Scandinavian economies were beginning to feel insecure. But, as Salmon observes, this is about the extent of British pressure in WWI. Britain was unwilling to violate Norwegian neutrality through direct military action, allowing Norway to continue to produce for both sides despite the lack of coal.[5]

According to Salmon, WWII witnessed much more blatant action by the belligerents in the North Sea, with Germany actively using Norwegian waters to torpedo British ships before the April 1940 invasion. Economic involvement was also more pronounced for Sweden, which managed to remain neutral, despite blockades and counter-blockades. Britain was particularly interested in exploiting Germany's dependence on Swedish iron ore.[6] Because of the occupation of Norway and Denmark, along with active fighting in Finland and economic warfare targeting Sweden from 1940 onwards, the negative economic effects for Nordic countries of WWII were much greater. The economic importance of Nordic countries should not be dismissed either. Milward asserts that Sweden could not have stopped World War II by withholding its iron ore from Germany.[7] Fritz reinforces Milward's position and demonstrates that Sweden's importance to the German steel industry was declining.[8] Golson's study contradicts Milward's view, by further demonstrating that both Sweden's iron ore and ball bearings were critical for Germany's war effort, while small segments of the Swedish economy were important for the Allies.[9]

There has been a considerable amount of economic history research on the Nordic countries in WWI and WWII. In one of the most famous, Fritz summarizes the Swedish wartime trade position with Germany.[10] Swedish-specific studies include Schön, Glete and Lindgren, suggesting that Swedish firms were actually in a fairly good position; nominally low indebted firms, which could attract savings through new mechanisms and reap profits from the war, would survive the downturn of the 1920s.[11] Covering the WWII period, a 1952 government report by Åmark measures authorized trade through the blockade of the Skaggerak.[12] The standard political work on the subject does not forge a unified understanding of the relationship between trade and the wider economic trends.[13] Accounts of Swedish trade relations in these and other works dependent on the same sources miss out illicit trade and reveal the use of exclusively aggregate nominal trade statistics, ignoring the changes in prices which help to explain the shifting power dynamics of the relationships and the potential aggregate economic changes which would result.

Building on these economic histories, Golson has provided some comparative statistics which attempt to evaluate Sweden's trade and capital flows in WWII on an evidential basis, from which more robust conclusions can be formed. Golson's statistical work suggests that the Swedish government was able to assuage the belligerents' political demands by exporting various material goods, most notably iron ore and ball bearings. To counter belligerent military pressure, the Swedish government provided iron ore, ball bearings, machine tools and other items. Prices of goods give an idea of the relative changes in power over time. In 1940 and 1941, Germany extracted better prices for exports to Sweden. In 1942, Sweden extracted price concessions from Germany, charging more for its exports than were charged for German goods sold to Sweden. The pricing situation reversed in 1943, perhaps suggesting that the Swedish reduction in export traffic relative to imports gave Germany the pricing advantage. Allied–Swedish trade saw sizeable price increases in favour of the Allies. At their peak in 1943, the gains in import prices outstripped export prices by about 35%. This increase in prices can be at least partially attributed to the restriction of imports via the blockade.[14]

Economic histories looking at other areas of Nordic economic behaviour agree with this timeline. Frey and his various co-authors use economic choices by bond investors to assess the perception of threats against belligerents and neutrals. On the basis of bond prices, Frey shows the turning points in the perceived threat against a neutral and which countries the markets believed would be successful in maintaining their independence through concessions. In particular, Frey is able to demonstrate that the price levels of Swedish bonds after June 1940 suggest the effectiveness of the concessions, with markets perceiving little risk of invasion after 1942.[15] The results from these capital market studies concur with the revised trade statistics from Golson, suggesting that from late 1942 onwards, the intensity of the economic warfare and the disintegration of Germany's economic machine gave a political economy advantage to the Allies. However, this also further constrained the Nordic economies as German trade disintegrated, but the maintenance of a strict blockade limited the amount of potential trade with the Allies and other neutral countries.

Finally, Golson has also reviewed movements of the Swedish current and capital accounts in WWII. Sweden was the Nordic country least affected by

WWII, in part because its capital account balance was generally better than the others'. Throughout, there were consistent merchandise deficits with Germany (totalling £98.1 million) and only small surpluses with Britain (£6.4 million). Sweden provided services to both countries, giving it an overall current account deficit with Germany of £9.9 million and a surplus with Britain of £37.9 million. The capital account provided Sweden with earnings from both countries. Before government transfers, this meant an overall balance of payments deficit with Germany in 1939-40 and earnings for Sweden from 1941 to 1944, totalling a net of £21.6 million (3.4% of Swedish GDP). Consistent surpluses were also gained from relations with Britain, totalling some £55.2 million, paid in monetary gold (around 8% of Swedish GDP). Overall, in its relations with all countries combined, Sweden had consistent current account deficits because the need to buy goods on international markets exceeded Sweden's capacity to sell to those markets.[16] While other Nordic relationships are not known in such detail, Sweden had a more advantageous trading position than any other Nordic country in WWII.

Methodology and data

There are several potential methodologies for measuring the economic effect of crises such as wars. However, given the little N and little T arising from there being few Nordic countries and only two world wars, the range of options in this instance is restricted. As in other studies, we measure the cost of crisis in terms of lost output.[17] Our conceptual framework is the following:

$$\tilde{y}_t = y_t - \bar{y}_t \tag{1}$$

where lost output or the output gap in period t is equal to the natural logarithm of real GDP (y_t) minus the natural logarithm of the trend of real GDP ($\bar{y}_t$), otherwise known as potential output.

The Hodrick-Prescott (HP) filter is one of the most common methods for estimating the trend of a time series ($\bar{y}_t$).[18] It is calculated by minimizing the cyclical component ($y_t - \bar{y}_t$) in the first summand of Equation (2) and the variability of the trend component, subject to the parameter λ, in the second summand. In the extreme case of $\lambda = 0$, the trend will track GDP one for one as $\bar{y}_t = y_t$ for $t = 1, 2, \ldots, T$. At the other extreme, as λ tends to infinity, the cyclical component carries no weight and $\tilde{y}_t$ will be constant. Thus, the trend component is sensitive to the chosen value of λ, with a higher value of λ resulting in a smoother series. We follow Backus and Kehoe in their study of historical international business cycles in setting $\lambda = 100$, although we also report the results for $\lambda = 6.25$, as suggested by Ravn and Uhlig and for $\lambda = 400$, as in Correia, Neves and Rebelo and Cooley and Ohanian in the results section.[19]

$$\sum_{t=1}^{T}(y_t - \bar{y}_t)^2 + \lambda \sum_{t=2}^{T-1}\left[(\bar{y}_{t+1} - \bar{y}_t) - (\bar{y}_t - \bar{y}_{t-1})\right]^2 \tag{2}$$

In terms of y_t, the Nordic countries have rich historical national accounts (HNA) thanks to a long tradition of constructing them and a longer tradition of diligent data collection. The data is sourced from the most recent vintages of HNAs for each country. Although the Nordic HNAs are of a relatively high quality, they are not exempt from the normal disclaimers. In particular, the Danish series relies heavily on interpolation before 1914.[20] If the interpolation technique yielded results different from the true series, then the error will clearly be passed on to $\tilde{y}_t$. However, given that our focus is on the post-1914 period, there should be little effect on the subsequent results, given reasonable values of λ.

Before filtering, the data were converted to 1990 international dollars.[21] This had the effect of removing misleading price trends and standardizing the units so that cross-country comparisons could be made. In addition, this conversion allowed us to sum the four HNAs to give Nordic GDP, from which we could calculate aggregate lost output. Subsequently, the data were also transformed into natural logarithms. This transformation eased interpretation, allowing the output gaps shown in Figures 10.2 and 10.3 to be understood as approximate percentage deviations from trend. Although the data are available for significant spans of time, the sample is limited to the years 1900–1960. In leaving over a decade before and after the world wars, there is little danger of the endpoint problem.[22] However, we explore the impact of the choice of sample period in the results section.

Finally, the cumulative output gap for each country during each war is simply the sum of the respective *linearized* output gaps:

$$\sum_{t=1}^{T}(e^{\tilde{y}_t} - 1)e^{\bar{y}_t} \tag{3}$$

for $t = 1, 2, \ldots, T$, where 1 is the first year of the war and T is the last.

Before a discussion of the results of this exercise, one should bear in mind that this methodology, though informative, does not yield causal results. Indeed, this is a general limitation of all studies that measure the effect of crises in this way. The cumulative output gaps that we estimate may be a consequence of "business as usual", since output gaps are also a feature of peacetime or are the outcome of other events. However, in parallel with the historical discussion below, the results are a step towards firmer quantification of the effects of two colossal wars on a group of neutral countries at the margin.

Results

In Figure 10.1, log real GDP and the log trend of real GDP are plotted for each of the countries for the years 1900–1960. In all cases the countries enjoyed strong growth during this period due to significant structural change. In Sweden, the share of the labour force in agriculture decreased from 52% in 1900 to 14% in 1960.[23] Industrialization was similar, though slower, in Denmark, Finland and Norway.[24] Total Nordic output grew during this period at an average rate of 2.83%, with the fastest growth in Finland at 2.98%

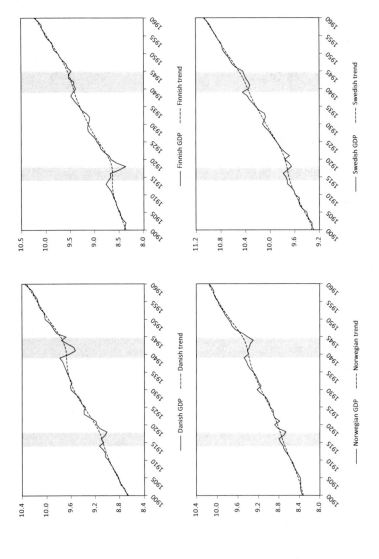

Figure 10.1 Actual and trend real output in Denmark, Finland, Norway and Sweden, 1900–1960.

Sources: Denmark: Hansen (1974); Finland: Hjerppe (1996); Norway: Grytten (2004b); Sweden: Edvinsson (2013).

Notes
Log scale. Shaded areas represent world wars. λ = 100.

and the slowest in Norway at 2.79%.[25] The existence of strong trend growth is a justification for filtering the data.

Table 10.1 presents summary statistics of the paper's main results. The table shows that in the benchmark case of $\lambda = 100$, the Nordic countries suffered *cumulative* output losses of Int $0.78 billion during WWI. While this number is large in absolute terms, it is only equivalent to about 2% of one year's output. In the alternative cases of $\lambda = 6.25$ and $\lambda = 400$, this figure is 2% and 4% respectively, which gives us approximate upper and lower bounds. However, the Nordic countries had heterogeneous experiences of WWI, which give a misleading impression of business as usual when averaged out. In fact, it was only in Norway that this was the case. Norway suffered losses of only Int $20 million or 0.33% of a year's output. In contrast, Sweden was above trend, with output *gains* worth 10% of one year's output. At the other extreme, Denmark and Finland were both below trend, with cumulative losses worth 12% and 17% of one year's output respectively.

This is consistent with the overall experiences in WWI, when Norway and Sweden benefited from increased trade with the two belligerent groups. Geographic position goes a long way to explaining the relative performance. Norway increased trade significantly with the victorious Allies. Because the western part of the Baltic Sea was almost completely under the control of Germany, Sweden's main trading partner remained Germany and the Central Powers. Hence, as Germany weakened, so too did Sweden's overall trade potential. Denmark found practically all of its international trade cut off. Until the end of the war Finland remained a Grand Duchy within the Russian Empire, and its economy was very much dependent on the travails of the Russian war effort.[26]

In Figure 10.2, which plots the dynamic path of the output gap, it is clear that WWI was a war of two halves. In 1916 the four countries were actually above trend, Denmark was 1.18% above, Finland 4.96%, Norway 7.04% and Sweden 8.45%. Thus, it appears that the outbreak of war was an initial stimulus to the Nordic economies. In 1917, however, the four countries sank deeply below trend. In February of that year, submarine warfare began in the Baltic and the North Sea, sinking 2,639 civilian ships, of which 26% were neutral.[27] The contemporaneous switch to a negative output gap suggests that trade was an important mechanism through which the war affected the neutral Nordic economies.

It is clear from Figure 10.2 that, with the exception of Norway, the Nordic economies did not immediately return to trend following the Armistice. A better measure of the true cost of war is to measure the cumulative output gap until the return to trend. For Norway, the figure clearly remains the same, but for Denmark, Finland and Sweden, the period was bleaker than suggested above. Finland returned to trend in 1922 with accumulated losses worth 33% of a year's output, caused by dislocation from the Sovietization of Russia and the consequent reorientation of the Finnish economy towards the West. Denmark also returned to trend in 1922 with losses equivalent to 23% of a year's output,

Table 10.1 Real output gains, WWI and WWII

	Denmark	Finland	Norway	Sweden	Total
WWI					
a Prewar output, 1913 (million 1990 Int. GK$)	8,690	6,390	5,984	16,612	37,676
b Return to trend	1922	1922	1919	1920	1920
	(1919, 1922)	(1920, 1923)	(1919, 1919)	(1920, 1926)	(1920, 1923)
c Cumulative sum of output gap, 1914–1918 (million 1990 Int. GK$)	−1,020	−1,111	−20	1,582	−780
	(−257, 1,659)	(−371, 1,693)	(−315, 81)	(277, 1,942)	(−784, 1,543)
d Cumulative sum of output gap, return to trend (million 1990 Int. GK$)	−1,980	−2,110	−20	815	−2,394
	(−257, 3,251)	(−459, 3,457)	(−315, 81)	(45, 3,474)	(−817, 9,540)
e Years of output gained, 1914–1918	−0.12	−0.17	0.00	0.10	−0.02
	(−0.03, 0.19)	(−0.06, 0.27)	(−0.05, 0.01)	(0.02, 0.12)	(−0.02, 0.04)
f Years of output gained, return to trend	−0.23	−0.33	0.00	0.05	−0.06
	(−0.03, 0.37)	(−0.07, 0.54)	(−0.05, 0.01)	(0.00, 0.21)	(−0.02, 0.25)
WWII					
a Prewar output, 1938 (million 1990 Int. GK$)	16,938	13,123	12,510	31,963	74,533
b Return to trend	1946	1949	1947	1946	1947
	(1946, 1946)	(1948, 1951)	(1947, 1947)	(1946, 1947)	(1946, 1947)
c Cumulative sum of output gap, 1939–1945	−5,244	−1,590	−3,612	−5,967	−16,793
	(−860, 8,248)	(−746, 2,268)	(−884, 5,365)	(−1,708, 7,700)	(−4,507, 24,023)
d Cumulative sum of output gap, return to trend (million 1990 Int. GK$)	−5,244	−2,809	−4,157	−5,967	−17,033
	(−860, 8,248)	(−1,081, 4,612)	(−902, 6,273)	(−1,708, 7,742)	(−4,507, 25,643)
e Years of output gained, 1939–1945	−0.31	−0.12	−0.29	−0.19	−0.23
	(−0.05, 0.49)	(−0.06, 0.17)	(−0.07, 0.43)	(−0.05, 0.24)	(−0.06, 0.32)
f Years of output gained, return to trend	−0.31	−0.21	−0.33	−0.19	−0.23
	(−0.05, 0.49)	(−0.08, 0.35)	(−0.07, 0.50)	(−0.05, 0.24)	(−0.06, 0.34)

Sources: see Figure 10.1.

Notes
Figures outside parentheses: $\lambda = 100$, first figure in parentheses: $\lambda = 6.25$, second figure in parentheses: $\lambda = 400$. 1913 and 1938 are expansionary years for all countries. $e = c/a$. $f = d/a$.

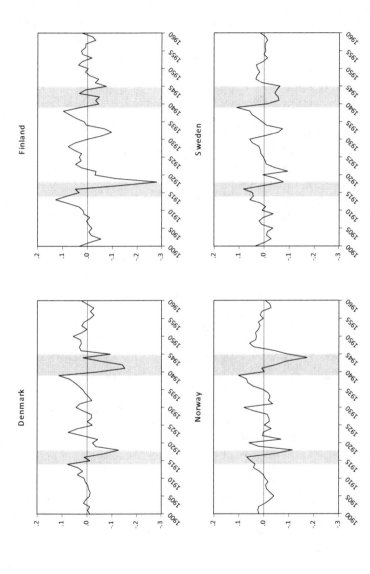

Figure 10.2 Real output gaps in Denmark, Finland, Norway and Sweden, 1900–1960.
Sources: see Figure 10.1.

Notes
Log scale. Approximate percentage deviation of output from its trend. Shaded areas represent world wars. $\lambda = 100$.

mirroring losses in Germany, its closest trading partner. In Sweden, the return to trend happened in 1920, reducing their gains to 5%.

Table 10.1 and Figure 10.2 tell a dark story of the Nordic experience of WWII. In the benchmark case, the cumulative loss in Nordic GDP between 1939 and 1945 was Int $16.79 billion. In absolute terms, WWII was far more costly than WWI. However, we must also consider that output had risen during this interval. Using the more comparable metric in line e, WWII cost the Nordic countries 23% of a year's output. The alternative estimates of the losses for $\lambda = 6.25$ and $\lambda = 400$ are 6% and 32% respectively. Thus, WWII was clearly associated with below trend output, though the severity varies in relation to the assumptions made about λ. These figures also imply that WWII was more severe on aggregate than WWI for the Nordic countries, though this was not true in the exceptional case of Finland.

Unlike WWI, WWII saw output below trend in each of the four Nordic economies by the end of the war. Denmark suffered the greatest losses, equivalent to 31% of a year's output, because of its links to the collapsing German war effort, the general strikes and the complete blockade by the Allies due to the occupation. Despite this, Denmark returned to trend in 1946 after an early trough. Norway suffered losses on a similar scale, with 29% of a year's output foregone, and took longer to recover, again because of the occupation and blockade. However, its return to trend was slower, reflecting the annexation of its naval shipping capacity. By the time it returned to trend in 1947, the losses exceeded even those of Denmark at 33%. In contrast to its relatively favourable experience of WWI, Sweden suffered losses of 19% of a year's output during WWII, reflecting its inability to sell to the Allies and the constraints on imports. Sweden's recovery was quick, returning to trend in 1946. Finland suffered less heavily than in WWI, with output losses of 12% up until 1945. However, it did not return to trend until 1949, by which point it had accrued output losses of 21%.

But how big is big? In order to guide our interpretation of the figures presented in Table 10.1, it is useful to have a benchmark against which to judge whether the 23% of lost output during WWII is big or small. A useful benchmark is the Nordic four's "mild" experience of the Great Depression in the 1930s.[28] The Nordic countries accumulated Int $6.5 billion of lost output between 1931, which was the first year of below-trend output, and 1933, the last year of below-trend output, which is equivalent to 11% of the level in 1930. In this context, WWII was about twice as severe as the Great Depression for the Nordic economies. WWI, in contrast, brought only a fraction of the severity of the Great Depression.

Another way to contextualize these output gaps is in terms of society's loss of welfare. Consider the linearized form of a classic social welfare function:

$$W = \alpha_y (y_t - \bar{y}_t)^2 + \alpha_\pi (\pi_t - \pi^*)^2 \tag{4}$$

where $y_t - \bar{y}_t$ is the output gap $(\hat{y}_t)$ as defined above, π_t is inflation, π^* is the central bank's target inflation and α_y and α_π are weights that measure the marginal welfare loss arising from the square of the two gaps.[29] Thus, we can see that society's average welfare loss increases with the variance of the output and inflation gaps. The general public are averse to fluctuations in the output gap, due to its link to consumption and employment, and to fluctuations in the inflation gap, due to relative price distortions.

It is beyond the scope of this chapter to empirically estimate the parameters α_y and α_π, so we limit our analysis to a plot of the output and inflation gaps. This is still a valid exercise in the case that the two gaps move in the same direction. If both increased during the wars, then so did the welfare loss; the reverse also holds. It is only in the case where the gaps moved in opposite directions that the weights determine the sign of the overall welfare effect. In what follows, we assume that the inflation target, π^*, was 0, although the variance is unaffected by this assumption.

To ease the interpretation, Figure 10.3 displays the standard deviation, as opposed to the variance, of the log real output gap and the log inflation gap for the four Nordic countries. The graphs reveal that the two world wars are clearly associated with higher volatility in both the output and inflation gaps. This is true in all 16 cases (4 countries x 2 wars x 2 variables) except for the Finnish output gap during WWII, where the conflict appears to have had no destabilizing effect on the march towards moderation. Even in Sweden during WWI, when small gains in output were made, there were marked increases in the variance of the output gap, and in particular of the inflation gap, which implies lower average welfare. As with the belligerents, for the four neutral Nordic economies the two world wars were almost certainly negative experiences.

Finally, in the interest of robustness, we display the results for the three values of λ commonly used to filter annual data in Table 10.1. In Figure 10.4 we also show the sensitivity of the HP filter to the sample period. If λ was extremely high, the trend would tend towards a straight line. In this instance, altering the sample period may change the slope of the line, which would affect the estimation of the cyclical component. However, for λ = 400, the largest reasonable value, we see that the output gap is almost identical for the overlapping period in the 1890–1970 sample and the 1900–1960 sample. The same is true for the 1910–1950 sample, with the exception of the endpoints. This is a classic example of the endpoint problem discussed above. Thus, a longer sample size is justified, though it does not appear to matter how much longer, as long as the endpoint problem is avoided.

Conclusions

This chapter has investigated the effects of the world wars on the Nordic economies. As a collective unit, the Nordic countries suffered only mildly in WWI and generally recovered quickly. However, they suffered significantly

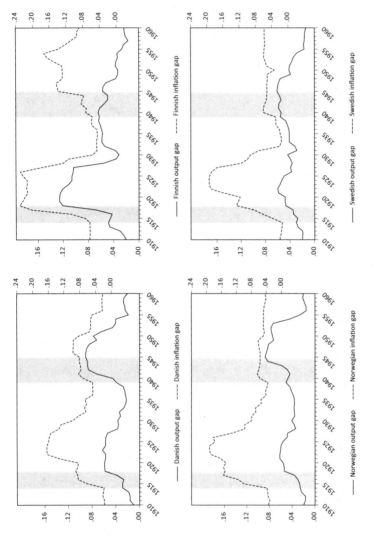

Figure 10.3 Volatility of output and inflation gaps, 1910–1960.

Sources: Output gap: see Figure 10.1. Inflation gap: Danish, Finnish and Swedish series calculated from GDP deflator from the same sources as Figure 10.1. Norwegian deflator unavailable for full period, so CPI used instead, from Grytten (2004a).

Notes

y-axis: output gap. z-axis: inflation gap. 10-year rolling standard deviation. $\lambda = 100$. Shaded areas represent world wars.

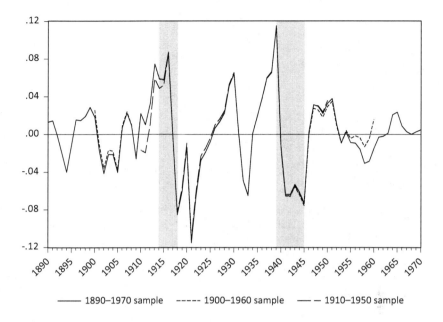

Figure 10.4 Sensitivity of Swedish output gap to choice of sample period, 1890–1970.
Sources: see Figure 10.1.

Notes
$\lambda = 400$. Shaded areas represent world wars.

in WWII, losing almost twice as much output as they lost in the Great Depression. Yet the time taken for them to recover to the long-run trend out of WWII was generally less than after WWI; much of the lost economic activity on the wartime current accounts was mitigated as trade quickly increased. Certain countries were in particularly bad circumstances and suffered in both wars; occupation was a sure reason for a steeper decline, and so too was isolation from traditional trading partners.

While we have focused on the short-term implications of the world wars on the Nordic economies, it is possible that there were also long-term implications. There is an empirical link between high volatility and low economic growth.[30] If investment decisions are costly to reverse, then volatility can lead to depressed investment spending. Given the magnitude of economic fluctuations during World War II, in particular, it is possible that there were indeed negative long-term spillovers.

Notes

1 Golson and Lennard, 2016.
2 Ibid.

3 Wylie, 2002.
4 Ibid.
5 Salmon, 1997.
6 Ibid.
7 Milward, 1967.
8 Fritz, 1974.
9 Golson, 2012.
10 Fritz, 1982.
11 Schön, 2010.
12 Åmark, 1952: 996.
13 Calgren, 1977.
14 Golson, 2011.
15 Frey and Kucher, 2000, 2001; Waldenström and Frey, 2006.
16 Golson, 2011.
17 Hagberg and Jonung, 2009; Laeven and Valencia, 2010; Turner, 2014.
18 See, for example, Mendoza, 2010; Campbell and Ó Gráda, 2011; Edvinsson, 2013.
19 Cooley and Ohanian, 1991; Backus and Kehoe, 1992; Correia, Neves and Rebelo, 1992; Ravn and Uhlig, 2002.
20 Christensen, Hjerppe, Krantz and Nilsson, 1995.
21 Conversion factors from Maddison, 2001: 189.
22 Mise, Kim and Newbold, 2005.
23 Krantz and Schön, 2012.
24 Mitchell, 1992: 143–150.
25 Average annual growth rates are calculated econometrically.
26 Salmon, 1997.
27 Findlay and O'Rourke, 2007: 430.
28 Grytten, 2008.
29 See Sørensen and Whitta-Jacobsen, 2010.
30 Ramey and Ramey, 1995.

References

Åmark, K. (1952), "Kristidspolitik och kristidshushållning i Sverige under och efter andra världskriget", *Statens Offentliga Utredningar: Handelsdepartment*, Stockholm: Handelsdepartment.
Backus, D. K. and Kehoe, P. J. (1992), "International Evidence on the Historical Properties of Business Cycles", *American Economic Review*, 82(4), 864–888.
Calgren, W. M. (1977), *Swedish Foreign Policy during the Second World War*, London: St Martin's Press.
Campbell, B. M. S. and Ó Gráda, C. (2011), "Harvest Shortfalls, Grain Prices, and Famines in Preindustrial England", *Journal of Economic History*, 71(4), 859–886.
Christensen, J. P., Hjerppe, R., Krantz, O. and Nilsson, C.-A. (1995), "Nordic Historical National Accounts since the 1880s", *Scandinavian Economic History Review*, 43(1), 30–52.
Cooley, T. F. and Ohanian, L. E. (1991), "The Cyclical Behavior of Prices", *Journal of Monetary Economics*, 28(1), 25–60.
Correia, I. H., Neves, J. L. and Rebelo, S. (1992), "Business Cycles from 1850 to 1950: New Facts About Old Data", *European Economic Review*, 36(2–3), 459–467.
Edvinsson, R. (2013), "New Annual Estimates of Swedish GDP, 1800–2010", *Economic History Review*, 66(4), 1101–1126.

Findlay, R. and O'Rourke, K. H. (2007), *Power and Plenty: Trade, War, and the World Economy in the Second Millennium*, Princeton, NJ: Princeton University Press.

Frey, B. S. and Kucher, M. (2000), "History as Reflected in the Capital Markets: The Case of World War II", *Journal of Economic History*, 60(2, June), 468–496.

Frey, B. S. and Kucher, M. (2001), "Wars and Markets: How Bond Values Reflect the Second World War", *Economica*, 68(271, August), 317–333.

Fritz, M. (1974), *German Steel and Swedish Iron Ore*, Gothenburg: Institute of Economic History of Gothenburg University.

Fritz, M. (1982). *The Adaptable Nation: Essays in Swedish Economy during the Second World War*. Stockholm: Almqvist & Wiksell International.

Golson, E. (2011), "The Economics of Neutrality: Spain, Sweden and Switzerland in the Second World War", D.Phil. dissertation, London School of Economics.

Golson, E. (2012). Did Swedish Ball Bearings Keep the Second World War Going? Re-evaluating Neutral Sweden's Role. *Scandinavian Economic History Review*, 60(2, June), 165–182.

Golson, E. and Lennard, J. (2016), "Swedish Business in the First World War: A Case Study of Ball Bearings Manufacturer SKF", in A. Smith, K. Tennant and S. Mollan (eds.), *The Impact of the First World War on International Business*, London: Routledge.

Grytten, O. H. (2004a), "A Consumer Price Index for Norway 1516–2003", in Ø. Eitrheim, J. T. Klovland and J. F. Qvigstad (eds.), *Historical Monetary Statistics for Norway 1819–2003*, Oslo: Norges Bank.

Grytten, O. H. (2004b), "The Gross Domestic Product for Norway 1830–2003", in Ø. Eitrheim, J. T. Klovland and J. F. Qvigstad (eds.), *Historical Monetary Statistics for Norway 1819–2003*, Oslo: Norges Bank.

Grytten, O. H. (2008), "Why Was the Great Depression Not So Great in the Nordic Countries? Economic Policy and Unemployment", *Journal of European Economic History*, 37(2–3), 369–403.

Hagberg, T. and Jonung, L. (2009), "How Costly Was the Crisis in Finland and Sweden?", in L. Jonung, J. Kiander and P. Vartia (eds.), *The Great Financial Crisis in Finland and Sweden: The Nordic Experience of Financial Liberalization*, Cheltenham, UK: Edward Elgar Publishing.

Hansen, S. (1974), *Økonomisk Vækst I Danmark*, Copenhagen: Akademisk Forlag.

Hjerppe, R. (1996), *Finland's Historical National Accounts 1860–1994: Calculation Methods and Statistical Tables*, Jyvaskyla: Department of History, Jyvaskala University.

Krantz, O. and Schön, L. (2012), "Swedish Historical National Accounts 1560–2010", *Lund Papers in Economic History*, 123, 1–34.

Laeven, L. and Valencia, F. (2010), *Resolution of Banking Crises: The Good, the Bad, and the Ugly*, IMF Working Paper 10/146.

Maddison, A. (2001), *The World Economy: A Millennial Perspective*, Paris: OECD.

Mendoza, E. G. (2010), "Sudden Stops, Financial Crises, and Leverage", *American Economic Review*, 100(5), 1941–1966.

Milward, A.S. (1967), "Could Sweden have Stopped the Second World War?", *Scandinavian Economic History Review*, 15, 127–138.

Mise, E., Kim, T.-H. and Newbold, P. (2005), "On Suboptimality of the Hodrick–Prescott Filter at Time Series Endpoints", *Journal of Macroeconomics*, 27(1), 53–67.

Mitchell, B. R. (1992), *European Historical Statistics 1750–1988*, Basingstoke: Macmillan.

Ramey, G. and Ramey, V. A. (1995), "Cross-Country Evidence on the Link Between Volatility and Growth", *American Economic Review*, 85(5), 1138–1151.

Ravn, M. O. and Uhlig, H. (2002), "On Adjusting the Hodrick-Prescott Filter for the Frequency of Observations", *Review of Economics and Statistics*, 84(2), 371–380.

Salmon, P. (1997), *Scandinavia and the Great Powers, 1890–1940*, Cambridge: Cambridge University Press.

Schön, L. (2010), *Sweden's Road to Modernity: An Economic History*, Stockholm: SNS Förlag.

Sørensen, P. B. and Whitta-Jacobsen, H. J. (2010), *Introducing Advanced Macroeconomics: Growth and Business Cycles*, Maidenhead: McGraw-Hill.

Turner, J. D. (2014), *Banking in Crisis: The Rise and Fall of British Banking Stability, 1800 to the Present*, Cambridge: Cambridge University Press.

Waldenström, D. and Frey, B. S. (2006), *Using Markets to Measure Pre-War Threat Assessments: The Nordic Countries Facing World War II*, IFN Working Paper 676. Stockholm: Research Institute of Industrial Economics.

Wylie, N. (2002), *European Neutrals and Non-Belligerents during the Second World War*, Cambridge: Cambridge University Press.

11 No room for neutrality?

The uncommitted European nations and the economic Cold War in the 1950s

Niklas Jensen-Eriksen

When the United States and its leading Western European allies decided at the end of the 1940s to limit exports of strategic raw materials, products, and technology to communist countries, this policy came into conflict with the desire of many non-communist European countries not to take part in the East-West conflict. Many of these nations were also eager to trade with Eastern Europe. In this chapter, we explore the role of neutral countries in the context of Western embargo. Such an exercise was last completed in 1968, although many scholars have since looked at individual countries. We seek answers to a few interrelated key questions: How did the Western alliance, and in particular the United States, try to incorporate Austria, Switzerland, Sweden, Finland, and Ireland within the Western alliance's export control system, usually known as the CoCom?[1] How did these neutral countries respond? How successful were the Americans and their allies in their efforts?

According to Harto Hakovirta, "the most reliable indicators of a political actor's real policies, or at least its freedom of action, are the choices it makes in dilemmatic test conditions and situations."[2] The establishment of CoCom created this kind of dilemma to the neutrals, but whether or not they were incorporated within the embargo is also significant for wider European history. Michael Mastanduno, one of the leading authorities on the history of CoCom, has stated that "export control policies and their coordination in CoCom have been an integral part of the postwar international system."[3]

As Bengt Sundelius highlighted, there are two ways of studying European neutrality: one can do so in an idiosyncratic fashion by studying and emphasizing the specific characteristics of individual countries or one can treat the neutral countries as a group, and try to establish general patterns and structures among them.[4] The idiosyncratic approach has been considerably more popular among the students of neutrality,[5] and certainly there were differences between the neutral countries. The Swiss and Swedish foreign policies were based on long traditions of neutrality. Austria declared itself neutral in 1955, when the independent Austrian state was re-established after a long period of occupation by US, British, French, and Soviet troops. In the Finnish case, the closeness of the Soviet Union and the latter's influence on Finnish affairs forced the small country to refrain from actions that the Soviets might find objectionable.

Ireland, in turn, was located far from the frontlines of the Cold War and was eager to emphasize its independence vis-à-vis the United Kingdom.[6]

In this chapter, I will adopt the second approach, because I am arguing that, in the context of the Western export control policies, similarities were more important than the differences. In all cases, the US government feared that the neutrals could undermine Western policies by exporting or re-exporting strategic goods to the Eastern bloc, and hence the Americans pressured these countries to limit trade with communist countries. The neutrals, with the partial exception of Ireland,[7] tried to defend their right not to participate in the Western economic embargo against the communist bloc, but all eventually gave up.

It has to be underlined that the neutral countries did not act as a group in the same way that the NATO or Eastern bloc members often did.[8] In this article, "the neutrals" is used as conceptual category to describe countries that, in public, did their best to underline that they did not belong to either of the two alliances (US-led NATO and the Soviet-led Eastern bloc).

The only scholar who has looked at the role of all non-communist neutral European countries together in the context of Western embargo was Gunnar Adler-Karlsson. In 1968, he published the first comprehensive book on the CoCom, in which he also discussed the role of the neutrals.[9] Adler-Karlsson did not have access to confidential government documents, and often had little information on what was going on behind the scenes.[10] Since the late 1980s, many scholars have been able to access previously closed collections. Therefore, this chapter is able to draw on a number of significant works that have looked at individual countries or groups of countries. These include Birgit Karlsson's and Mikael Nilsson's works on Sweden,[11] André Schaller's and Klaus Ammann's on Switzerland,[12] Till Geiger's on Ireland,[13] Niklas Jensen-Eriksen's on Finland,[14] and Hendrik Roodbeen's Ph.D. thesis, which looks at a number of small allied or neutral countries, including Switzerland and Austria.[15] In addition, information for this chapter has been collected from US, British, Swedish, and Finnish archives, as well as from the archives of CoCom, which are located in Paris, France.

Compromising neutrality

During the Cold War decades, the European states were commonly divided into three groups. First, there were those that had joined the North Atlantic Treaty Organization (NATO) and hence had established a close political and military alliance with the US. Second, there were countries that formed what outsiders often called the "Eastern" or "Soviet" bloc and, since 1955, were members of the Warsaw Pact. Third, there were countries that had joined neither of these two competing alliances, and had professed their willingness to stay neutral in the Cold War, which could at any time escalate into a World War III.

Some contemporary observers were not impressed by the statements made by the leaders of these countries. For example, Harto Hakovirta argued in 1988, in what became a classic study on this subject, that "European neutrality has suffered from an inherent and chronic problem of credibility since the emergence of the East-West conflict."[16] He and some other scholars pointed out that, in ideological terms, Switzerland, Austria, Sweden, Finland, and Ireland were not uncommitted but a part of the Western world.[17] Their political and economic systems were based on Western ideas of democracy and capitalism. Furthermore, their trading patterns revealed that they were economically more dependent on the West than the East. Most later joined Western European regional organizations like the Organisation for European Economic Co-operation (OEEC) and the European Free Trade Association (EFTA).[18]

During the 1970s and the 1980s, the links between neutrals and the United States did, however, become somewhat weaker when many Europeans criticized strongly US participation in the Vietnam War and, later, President Ronald Reagan's foreign policies.[19] Neutral powers could then represent themselves as supporters of world peace and the joint interests of world community in a divided planet. In short, they occasionally implied that they were in some ways morally superior to the NATO and Warsaw Pact countries.[20] Neutrality could also become a part of national identity or self-image, even if it had originally been adopted for pragmatic reasons.[21]

Supporting neutral tendencies in non-communist countries benefited the Soviets if such neutrality weakened the Western alliance.[22] The Soviets nevertheless continued to harbor suspicions about the policies of the countries that had actually chosen a neutral path. "In general, it is obvious that the credibility of wartime neutrality by the Western European neutrals is fairly low in Soviet eyes," Hakovirta wrote in 1987.[23] Since then, a substantial amount of previously closed archival sources has become available for research, and from these sources we have learned that the Soviet suspicions were well founded. Sweden provides a case in point. As Mikael Nilsson summarized,

> Between 1945 and 1952 the Swedish government tried to combine US demands for solidarity with the West with a credible policy of neutrality. The end result was Swedish consent to American hegemony in Western Europe. Sweden participated in the Marshall Plan, agreed secretly to abide by the CoCom trade embargo, and embarked on an extensive, secret, military cooperation with the US and Britain.[24]

In short, Sweden became "a trusted ally."[25] Another scholar, Simon Moores, has written, that Swedish weapons were pointing East.[26] The same was true in the Swiss case,[27] and Oliver Rathkolb found evidence that Austria tended to behave like a "secret ally" of the West, although the country also tried to form links with the Soviet Union.[28] Even Finns, who were often believed to be under the thumb of the Soviets, formed secret links with the West during the early Cold War period. The Finnish Security Policy (*Suojelupoliisi*) identified Finnish communists and the Soviet KGB as its main opponents, and cooperated with US and British intelligence agencies in order to contain the communist threat.[29] Norwegian intelligence sent Finnish war veterans to the Soviet Union to gather information about the Red Army, while the Americans got photos and information from Finnish officials and soldiers. These links formed the basis for a more extensive exchange of intelligence.[30] When the British and US officials spread propaganda to Finland, they found locals eager to help them.[31]

Need to secure "parallel action"

The Americans and, to a lesser degree, their allies believed that it was in the interest of the West to stop the flow of sophisticated new technologies, as well as valuable strategic items like weapons, machine tools, and important raw materials, to the communist countries. The embargo would reduce the growth of the Eastern bloc's military potential, and hence it was a "necessary adjunct to the build-up of the North Atlantic Treaty Organisation,"[32] as *The Economist* wrote in 1954. The United States introduced strict controls on its trade with the communist countries in 1948, and in meetings held in Paris in November 1949 and January 1950, the Americans and the European members of NATO (except Iceland) set up a joint export control organization. The system was originally secret and had no official name. Two committees were set up to coordinate the activities of member countries: the Consultative Group and the Coordinating Committee (CoCom). As the first gradually lost its significance, the system as a whole became known simply as the CoCom.

It was understandable that Austria, which was still partly occupied by Soviet troops, and Finland, which was now living under the Soviet shadow, did not join CoCom when the association was set up in 1949–1950. Ireland was only involved in East-West trade to a very limited degree. It was therefore no surprise that these countries were not present at the creation of the multilateral Western export control system.

The Swiss and Swedes were free to join CoCom but refused to do so. International law placed no restrictions on neutrals' foreign trade, particularly in the case of the Cold War, which was not a war at all in the formal sense.[33] These legal points were probably not going to impress most foreigners, and both the Swedes and the Swiss argued that membership would be incompatible with their non-aligned and neutrality policies. The latter warned as early as 1949 that "public knowledge [of US-Swiss discussions] would force Swiss government to deny flatly any intention [of] cooperating."[34]

CoCom countries recognized that Sweden and Switzerland could effectively undercut the Western export control system. Both had managed to stay out of World War II, were important exporters of industrial goods, and could manufacture many items that the members of the Western alliance were no longer willing to sell to the East. Hence, the CoCom members gave considerable thought to how the neutrals could be persuaded to adopt export controls against the socialist countries.[35] There was an "urgent need" to ensure that the Swiss and Swedes would introduce "parallel" controls on East-West trade.[36]

The representatives of small neutral governments sometimes ridiculed claims that their exports could have substantial impact on the large Soviet economy,[37] but the CoCom's concern was in fact understandable. As Klaus Knorr, a well-known student of international political economy, stated, "Once there are holes in the embargo, futility is a foregone conclusion."[38] The socialist countries knew this well. The Czechoslovakian authorities made considerable efforts during the early 1950s to import via Switzerland and Sweden goods that the socialist countries were no longer allowed to buy directly from CoCom countries.[39] In the late 1950s and early 1960s, US officials complained that goods sent to Sweden were redirected to Eastern bloc destinations and approached many Swedish companies to stop them from selling embargoed US electronics to the East.[40]

Sales made by neutral countries could undermine export control policies, but they could also jeopardize the cohesiveness and effectiveness of the Western alliance. European CoCom members were therefore unwilling to include in the export control lists items that the communist countries could buy from alternative suppliers. The US officials recognized that if neutral countries could export strategic items freely to the Soviet Union, it would be hard to ensure that European CoCom countries maintained strict controls on their exports to the communist bloc.[41]

Neutral countries depended on American technology and raw materials, and the United States government could use this dependence as a tool to persuade neutrals to participate unofficially in Western export control policies. In October 1950, the Swedes agreed to prevent re-exports of Western strategic goods to the Soviet Union. They also stated that Swedish-made "war materials" were only exported to "traditional" destinations, none of which were located behind the Iron Curtain.

The Americans, however, wanted more: the US government decided to put pressure on the Swedes by limiting and delaying the sales of strategic materials to them. The Swedes gave in, and in June 1951, Walton Butterworth, the US Ambassador to Stockholm, and Dag Hammarskjöld, a State Secretary of the Swedish Cabinet, concluded an unofficial agreement. The Swedes gave general assurances that strategic goods from the US would not be re-exported to East and that sales of Swedish strategic goods to socialist countries would be avoided if possible. The ball bearing maker SKF, which had been a target of direct US pressure, went even further than its competitors in the CoCom counties in its efforts to limit trade with the socialist countries.[42] These concessions were not meaningless: export control issues became, according to Wilhelm Agrell, "a central component" of bilateral US-Swedish relations,[43] while Charles Silva concluded that export control cooperation "became a benchmark for how Sweden could be incorporated into a key area of strategic policy."[44]

For Switzerland, trade with the socialist countries was of limited importance in economic terms.[45] However, by trading with them, the Swiss could demonstrate their impartial attitude to the Cold War and their willingness to treat both sides equally.[46] Following an approach from the CoCom countries, Switzerland nevertheless introduced an effective system of import and re-export control and limited its exports of strategic goods to Eastern Europe to "normal level" (*courant normal*). In practice, this meant that they would not exceed the level of exports in 1949–1950. Therefore, the Swiss agreed not to seize the opportunity to benefit from restrictions imposed by CoCom countries. The British and French governments regarded the Swiss measures as satisfactory, but the US did not. In order to put pressure on the small country, it blocked a large number of Swiss attempts to buy essential goods from the US. The "Americans' high-handed tactics," as the British diplomats called them, worked. The Swiss invited a US delegation to Bern and, following intensive negotiations, a compromise was reached in July. In this Hotz-Linder agreement, an oral "gentlemen's agreement," the Swiss agreed to limit further their exports of many strategic goods to an "essential" (*courant essentiel*) level. The Americans could accept this, even if the restrictions were not quite as tight as the ones introduced previously by the CoCom countries.[47] Switzerland thereby "became a secret member of NATO's economic warfare system."[48]

Both the Swedes and Swiss were now partly integrated within the Western export control system, although they could conveniently argue that they still had "autonomous" policies (albeit policies that satisfied CoCom's wishes);[49] the latter later claimed that, actually, their neutrality applied only to political and military spheres.[50]

Finland and Austria

Austria and Finland were more difficult cases for Western export control authorities than Sweden or Switzerland. The Swiss and Swedes could, if they were willing to compromise their neutrality, cooperate with the Western alliance, but the Finns and Austrians had less freedom. Up to 1955, Austria was occupied by both Western and Soviet troops, and the latter could undermine the effectiveness of Austrian export control mechanisms.[51] Finland was a neighbor of the Soviet Union and, although it had managed to avoid Soviet occupation during World War II, the Soviets might try again or help Finnish communists to arrange a coup. The Finns also had to ship large war reparations deliveries to the Soviet Union between 1944 and 1952, which formed the basis of extensive commercial trade between the two countries.

On the other hand, strict export control policies toward Finland and Austria could harm their economies, help communists attract more support from local populations, and push these countries closer to the Eastern bloc. A British official therefore concluded that "we should be reluctant to deny to Austria many of the prohibited items as to do so would be contrary to our general policy of building up her economic strength."[52] In addition, the British were eager, for commercial reasons, to protect what was a traditionally extensive Anglo-Finnish trade.[53]

Finland and Austria became targets of the British and the US, and later also of CoCom's export control policies, but the Western regulations concerning them were considerably more relaxed than those concerning trade with the communist countries. The two countries were allowed to buy goods they needed for normal peacetime use, but shipments were tightly scrutinized in order to stop diversion to communist hands. Sales of munitions were mostly prohibited. The CoCom countries underlined their sympathetic attitudes towards Finland and Austria, but because of Finland's "unfortunate geographical and economic position" and the Soviets' occupation of part of Austria, restrictions were deemed necessary.[54]

CoCom countries submitted regular reports of their strategic exports to these countries to the secretariat of the organization.[55] Communist Yugoslavia, which in 1948 broke away from the Soviet bloc, was treated in the same way as Austria and Finland. In 1951, the leading Western nations of the US, UK, and France mostly eliminated their restrictions of trade with Yugoslavia, because they had adopted a policy of supporting the country against the increasing Soviet military threat.[56] CoCom's reporting requirements were also abolished in regards to the Balkan country.[57]

Finland and Austria were targets of export control policies, but also cooperated with Western authorities. As early as 1948, US and Austrian authorities jointly set up a system to prevent the sales of strategic goods to communist countries.[58] The Finns concluded neither official nor unofficial agreements with the Americans. Gunnar Adler-Karlsson believed, erroneously, that the Finnish-Soviet "special relationship . . . made any cooperation with the CoCom policy unthinkable."[59] The US and Finnish documents indicate, however, that the US diplomats who administered export controls formed close relations with key Finnish officials and industrialists and, as a result of these links, the Americans gradually began to trust that the Finns were not re-exporting confidential Western goods or technology to the Eastern bloc.[60] The Americans reported to the CoCom in early 1950 that they had found "no evidence of diversions" of US strategic goods that had been sold to Finland.[61] In a CoCom meeting in June 1952, the Danes summarized that the Finns and Austrians were both "co-operating in the Committee's controls."[62]

There were clear similarities between US cooperation with the Austrians on the one hand and with the Finns on the other hand. Export control was based on informal methods.[63] Both in Helsinki and in Vienna, there was an American Screening Committee that monitored US shipments to the country in question.[64] In both countries, a number of officials cooperated unofficially and secretly with the US and British officials who were responsible for the embargo.[65] For example, in February 1956, the chairman of a Whitehall committee responsible for security controls stated that "during the Occupation we had received a good deal of informal co-operation from the Austrians in preventing the supply of strategic goods to the Soviet zone and the Bloc."[66] There was, however, one crucial difference between the small countries: in December 1955, the Austrian government lost its ability to monitor carefully its imports and exports when the country's trade was liberalized.[67] In the case of Finland, however, similar liberalization never applied to Finnish-Soviet trade.

The Americans were also concerned about the exports of Finnish-made strategic goods, such as tankers and copper, to the Soviet Union. The Finns cooperated with the Western export control authorities in order to prevent the re-export of Western strategic goods to the Soviet bloc but refused to halt the sales of Finnish-made strategic goods. Many of the items that the Finns sold to the Soviet Union were, however, removed from the CoCom embargo lists in 1954 and 1958; hence, at the end of the 1950s, the Finnish exports no longer undermined the Western embargo in a substantial way.[68]

Why cooperate?

Why did the neutrals cooperate with the Americans? The simple answer was that they had to, because otherwise the Americans would retaliate. If Europeans rejected the US's demands, the latter could refuse to sell them strategic materials or to give them economic aid.[69] Yet, this reason is not sufficient to explain all the cooperation, because it does not take into account the fact that many neutrals did see the Soviet Union and communism as threatening forces. For example, E. A. W. Bullock, of the British Foreign Office, recognized that the Swiss were of course determined to protect their trading relations with the West, but he suspected that they were also "genuinely anxious not to help the Russians."[70] Research by Till Geiger suggests that, by limiting exports to the Eastern bloc, Irish politicians could demonstrate their anti-Communist credentials in a cost-effective way.[71]

Something similar happened in Finland. The Finns needed US and Western European supplies and technologies and were not willing to endanger their essential trading links with these countries, but Finnish companies had another motive to cooperate with Western powers, as well. The owners and managers of Finnish companies were usually strongly anti-communist. The companies, including many of those that traded extensively with the Soviets, funded anti-communist struggle in Finnish political life, and tried to strengthen Finnish economic and cultural links with the Western world. During the Cold War, they worked hard to project an image of Finland as a democratic market economy to the Western world.[72] By cooperating with the US and British export control administrations, Finnish industrialists could not only make sure that they received goods and technology, but they also were able to show that they regarded themselves as a part of the Western world, even though Finland could not join the Western alliance. Policymakers in Washington were eager to receive such pro-Western and anti-communist messages. Niklas Stenlås and Mikael Nilsson have suggested that the Western embargo policy could be seen as "a touchstone which could be used to probe the alignment of hesitant or refractory countries such as Sweden and Switzerland."[73]

The Irish did not have to pay high price for their strict attitude on East-West trade, because the country's trade with socialist countries was already very limited.[74] Finnish trade with the communist countries was, in contrast, extensive, as the latter bought a quarter or a fifth of Finland's exports during the early part of the Cold War. The trade was not only extensive, but also particularly profitable for Finnish companies.[75] Nevertheless, the Finns often had an economic motive to comply with the Western re-export regulations. They had to ensure that the goods sold to the Soviet Union by Finland did not contain too many Western components. Finland had to pay for these components with hard currencies but itself received payment from the Soviet Union in inconvertible clearing rubles. Extensive use of Western items would therefore cause balance of payments problems for Finland.[76]

Disadvantages and advantages of neutrality

The Western alliance had introduced the embargo in order to minimize the Soviet threat to their security. The neutral countries mostly saw the issue differently. At least to some of them, the strategic embargo was not an East-West problem, but rather a West-West problem.[77] In other words, the threat that provoked the neutral countries to limit their exports of strategic goods did not always come from Soviet Union, but sometimes from the West – in particular, from the US.[78] The neutral countries were concerned that the US and its allies would use economic sanctions against them or force them to adopt policies that undermined their efforts to stay out of the global confrontation between the Western and Eastern alliances.

Although the Americans were eager to stop the flow of strategic materials to the East, they were not trying to force neutral countries to become full members in the Western embargo. As Birgit Karlsson concluded, for "the USA the *contents* of policy were more important than the form it was given in, while for Sweden the opposite was the case."[79] The informality of the arrangements between the US and the neutrals gave the latter a chance to claim that they had not diverted from the policy of neutrality, while in practice they had done just that. Swedish companies were instructed to refuse to sell items on CoCom lists to the communist countries unless the Swedish government approved these deals. If the order was rejected, the companies were told not to disclose the real reason to their potential customers, but instead claim that they lacked necessary production capacity or raw materials.[80]

Informal cooperation with the Americans had some disadvantages. As neutral countries were not formally members of CoCom, they had to continuously prove that they could be trusted. As a result, they could even become "more Catholic than the Pope," as the Polish concluded when they failed to buy ball bearings from Sweden but got them from NATO countries instead.[81] CoCom members often defended their interests against US demands. One such country was Denmark. According to Karlsson, the "Danish example seems to imply that it was possible to combine formal adherence to CoCom with a relatively independent trade policy, whereas Swedish formal independence was combined with extensive concessions in practice."[82]

Furthermore, since each neutral country negotiated independently with the US government, they could not get support from other neutrals that were facing similar pressure. In contrast, small CoCom countries could join forces with each other in order to block US initiatives that they opposed.[83] The Swiss and Swedes consulted each other,[84] but the neutrals did not form a wider bloc, even though such extensive cooperation could have strengthened their bargaining position vis-à-vis the US. The Swedes even sent reports to the CoCom of their exports of strategic goods to Finland.[85] Building a "third bloc" was probably an alien idea to countries underlining their neutrality or non-aligned status, but such a cooperation could have brought benefits. Thomas Fischer has studied the role of "N+N states" in the process that led to the Conference on Security and Cooperation in Europe in 1975. In this case, the ability of neutral and non-aligned countries, for the first time, to build a "third force" helped to change their position "from objects to subjects in European Cold War affairs."[86]

There was, however, some Nordic cooperation in the field of export controls. The Danes and Norwegians were members of CoCom and supplied information about its internal discussions to the Swedes.[87] In 1951, the Danes resisted attempts to put pressure on Sweden and Switzerland.[88] The Norwegians and Danes also jointly opposed restrictions on Western trade with Finland,[89] and later tried to have the reporting requirements concerning Finland abolished.[90]

Politically, the neutrals had "sinned." But did this matter economically? A group of scholars have argued that they nevertheless become "path-breakers in building East-West contacts."[91] During the Korean War (1950–1953), when relations between the Western and Eastern blocs were tense, the neutrals sold roughly half of all goods exported by non-communist countries to socialist countries in Europe. At the end of the decade, the market share of the neutrals was still close to 40 percent. These figures reflect, to a large degree, an overall decline in East-West trade, but they nevertheless indicate that the neutrals could protect their trade interests in the socialist countries better than the CoCom countries. How was this possible? There are two key reasons. First, as the neutral countries were not full members, their export restrictions were more relaxed than those of full CoCom members. Second, communist countries seemed to feel that small neutral countries were, to some degree, less dangerous trading partners than other capitalist states.[92]

However, we have to recognize that neutrality itself did not automatically make a country an intermediary in the Cold War: the Swiss had relatively little interest in trade with the socialist countries, and the Irish even less. The Swiss could show that the Hotz-Linder agreement had only a small impact on the country's foreign trade, except in the case of machine exports, which suffered. A fear of US countermeasures, but also the increasingly complicated Soviet foreign trade bureaucracy, the communists' striving for autarky, and lack of interest in Eastern European products encouraged Swiss traders to divert their business to non-communist countries. Swiss trade with the Soviet Union had been declining since 1949 and, in 1952, essential quotas were filled only partly.

In September 1954, following relaxation of the general CoCom embargo, the Swiss Federal Council terminated the Hotz-Linder agreement, but continued to restrict trade – too strictly, according to the Soviets.[93] Austria, however, had a strong interest in trading with other parts of the former Habsburg Empire, while the large war reparations shipments formed the basis of Finnish-Soviet trade, which was also seen as a symbol of new postwar "friendship" between the two countries.

Conclusions

If the establishment of CoCom is analyzed as "a test" for European neutrals, it is clear that they failed it. In the 1950s, each of these countries cooperated with the Western alliance in the latter's efforts to limit strategic exports from non-communist countries to the Soviet bloc. Some of the officials and companies of the neutral countries shared the desire of CoCom to limit the flow of military useful goods to the East, while others tried to maintain the appearance of neutrality even though there was a lot of practical cooperation between CoCom and uncommitted countries. This cooperation was often based on informal links and agreements, which shows how important it is to look at low-level interaction instead of focusing on "high politics" and public statements.

In his recent study on Finnish security police (*Suojelupoliisi*), Kimmo Rentola concluded that there was little room for neutrality in Cold War intelligence activities.[94] The same could be said about the field of export controls. If neutral countries continued to sell communist countries items embargoed by the Western alliance, this trade helped the Soviet Union and its allies to undermine the embargo. If, on the other hand, the neutrals stopped this trade, they participated in the efforts of the Western alliance to weaken the military and economic potential of the communist countries. We know now that, in most cases, the neutrals chose the latter option regardless of whether it was compatible with the declared guidelines of their neutrality policy.

All neutrals, including the ones located closest to the Soviet bloc, were living in the "American century."[95] None of the countries – not even frontline ones like Austria and Finland – could resist US demands for cooperation. Some of their policymakers and industrialists did not even want to try. During previous conflicts, neutral countries had often reaped economic benefits from their uncommitted status. During the early Cold War, however, the US was economically strong enough to limit, although not totally eliminate, such benefits.

Acknowledgments

I would like to thank Thomas Fischer, Johanna Rainio-Niemi, and Marianne Rostgaard for their useful comments and suggestions.

Notes

1 The chapter does not discuss the role of mini-states like Liechtenstein. We will also ignore Spain, which joined NATO and CoCom in the 1980s, but had close military links with the USA already in the 1950s.
2 Hakovirta 1988, 7.
3 Mastanduno 1992, 5.
4 Sundelius 1990, 207.
5 Hakovirta 1988, 2.
6 For a convenient summary of the characteristics of these countries, see Fischer 2009, 32–55.
7 Geiger 2009.
8 In fact, as we will see, this had a clear negative impact on their ability to defend themselves against US pressure.
9 Adler-Karlsson 1968.
10 For a long time, there was so little information available on CoCom that, although Adler-Karlsson's book was highly critical on CoCom, a British diplomat in charge of export control issues recommended it as useful reading when a British ambassador asked for information on the organization. National Archives, Kew, London (NA). FCO69/558. Minute by T. J. Alexander, 27 February 1975.
11 Karlsson 1992, 1995; Nilsson 2007, 2009; Nilsson 2010; Nilsson and Wyss 2016.
12 Schaller 1987; Ammann 2005.
13 Geiger 2008.
14 Jensen-Eriksen 2011, 2013.
15 Roodbeen 1992.
16 Hakovirta 1988, 52–53.
17 For example, Fischer 2009, 31.
18 For example, Enderle-Burcel et al. 2009, 2; Rathkolb 2009, 17.
19 Zakheim 1998, 124; Sundelius 1987, 15.
20 Sundelius 1987, 15–16.
21 Rainio-Niemi 2014.
22 Zubok 2009, 110.
23 Hakovirta 1987, 201.
24 Nilsson 2009, 273.
25 Nilsson 2010, 291.
26 Moores 2002, 29.
27 Wyss 2012.
28 Rathkolb 2009, 18.
29 Rentola 2009, 20–24, 28, 78.
30 Rislakki 2011; Heikka 2005, 107.
31 Fields 2015.
32 "Butter for Soviet Guns". *The Economist*, 23 January 1954.
33 Aalders 2009, 60; Karlsson 1992, 130.
34 Foreign Relations of United States 1949, volume V, p. 68: The Minister in Switzerland (Vincent) to the Acting Secretary of State, 19 January 1949.
35 See, for example, NA. FO371/87193. UR3424/13. Telegram no. 423 from Hall-Patch, Paris, to Foreign Office (FO), 3 June 1950; FO371/87195. UR3424/55. A minute by E. A. W. Bullock, 1 December 1950; UR3424/57. "Report of the Sub-committee on the question of Sweden and Switzerland." CoCom Doc. 176, 26 October 1950; FO371/94288. M3415719. "Meeting of the Consultative Group

No room for neutrality? 225

16 January 1950." CoCom Document no. 258B; Ministère des Affaires Étrangères. Archives diplomatiques, La Courneuve. CoCom Archives (hereafter MAE. CoCom). Early miscellaneous documents, File 21. CoCom doc 303: "Report of the Coordinating Committee on the UK statement on Sweden and Switzerland and Subsequent Decisions," 9 March 1951.
36 MAE. CoCom. Early miscellaneous documents, File 21. CoCom doc 303: "Report of the Coordinating Committee on the UK statement on Sweden and Switzerland and subsequent decisions," 9 March 1951.
37 See, for example, Nilsson 2009, 278.
38 Knorr 1975, 146.
39 Brom and Kubů 2009, 168, 175–176, 184.
40 MAE. CoCom. File 658. CoCom Document 3965. Memorandum from the United States Delegation on non-member country cooperation and relations – Sweden. Subcommittee on export controls, 22 April 1960; CoCom Document 4620: A US memorandum on the same topic, 21 September 1961.
41 Mastanduno 1992, 19, 21.
42 Karlsson 1992, 171–181, 188–189; MAE. CoCom. Early miscellaneous documents, File 21. CoCom doc 303: "Report of the Coordinating Committee on the UK statement on Sweden and Switzerland and subsequent decisions," 9 March 1951; Riksarkivet, Stockholm. Utrikesdepartementet 1920 års dossiersystem. HP 65 Ea, File 3109. A memo by Sverker Åström, 31 July 1951, and the attached memos; HP 64 Ea, File 2684. Telegram from Swedish Cabinet to Embassies in London, Paris and Washington, 28 January 1951.
43 Agrell 2000, 199.
44 Silva 1999, 317; See also Nilsson 2010, 290, 292, 297.
45 Ammann 2005, 119–120.
46 Lohm and Fritzsche 2009, 26.
47 The classic study on this agreement is Schaller 1987; See also Ammann 2005, 126–127; Roodbeen 1992, 236–243; Lohm and Fritzsche 2009, 31–33; NA. DEFE10/254. J.W.P.C.(SX)/P(51)27. Copy of a letter from U.K. Delegation to O.E.E.C. to Foreign Office dated 16th February, 1951" (quote); The agreement received its name from Harold F. Linder, US Deputy Assistant Secretary of State for Economic Affairs and Jean Hotz, Director of the Swiss Division of Commerce.
48 Gabriel 1998, 19.
49 Riksarkivet, Stockholm. Utrikesdepartementet 1920 års dossiersystem. HP 64 Ea, File 2685. Telegram from Swedish Cabinet, to Embassy in Washington, 7 June 1951; Silva 1999, 314; Karlsson 1992, 178; NA. FO371/111295. M3423/12. L.H. Lamb, Berne, to J. E. Coulson, FO, 27 October 1954.
50 Vogel 1987, 105.
51 NA. FO371/87186. UR348/1. "Paris (U.K. Delegation) Tel. No. 32". C.B. Duke, 11 January 1950.
52 NA. FO371/87186. UR348/1. "Paris (U.K. Delegation) Tel. No. 32". C.B. Duke, 11 January 1950.
53 NA. FO371/87186. UR348/4. "East/West Trade. Note for the U.K. Delegate" 5 January 1950.
54 NA. FO371/87193. UR3424/10. "Report of Coordinating Committee on Exports to Austria and Finland," 12 May 1950; FO371/100223. M3410/2. CoCom Doc. 553: Coordinating Committee. Record of Discussion, 6 December 1951 (quote) and annexes to this document; DEFE10/395. J.W.P.S.(W.P.)/P(50)49. Briefs for the UK representative on security controls on exports to Austria and Finland, 1 May 1950; Hanhimäki 1997, 60–61.

55 MAE. CoCom. Early miscellaneous documents, File 19. V. Price, UK Delegation, Paris, to G. d'Orlandi, Chairman of the CoCom, 28 August 1950; See also, for example, the reports in Early miscellaneous documents, Files 18–20 and 22, and CoCom Secretariat Papers, File 14, Paper No. 78: "Exports to Finland of List I and List II items and items of the Munitions and Atomic Lists During the first half of 1955."
56 MAE. CoCom. Early miscellaneous documents, File 20. Doc. 231. "Statement by United Kingdom on Export Policy to Yugoslavia"; CoCom Doc 268: "Statement of U.S. Export Policy Toward Yugoslavia," 6 February 1951; File 22. CoCom Doc. 347B. "Declaration by the French Delegate on policy regarding exports to Jugoslavia," 5 April 1951; Mehta 2011, 125.
57 MAE. CoCom. Early miscellaneous documents, File 20. CoCom Document 785. "Report of the Coordinating Committee to the Consultative Group Covering the Period July 20th 1951–June 17th 1952".
58 Rathkolb 2009, 12–13.
59 Adler-Karlsson 1968, 58. He did suspect that they may have been a "secret transhipment agreement" between Finland and the Western countries, but believed that even this was "doubtful."
60 Jensen-Eriksen 2011.
61 MAE. CoCom. Early miscellaneous documents, File 22. CoCom Doc. 306: "Control Over Reexports and Transit Trade in Finland," U.S. Delegation [1951].
62 MAE. CoCom. Early miscellaneous documents, File 30. CoCom Doc. 787: Record of Discussion, 10 June 1952.
63 Roodbeen 1992, 296; NARA. SD. RG59. Decimal Files on Finland 1950–1954, box 2120. 460E.119/8-2251. "Memorandum of Discussion with Foreign Ministry officials on application of U.S. export controls and allocation procedures to Finland," W. Barnes, 22 August 1951.
64 Roodbeen 1992, 289.
65 Stankovsky and Roodbeen 1991, 73–74; MAE. CoCom. Early miscellaneous documents, File 21. CoCom doc 280. Report of the Coordinating Committee on the question of Third Countries (i.e., non-participating countries) 16 February 1951; File 22. CoCom doc. 313: "Report of the Coordinating Committee on the U.S. Proposal on Austria," 13 March 1951.
66 NA. DEFE10/340. Security Export Controls Working Party, SX/M(56)1, 2 February, 1956. The Chairman was H. Gresswell from the Ministry of Defence.
67 Roodbeen 1992, 299.
68 Jensen-Eriksen 2011.
69 Roodbeen 1992, 5; Lohm and Fritzsche 2009, 32.
70 NA. FO371/87195. UR3424/55. A minute by E.A.W. Bullock, 1 December 1950; see also FO371/87194. UR3424/36. Telegram no. 242 from Scrivener, Bern, to FO, 23 October 1950.
71 Geiger 2008, 124.
72 Vesikansa 2004; Jensen-Eriksen 2007, 84–85, 87–88, 99–100, 110–111.
73 Stenlås and Nilsson 2005, 151.
74 Geiger 2008, 122, 124.
75 Viita 2006, 39.
76 Sutela 2005, 4.
77 Stankovsky and Roodbeen 1991, 72.
78 Roodbeen 1992, 246; Agrell 2000, 199.
79 Karlsson 1995, 45.
80 Karlsson 1995, 45; Nilsson 2007, 191.
81 Nilsson 2009, 281 (quote), 283; Nilsson 2007, 253–254.

82 Karlsson 1992, 256.
83 Førland 1994, 178.
84 Riksarkivet. HP 64 Ea, File 2683. Erik von Sydow, Paris, to Dag Hammarskjöld, Utrikesdepartmentet, 9 January 1950; HP 64 Ea, File 2684. Telegram from Swedish Cabinet to Bern, 15 January 1951; Karlsson 1992, 170.
85 Riksarkivet. HP 64 Ea, File 2685. "Revised International Lists 1952. Export Licenses granted to Finland in October 1952; "Revised International Lists 1951. Export Licenses granted to Finland in February 1952." The fact that these reports were written in English suggests that they were sent to the West. Some of the lists can also be found from US archives. NARA. SD. RG59. Decimal Files on Finland 1950–1954, box 2119. 460C.589/1-2753. DuWayne G. Clark, Stockholm, to State Department, 27 January 1953. The Swedes agreed in 1951 to give British information about the exports of strategic goods to Eastern Europe. This may have included Finland; Nilson 1991, 56.
86 Fischer 2009, 18.
87 Riksarkivet, Stockholm; Utrikesdepartementet 1920 års dossiersystem. HP 64 Ea, File 2685. Erik von Sydow, Paris, to Sverker Åström, Utrikesdepartementet, 28 June 1951.
88 NA. FO371/94288. M3415/19. "East/West Trade," A British record of the Consultative Group meeting on 16 January 1951.
89 NA. FO371/87186. UR348/6. E. Hall-Patch, Paris, to Ernest Bevin, 26 January 1950.
90 MAE. CoCom. Early miscellaneous documents, File 30. CoCom Doc. 787: Record of Discussion, 10 June 1952.
91 Enderle-Burcel et al. 2009, 1.
92 Komlosy 2009, 115.
93 Lohm and Fritzsche 2009, 32–33.
94 Rentola 2009, 45, 159.
95 Compare with Gabriel 1998.

References

Aalders, Gerard, The Second World War and the Cold War: Influences on the Swedish Post-war Economy. In *Gaps in the Iron Curtain: Economic Relations between Neutral and Socialist Countries in Cold War Europe*. Edited by Gertrude Enderle-Burcel, Piotor Franaszek, Dieter Stiefel and Alice Teichova. Jagiellonian University Press, Kraków 2009, 60–72.

Adler-Karlsson, Gunnar, *Western Economic Warfare 1947–1967: A Case Study in Foreign Economic Policy*, Stockholm economic studies. New series 9. Almqvist & Wiksell, Stockholm 1968.

Agrell, Wilhelm, *Fred och fruktan: Sveriges säkerhetspolitiska historia 1918–2000*. Historiska media, Lund 2000.

Ammann, Klaus, Swiss Trade with the East in the Early Cold War. In *East-West Trade and the Cold War*. Edited by Jari Eloranta and Jari Ojala. University of Jyväskylä, Jyväskylä 2005, 113–131.

Brom, Bohumír, and Kubů, Eduard, The Role of Czechoslovak Trade with Neutral Countries in the Period of Escalating Cold War: The Cases of Switzerland and Sweden, 1949–1953. In *Gaps in the Iron Curtain: Economic Relations between Neutral and Socialist Countries in Cold War Europe*. Edited by Gertrude Enderle-Burcel, Piotor Franaszek, Dieter Stiefel and Alice Teichova. Jagiellonian University Press, Kraków 2009, 165–190.

Enderle-Burcel, Gertrude, Franaszek, Piotor, Stiefel, Dieter, and Teichova, Alice, Introduction. In *Gaps in the Iron Curtain: Economic Relations between Neutral and Socialist Countries in Cold War Europe*. Edited by Gertrude Enderle-Burcel, Piotor Franaszek, Dieter Stiefel and Alice Teichova. Jagiellonian University Press, Kraków 2009, 1–7.

Fields, Marek, *Reinforcing Finland's Attachment to the West – British and American Propaganda and Cultural Diplomacy in Finland, 1944–1962*. University of Helsinki, Helsinki 2015.

Fischer, Thomas, Neutral Power in the CSCE: The N+N States and the Making of the Helsinki Accords 1975, *Wiener Schriften zur Internationalen Politik* 12. Nomos, Baden-Baden 2009.

Førland, Tor Egil, Foreign policy profiles of the Scandinavian countries: Making Use of CoCom. *Scandinavian Journal of History* 19, no. 2 (1994), 165–184.

Gabriel, Jürg Martin, Swiss Neutrality and the "American Century": Two Conflicting Worldviews, *Beiträge* 14. Forschungsstelle für Internationale Beziehungen, Eidgenössische Technische Hochschule Zürich, Zürich 1998.

Geiger, Till, Trading with the Enemy: Ireland, the Cold War and East-West Trade, 1945–55. *Irish Studies in International Affairs* 19 (2008), 119–142.

Geiger, Till, Neutral Ireland and East-West trade, 1945–1955. In *Gaps in the iron curtain: Economic Relations between Neutral and Socialist Countries in Cold War Europe*. Edited by Gertrude Enderle-Burcel, Piotor Franaszek, Dieter Stiefel and Alice Teichova. Jagiellonian University Press, Kraków 2009, 43–59.

Hakovirta, Harto, East-West Tensions and Soviet Policies on European Neutrality. In *The Neutral Democracies and the New Cold War*. Edited by Bengt Sundelius. Westview Press, Boulder, CO and London 1987, 198–217.

Hakovirta, Harto, *East-West Conflict and European Neutrality*. Clarendon Press, Oxford 1988.

Hanhimäki, Jussi M., *Containing Coexistence: America, Russia, and the "Finnish Solution," 1945–1956*. Kent State University Press, Kent, OH and London 1997.

Heikka, Henrikki, Republican Realism: Finnish Strategic Culture in Historical Perspective. *Cooperation and Conflict* 40, no. 1 (2005), 91–119.

Jensen-Eriksen, Niklas, *Läpimurto: Metsäteollisuus kasvun, integraation ja kylmän sodan Euroopassa 1950–1973*, Metsäteollisuuden maa 4. Suomalaisen Kirjallisuuden Seura, Helsinki 2007.

Jensen-Eriksen, Niklas, CoCom and Neutrality: Western Export Control Policies, Finland and the Cold War, 1949–58. In *Reassessing Cold War Europe*. Edited by Sari Autio-Sarasmo and Katalin Miklóssy. London and New York, Routledge 2011, 49–65.

Jensen-Eriksen, Niklas, Lost at Sea: Finnish Government, Shipping Companies and the United Nations Embargo against China during the 1950s. *Scandinavian Journal of History* 38, no. 5 (2013), 568–589.

Karlsson, Birgit, *Handelspolitik eller politisk handling. Sveriges handel med öststaterna 1946–1952* Meddelanden från Ekonomisk-historiska institutionen vid Göteborgs universitet 66. Göteborgs universitet, Göteborg 1992.

Karlsson, Birgit, Neutrality and Economy: The Redefining of Swedish Neutrality, 1946–1952. *Journal of Peace Research* 32, no. 1 (1995), 37–48.

Knorr, Klaus, *The Power of Nations. The Political Economy of International Relations*. Basic Books, Inc., New York 1975.

Komlosy, Andrea, Austria and the Permeability of the Iron Curtain: from Bridge-Building to Systemic Change. In *Gaps in the Iron Curtain: Economic Relations between Neutral and Socialist Countries in Cold War Europe*. Edited by Gertrude Enderle-Burcel, Piotor Franaszek, Dieter Stiefel and Alice Teichova. Jagiellonian University Press, Kraków 2009, 107–124.

Lohm, Christina, and Fritzsche, Bruno, Swiss Economic Relations with the Soviet Union during the Cold War. In *Gaps in the Iron Curtain: Economic Relations between Neutral and Socialist Countries in Cold War Europe*. Edited by Gertrude Enderle-Burcel, Piotor Franaszek, Dieter Stiefel and Alice Teichova. Jagiellonian University Press, Kraków 2009, 26–42.

Mastanduno, Michael, *Economic Containment: CoCom and the Politics of East-West Trade*. Cornell Studies in Political Economy. Cornell University Press, Ithaca, NY 1992.

Mehta, Coleman, The CIA Confronts the Tito-Stalin Split, 1948–1951. *Journal of Cold War Studies* 13, no. 1 (2011), 101–145.

Moores, Simon, "Neutral on our Side": US Policy towards Sweden during the Eisenhower Administration. *Cold War History* 2, no. 3 (2002), 29–62.

Nilson, Bengt, No Coal Without Iron Ore: Anglo-Swedish Trade Relations in the Shadow of the Korean War. *Scandinavian Journal of History* 16, no. 1 (1991), 45–72.

Nilsson, Mikael, *Tools of Hegemony: Military Technology and Swedish-American Security Relations, 1945–1962*. Santérus Academic Press Sweden, Stockholm 2007.

Nilsson, Mikael, Limiting Diplomatic Friction: Sweden, the United States and SKF's Ball Bearing Exports to Eastern Europe, 1950–52. *Scandinavian Economic History Review* 57, no. 3 (2009), 273–288.

Nilsson, Mikael, Aligning the Non-Aligned: A Re-interpretation of why and how Sweden Was Granted access to US military materiel in the early Cold War, 1948–1952 *Scandinavian Journal of History* 35, no. 3 (2010), 290–309.

Nilsson, Mikael, and Wyss, Marco, The Armed Neutrality Paradox: Sweden and Switzerland in US Cold War Armaments Policy. *Journal of Contemporary History* 51, no. 2 (2016), 335–363.

Rainio-Niemi, Johanna, *The Ideological Cold War: The Politics of Neutrality in Austria and Finland*. Routledge, New York and London 2014.

Rathkolb, Oliver, "Austria – Sieve to East": Austria's Neutrality during the East-West Economic War. 1945/8–1989. In *Gaps in the Iron Curtain: Economic Relations between Neutral and Socialist Countries in Cold War Europe*. Edited by Gertrude Enderle-Burcel, Piotor Franaszek, Dieter Stiefel and Alice Teichova. Jagiellonian University Press, Kraków 2009, 11–25.

Rentola, Kimmo, Suojelupoliisi kylmässä sodassa 1949–1991. In *Ratakatu 12: Suojelupoliisi 1949–2009*. Edited by Matti Simola. WSOY [Helsinki] 2009, 9–192.

Rislakki, Jukka. "Without Mercy": US Strategic Intelligence and Finland in the Cold War. 2011. Available at www.economist.com/blogs/easternapproaches/2011/12/finland-and-american-intelligence (accessed 23 October 2017).

Roodbeen, Hendrik, Trading the Jewel of Great Value: The Participation of the Netherlands, Belgium, Switzerland and Austria in the Western Strategic Embargo. Ph.D. thesis, Rijksuniversiteit, Leiden, 1992.

Schaller, André, *Schweizer Neutralität im West-Ost-Handel: Das Hotz-Linder-Agreement vom 23. Juli 1951*. Verlag Paul Haupt, Bern 1987.

Silva, Charles, *Keep Them Strong, Keep Them Friendly: Swedish-American Relations and the Pax Americana, 1948–1952*. University of Stockholm, Stockholm 1999.

Stankovsky, Jan, and Roodbeen, Hendrik, Export Controls Outside CoCom. In *After the Revolutions. East-West Trade and Technology Transfer in the 1990s.* Edited by Gary K. Bertsch, Heinrich Vogel and Jan Zielonka. Westview Press, Boulder, CO 1991, 71–91.

Stenlås, Niklas, and Nilsson, Mikael, Cold War Neutrality and Technological Dependence: Sweden's Military Technology and the East-West Trade. In *East-West Trade and the Cold War.* Edited by Jari Eloranta and Jari Ojala. University of Jyväskylä, Jyväskylä 2005, 133–151.

Sundelius, Bengt, Dilemmas and Security Strategies for the Neutral Democracies. In *The Neutral Democracies and the New Cold War.* Edited by Bengt Sundelius. Westview Press, Boulder, CO and London 1987, 11–32.

Sundelius, Bengt, Review Article: East-West Conflict and European Neutrality. *Cooperation and Conflict* 25, no. 4 (1990), 207–214.

Sutela, Pekka, Finnish Trade with the USSR: Why Was it Different? *BOFIT Online* 7. Bank of Finland, BOFIT – Institute for Economies in Transition, Helsinki 2005.

Vesikansa, Jarkko, *Salainen sisällissota: Työnantajien ja porvarien taistelu kommunismia vastaan kylmän sodan Suomessa.* Kustannusosakeyhtiö Otava, Helsinki 2004.

Viita, Pentti, *Kapitalismin ja sosialismin puristuksessa: Suomen ja Neuvostoliiton taloussuhteet 1944–1991.* BSV Kirja, Helsinki 2006.

Vogel, Hans, Switzerland and the New Cold War: International and Domestic Determinants of Swiss Security Policy. In *The Neutral Democracies and the New Cold War.* Edited by Bengt Sundelius. Westview Press, Boulder, CO and London 1987, 95–116.

Wyss, Marco, Neutrality in the Early Cold War: Swiss Arms Imports and Neutrality. *Cold War History* 12, no. 1 (2012), 25–49.

Zakheim, Dov S., The United States and the Nordic Countries during the Cold War. *Cooperation and Conflict* 33, no. 2 (1998), 115–129.

Zubok, Vladislav M., *A Failed Empire: The Soviet Union in the Cold War from Stalin to Gorbachev.* University of North Carolina Press, Chapel Hill 2009.

12 Bicycles in rush hour

Concluding neutrality and war

Toshiaki Tamaki and Jari Ojala

This anthology probes one of the fundamental questions of human history. How have wars affected societies? Wartime economies and businesses have recently attracted more attention among researchers.[1] In historiography, however, the focus is usually on the great powers directly involved in the conflicts.[2] Without a doubt, great powers have contributed to the history of the world and they have also been the main parties to global conflicts. Nevertheless, we should not ignore the role of small and medium-sized states which have also played an important role in human history: global history cannot be written without taking their roles into consideration. This book deals with two meta-themes, as suggested by Patrick K. O'Brien in the Foreword: small neutral states and their economies during (and after) great wars.

In the global economy today – and also in history – small and weak countries are important. The world has always been networked together between human actors, civilizations, trade, diplomacy, culture, religion and so on.[3] Different continents, states, and regions have utilized their comparative and competitive advantages in this global network, contributing their resources and products. Together, small states do play a role in these networks of the world economy. For example, their growth rates have been fairly high, as suggested by Joel Mokyr.[4] Small and medium-sized states have also been involved in wars – voluntarily or involuntarily. There is a plethora of examples where, especially during major wars (like the Napoleonic and Crimean Wars, or World Wars I and II) they have maintained, or at least tried to maintain, their neutrality. In wartime the role played by the neutral states may be pronounced as the demand for various products and resources may increase, and at the same time the warring parties may not necessarily be able to engage in trade. Thus, small and neutral countries are like bicycles during the rush hour: navigating the traffic jams which big cars cannot get through.

What is neutrality, especially for small and medium-sized countries? Neutrality as a concept is well defined in the introduction of this volume and the subsequent chapters. Namely, neutrality is first and foremost a concept of politics and diplomacy, but it does also affect economic affairs, primarily trade and international transport. In Chapter 7, Eric Golson presents an overview of the evolution of the concept.[5] Neutrality, according to Golson, is to remain "outside the conflict to exploit the situation for their [neutral states'] own benefit." Nevertheless, neutrality is a broad and perhaps ill-defined concept, as Golson suggests in his chapter. The content of the concept has also changed over time, as we will discuss below.

Was, then, neutrality beneficial for the weak countries during and after the war? A number of studies have previously suggested that those affected by wars may experience high growth figures due to reconstruction – as can be seen, for example, in Japan and Finland after World War II.[6] However, the chapters in this compilation do show that neutrality may be beneficial even during and especially after a war. Indeed, the chapter by Jason Lennard and Eric Golson (Chapter 9) shows that in all the Nordic countries GDP actually declined during both World War I and II – regardless of whether these countries remained neutral or not – but immediately after the war the growth rates were high. Thus, the reconstruction in devastated countries after the war increased demand for products produced in countries that were not exposed to the war in the first place.

Moreover, neutrality was certainly beneficial for several Western countries during the French Revolutionary and Napoleonic Wars in terms of an increase in demand for their products and (shipping) services. However, these conflicts were also detrimental to the businesses of neutrals in many ways. However, if the neutrals had been involved in the war, their economies would most probably have been harmed even more devastatingly than those of major powers.

Five partly overlapping arguments can be summarized as the outcomes of this anthology. The first argument is obvious: the role played by the small and medium-sized neutral states during wars has changed. The small neutral states had only limited potential to enhance trade and transport during the early modern era – for example, by establishing consular networks, signing trade agreements, and promoting overall diplomatic relationships. During this time, the individual merchants played a more important role, as suggested by Silvia Marzagalli in Chapter 3 of this volume. Nevertheless, small and medium-sized states could still play an active role in promoting their commercial interests by providing commercial information to individual merchants. During and after industrialization this commercial information was not enough, as businesses desired protection and public goods (like infrastructure). The cost of such infrastructure was higher than the information costs during the era of merchant capitalism, and thus more challenging for small and medium-sized countries to provide – whether they were neutral or not during the war. In wartime this was even more pronounced for neutral states as economic activities as a whole became more expensive – and also the gains and possible losses caused by the war may have been huge. Moreover, after the wars, new coalitions and trade agreements may be created. This was the case after World War I, for example, with the Norwegian-American Trade Agreement (Knut Ola Naastad Ström, Chapter 8 in this volume), in CoCom restrictions during the Cold War (Niklas Jensen-Eriksen, in Chapter 11), and in the free trade agreements and emergence of the European integration after World War II.

Even more extreme cases emerged due the war, as witnessed in the move of the Portuguese Court to Brazil in 1807 just before Napoleonic forces invaded Lisbon, as discussed in this volume by Rodrigo da Costa Dominguez and Angelo Alves Carrara (Chapter 5).

Second, international payment mechanisms did not necessarily change, even though commodity transfers changed during the wars. In. Chapter 4, Maria Cristina Moreira, Rita Martins de Sousa and Werner Scheltjens show how the financial market of Amsterdam remained the key operator for the neutral countries throughout the tempestuous times from the mid-18th to the mid-19th century. Similarly, Hamburg was able to retain its position as a financial center throughout the troubled decades[7].

The third major contribution of the volume is related to trade flows, which during wars may change temporarily or permanently. These changes may be especially beneficial for small neutral countries. War creates demands of which small neutral countries can take advantage. Sweden is a primary example of this, both during the Napoleonic era, during the Crimean War and during the First and Second World Wars I and II. This is witnessed in the chapter by Peter Hedberg and Henric Häggqvist (Chapter 6) and, in the case of SKF, by Eric Golson and Jason Lennard (Chapter 9). SKF, for example, increased its exports due to wartime demand. The investments in production capacity during wartime, however, may be long-lasting and lucrative even after the war, and enable market control and pricing power. Similarly, Finnish and Swedish tar overtook American tar in British markets during the American War of Independence, as previous providers of this product (the American colonies) were out of the markets. However, the Finns (and Swedes) were able to remain in these growing markets even after the war.[8]

The fourth argument concerns the prospects for neutral countries to participate in transportation. Freight rates in wartime are usually higher due to the high demand of transport capacity and the high risks involved. This was shown especially during the French Revolutionary and Napoleonic Wars, when the price of transport (freight) could double the price of the cargo. Thus, many entrepreneurs from neutral countries made fortunes during wartime – but also huge losses, as neutral ships were also captured or sunk by the belligerents. This happened both in early modern and modern times, as shown by Naastad Ström in the case of Norwegian shipping during World War I.[9] For example, US vessels became important players in European markets, especially during the French Revolutionary and Napoleonic Wars – as is shown in the contributions by Jeremy Land, Jari Eloranta, and Maria Cristina Moreira (Chapter 2) and Silvia Marzagalli (Chapter 3). This may have been important for the economic growth of the USA[10].

The fifth argument is the changing nature of neutrality: this concept created during the 17th century gained new meaning during the French Revolutionary and Napoleonic Wars, as a number of neutral countries were able to benefit from trade and shipping at the time. These issues are studied in this volume by Land, Eloranta, and Moreira (Chapter 2); Marzagalli (Chapter 3);

and Moreira, de Sousa, and Schletjens (Chapter 4). Neutrality, however, was still a rather a matter of practice. As noted by Golson, the Hague and Geneva Conventions provided legal justification for neutrality during the late 19h and early 20th centuries. This legally based neutrality was, in turn, disrupted during World Wars I and II, which both impeded or made it impossible even for neutral states to engage in trade. Thus, neutrality arose as an act of necessity during the Napoleonic era; it gained legal status during the late 19th century, was challenged by the global wars of the early 20th century, and has re-emerged ever since in international politics disturbed by series of conflicts. Furthermore, in the overwhelming shadow of the Cold War, the great powers (the USA and the USSR) aimed to engulf neutral and weak states into their spheres of interest.

The countries analyzed in this volume may be small or medium-sized, but they are also large enough. Moreover, they may belong to larger units, such as the EU, the OECD, NATO, ASEAN, or OPEC. In these larger units, even small states may collectively possess enough political and even economic power to have an effect in world politics. Nevertheless, the state is usually the unit for analyzing the current and historical world. We are now, however, entering a different world, where the unit of analysis is not necessarily a state but a community or union. Even so, studies of small and medium-sized states are still useful and important to draw an overall picture of global history; they were part of the connections of both the early modern and the modern world[11]. Therefore, this book helps readers to understand history also from a non-major power perspective. We would like to emphasize that our world consists of small, medium, and large states. The relationships between these three types of states will bring about new perspectives in historical studies. Small and neutral states may have benefited in wartime, but it is not an entirely easy task for small countries to remain neutral during massive wars, as seen during World War II.

In global history neutrality is a complex issue, as the whole concept of "neutrality" is Eurocentric. This relates to the fact that the idea of neutral (nation) states was created during the Napoleonic era in the European context. In Asia, in turn, there were no similar conflicts, and thus no need for neutrality to emerge in practice. However, the global conflicts of the early 20th century transformed neutrality into a global concept. Moreover, after numerous colonies gained independence in the aftermath of World War I, many of these newly independent states preferred to remain neutral in the emerging Cold War. An example of this was the Non-Aligned Movement, initiated by India (Jawaharlal Nehru), Egypt (Gamal Abdel Nasser), and Yugoslavia (Josip Broz Tito) during the 1950s.

In this volume, one country is especially noted as the one that benefited from neutrality: Sweden. But is Sweden a typical or rather exceptional case in the global history of neutrality? The chapters in this collection show that even similar neutral states (like the Nordic countries) did have different experiences during wartime. This collection of chapters may open discussion for future studies to evaluate the role played by neutrality in long-term growth. If a link between growth and neutrality does, indeed, exist – or the idea that war is bad for business – it may motivate countries today to avoid conflicts. This, in turn, would make the world a better place to live. What a marvelous result for historical research.

Notes

1. For an overview of the most recent research, see especially Eloranta (2007); Eloranta, Golson, Markevich, and Wolf (2016); Lakomaa (2017).
2. See especially Kennedy (1989).
3. For example, McNeill (2003).
4. Mokyr (2006).
5. See also especially Müller (2016).
6. See especially Tanaka, Tamaki, Ojala, and Eloranta (2015).
7. See, for example, Samuelson (1951).
8. Especially Airaksinen (1996); Hautala (1963).
9. On profits, see especially Ojala (1999); and on neutrality of shipping, see Müller (2016).
10. North (1961).
11. See especially O'Brien (2006).

References

Airaksinen, M. (1996). Tar Production in Colonial North America. *Environment and History*, 2(1), 115–125.

Eloranta, J. (2007). From the Great illusion to the Great War: Military Spending Behaviour of the Great Powers, 1870–1913. *European Review of Economic History*, 11(2), 255–283.

Eloranta, J., Golson, E., Markevich, A., & Wolf, N. (Eds.). (2016). *Economic History of Warfare and State Formation*. Singapore: Springer.

Hautala, K. (1963). *European and American Tar in the English Market during the Eighteenth and Early Nineteenth Centuries*. Helsinki: Suomalainen tiedeakatemia.

Kennedy, P. (1989). *The Rise and Fall of Great Powers*. New York: Penguin Books.

Lakomaa, E. (2017). The History of Business and War: Introduction. *Scandinavian Economic History Review*, 65(3), 224–230.

McNeill, J. R., McNeill, W. H. . (2003). *The Human Web: A Bird's-Eye View of World History*. New York: W. W. Norton & Company.

Mokyr, J. (2006). Successful Small Open Economies and the Importance of Good Institutions. In J. Ojala, J. Eloranta, & J. Jalava (Eds.), *The Road to Prosperity: An Economic History of Finland*. Helsinki: SKS.

Müller, L. (2016). Swedish Merchant Shipping in Troubled Times: The French Revolutionary Wars and Sweden's Neutrality 1793–1801. *International Journal of Maritime History*, 28(1), 147–164.

North, D. C. (1961). *The Economic Growth of the United States 1790–1860*. New York: W W Norton.

O'Brien, P. K. (2006). Historiographical Traditions and Modern Imperatives for the Restoration of Global History. *Journal of Global History*, 1(1), 3–39.

Ojala, J. (1999). *Tehokasta liiketoimintaa Pohjanmaan pikkukaupungeissa. Purjemerenkulun kannattavuus ja tuottavuus 1700–1800-luvulla. [Efficient Business Activities in Small Ostrobothnian Towns. Productivity and Profitability of Shipping by Sail during the 18th and 19th Centuries.]* Helsinki: SHS.

Samuelson, K. (1951). *De stora köpmanshusen i Stockholm 1730–1815. En studie i den svenska handelskapitalismens historia.* Stockholm: Ekonomisk-historiska institutet.

Tanaka, Y., Tamaki, T., Ojala, J., & Eloranta, J. (Eds.). (2015). *Comparing Post-War Japanese and Finnish Economies and Societies: Longitudinal Perspectives.* London: Routledge.

Index

Adams, Donald Jr. 33
Admiralty 58, 65, 69–80, 157–8
Algiers 55–7, 65, 68–9, 72
Alicante 55, 57
Allies 118, 145, 148–50, 165–9, 188–91, 198–9, 203, 206, 213, 216, 221, 223
American 8, 16, 21–2, 25, 30, 32–45, 47–50, 52–74, 92, 107, 114, 144, 146, 153–61, 164–8, 171, 183, 210–11, 215, 219, 223, 228–9, 232–3, 235; republic ix, 121; revolution 34; War of Independence 16, 71–4
Amsterdam 26, 86, 88–91, 93–5, 233
Appleby, Joyce 32
Appleton, Thomas 56
ASEAN 234
Asquith, Herbert Henry 158
Atlantic 23, 31, 35, 52, 55, 61, 69, 71, 99–101, 109, 155, 157, 159, 214, 216
Austria 143, 177, 213–14, 218–19, 223, 225–6, 229

balance of payments 72, 131, 178–9, 200, 221
ball bearings 15, 17–18, 148, 153, 173–5, 177, 179, 182–3, 186–96, 198–9, 211, 221
Baltic Sea region 16, 73–4
Bank of Brazil 103, 105, 109
Barbary 62, 68, 70–2; privateering 52; privateers, 55, 57; regencies 55–6, 65; states 52–3, 56–8, 60–1, 63, 66–7
Barcelona 55–6, 59, 64
Barclay, Thomas 54, 72
Barnes, Joseph 56
Belgium 143, 147, 154, 198, 229
blacklist 162
blockade 10, 15, 17, 20, 22–3, 76, 79, 88, 100, 111, 119, 120–2, 131, 133, 145, 149, 155–9, 161–6, 168–72, 187, 196, 199, 206

bond prices 199
Borchers, Johannes Anton 75
Brazil 3–9, 13, 45–6, 48, 74–5, 79, 84, 88, 95–101, 103–9, 111, 113–15, 167, 233
Brazilian Royal Treasury 100
Britain 2, 21, 23–4, 30–2, 35, 40–2, 47, 50, 52, 54, 57–8, 60, 69, 74, 77, 82, 90, 93, 100, 111, 117, 119, 122, 127, 135, 137, 144, 146, 148–50, 156–9, 164, 171–2, 175–6, 187–8, 191, 198, 200, 215

capital ix, 17–18, 26, 93, 103, 118, 131, 142, 147, 150–1, 180–7, 191–3, 196, 211; account, 150, 179, 200; investment 174, 181, 187, 192, 196
Cartagena 58
Castro, Martinho Melo 75, 92
Catalan, Etienne 56
Catherine II 75–6, 86
Cecil, (Lord) Robert 162–3
Central Powers 119, 155–9, 161–4, 167–9, 177–8, 188–90, 193, 203
Chiappe, Franceso and Guiseppe 54, 68
Christian states 55
CINC 3–4, 25, 37
civil war 4, 24, 33–4, 36, 39, 48–9, 54, 79, 144, 150, 154
COCOM 213–30, 232
Cold War 1–2, 13–14, 18, 21, 134, 214–17, 220–3, 227–30, 232, 234
communism 220
concessions 13, 147–51, 163, 166–9, 199, 217, 221
Constantinople 64
consular 57, 69, 90, 232; correspondence 58, 63; posts 55, 67; records, 53, 63; reports, 69; service 50, 53, 56, 66, 71, 137; system 53, 55

Index

Continental System 23, 31, 47, 50, 117, 121, 134, 137
cooperation 13, 15, 59, 98, 154, 161–2, 215, 217, 219–23, 225, 228, 230
Copenhagen 62, 21
copper 75, 103–6, 126, 129, 162–3, 166–7, 220
Coutinho Luis, de Sousa 75
COW 3, 9
Crimean War 11, 16, 21, 116, 118–23, 127–8, 130–7, 233
crises 20, 24–5, 29, 39, 45, 60, 181, 200–1, 211
current account 178–80, 196–200
customs revenue 116, 126–8, 130–3, 135

Danish Sound 11–12, 73, 94
Denmark ix, 3–5, 45, 47, 50, 59, 85, 117, 122, 135, 147, 156, 177–8, 196, 198, 201–6, 221

Early Republic (US) 31–2, 35, 39, 48–9, 51, 71–2
Eastern bloc 18, 214, 217–20
economic warfare 17–18, 120, 136, 142, 151, 155–8, 161–2, 169, 172, 197–9, 218, 227
Embargo Act of 1807 35
EU 234
exports ix, 13–14, 18, 25, 30, 33, 35–45, 49, 61–3, 66, 70, 73–4, 77–9, 82–5, 88, 92, 101, 121–4, 127–8, 133–5, 137, 145, 148, 156–7, 159–63, 165–70, 175–7, 180–3, 187, 189, 191, 193, 197, 199, 213, 217–23, 225, 227, 229, 233
Exports Administrative Board (EAB) 166

Federico, Giovanni 11–14
Filicchi, Fillippo 56
Finland 6, 13–15, 18, 25, 117–18, 122, 174, 193, 196–8, 201–6, 211–16, 218–23, 225–30, 232, 235
fiscal 3, 16, 19, 22, 25–6, 98–107, 109, 111, 126, 130–1, 133
fish 48, 55, 62, 162, 166–7, 170
fisheries 35, 162–3
Foreign Office (FO) 158, 161, 170–1, 220, 224–5
foreign trade 16, 23, 33–4, 40, 72, 88, 102, 116–17, 121, 127, 130, 133, 168, 216, 222
France, 3–7, 23–4, 30–5, 39–42, 50, 54, 57, 59, 60–2, 66, 69, 72, 77, 117, 121–2, 136–7, 142–3, 145–7, 161, 175, 177, 187–9, 214, 219
Franco-Prussian War 21, 143

freight rates 11–12, 23, 25, 65, 233
French Revolution 9, 71, 74
French Revolutionary Wars 25, 50, 55, 72, 134, 137, 235
French Wars 16, 52–3, 56–7, 60–1, 66–7, 71, 79, 82

Gallatin, Albert 61
Genoa 56, 59
Germany 4–7, 9, 15, 17, 20, 30, 39–41, 119, 122–3, 131, 145–50, 152–3, 156–9, 161–3, 165–70, 175, 177, 181–2, 187–8, 191, 198–200, 203, 206
Gibraltar 56, 58–62, 64–5, 60–71, 149
Gilpin, Robert 2
Goldin, Claudia 33
Golson, Eric 17, 231–3
Great Britain 2, 23–4, 30–1, 41, 47, 50, 53, 57–8, 60, 69, 74, 93, 117, 119, 122, 135, 144, 148–9 *see also* Britain
Great Depression 18, 192, 197, 206, 209, 211
Great War 17, 22–3, 119, 141, 143–7, 151–7, 172, 174–5, 182–3, 190–5, 235
Grotius, Hugo 142
Guisan, Henri 141

Hague Convention 13, 119, 144–5, 150–1, 234
Hamburg 75, 86, 233
Handel, Michael 2
Hasket Derby Jr., Elias 58, 64
Heckscher, Eli F. 117, 124
Humphreys, Davis 59, 68–9

Ihlen, Nils Claus 161
Indian Ocean 33–4, 69
industrialization 2, 32, 34, 48, 118, 122, 134, 175, 177, 201, 232
inflation 131, 134–5, 177–8, 183, 187, 207–8
Ireland 13, 147, 213–16, 228
Italian 56–7, 59, 61, 71, 101; peninsula 61–2; States 53
Italy 62, 70, 85, 143

Japan 192, 232
Jefferson, T. 54, 62, 68, 70, 32

Kennedy, Paul 2
Kirkpatrick, William 56, 58–9, 71
Knudsen, Gunnar 161

labour 142, 147–9, 151, 153, 181–2, 185, 191–2, 201
Lamb, John 55

League of Nations 146, 154, 191
Leghorn 50, 56, 62–6, 70–1
Lewis, Frank 33
Lindstrom, Diane 32
Lisbon 16, 62, 64, 68, 74, 76, 86, 90–1, 93, 95, 97, 100, 103–4, 110–13, 115, 233
Lisle, Robert 58
London 23–5, 49–52, 57–8, 62, 65, 69–71, 75, 86, 88, 90–1, 94, 137, 153–4, 157–9, 161, 165, 167, 193, 195, 210–11, 224–5, 228–30
Luxembourg 147, 198

Machado, Horta 75
Mahan, Alfred T. 32
Malaga 55–7, 59, 67, 69, 71
Malta 58, 60, 63–4, 69–70
Marseille 55–8, 64–5, 68–9, 71
Martinique 58
Mary I (Queen of Portugal) 76, 86
Massachusetts 34, 51, 64, 72
McCormick, Vance 166
merchant 20, 25, 50, 53, 55, 57–61, 64, 66, 88, 137, 157, 159, 162, 164, 232, 235; fleet, 11, 15, 117, 119, 156; marine 72, 120, 157
military spending 3–5, 22, 25, 49, 152, 235
Ministry of Blockade (MOB) 162, 170–1
Mokyr, Joel 231
Monroe, James 35
Morocco 54–6, 63
Müller, Leos 20–1, 24–5, 31, 44, 47–8, 50, 67, 70, 72, 134, 137, 235
Murphy, Michael 56, 69

Nansen, Fridtjof 165
Naples 56, 64, 66
Napoleonic Wars 15–16, 20, 24–6, 29–32, 36, 39, 41–43, 46, 49–50, 72, 73–4, 77, 82, 93, 95, 100, 106, 111, 116–24, 127–8, 131–5, 232–3
Nasser, Gamal Abdel 234
NATO 214–16, 221, 224, 234
"Navicert" 164
Nehru, Jawaharlal 234
Netherlands 3–5, 23, 90, 143, 146–7, 153, 177–8, 229
neutral 1–2, 14, 16–18, 20–1, 23, 32, 35, 49, 53–4, 59–60, 64–5, 69, 76, 82, 91, 100, 116–21, 134, 137, 142–50, 152–3, 157–65, 169, 172, 174–7, 188, 193, 195, 198–9, 203, 207, 211, 213–15, 228, 232; countries 10, 14, 18, 20, 53, 119, 142, 146–7, 150, 197, 201, 203–4, 217–29, 233; shipping 52, 57, 60, 66–67, 120, 157; states 1, 9, 15, 17, 30–1, 58, 67, 144, 231–2, 234; trade, 10, 20, 23, 31–2, 58, 60, 66; transport 56, 60
neutrality 1, 9, 13–21, 23–6, 31, 33, 35, 47, 49–50, 52–4, 56–62, 65–8, 71–3, 75–6, 86, 90–1, 93, 116–19, 133–4, 136–8, 141–7, 149–54, 156–8, 161, 167, 169, 171, 174–5, 188, 190, 196–9, 211, 213–19, 221–3, 228–30, 232, 234–5
non-aligned countries 222
Non-Aligned Movement 234
Nordic 5, 15, 18, 29–31, 44, 171, 196–201, 203, 206–7, 209–12, 22, 230, 234
North Sea 149, 157–9, 161, 163–4, 197–8, 203
Norway 3–7, 9, 15, 17, 147, 156–7, 158–68, 170–2, 177, 197–8, 201–6, 211

O'Brien, Patrick 19
OECD 211, 234
Olson, Mancur 147
OPEC 234
Ørvik, Nils 143

Palermo 64, 66, 70
Paraguay War 96
"parallel action" 216
Pax Britannica 117
Pedro II 96
Peninsular War 41, 45, 74, 82, 84, 90
Portugal 4–7, 9, 13–16, 30, 40–1, 43–6, 48, 55, 73–9, 82–6, 88, 90–1, 93–5, 97–100, 102–4, 109–11, 113–15, 147–8, 150–1
Portuguese Empire 74, 100, 106
protectionism 23, 124, 126, 134, 137, 191
Prussia 54, 82, 84, 90
pyrites (also "pyrite") 162–3, 166–7

Quasi-War 53, 57–8, 60–1, 68–9, 72

re-exports 32–3, 61, 134, 158, 161, 218, 220–1
realism 17, 144, 146–7, 228
revenues 96, 100–4, 106, 109, 133, 183
revolutionary war(s) 29–30, 55, 58
Rio de Janeiro 93, 95–104, 106, 109–15
Rome 56
Russia 5, 24–6, 36, 66, 83–9, 91–6, 98, 100–4, 127–8, 132, 147, 185, 187, 198–9, 204, 207, 213, 238

Scandinavia 14, 26, 155–6, 159, 171–2, 196–8, 212
Second World War 147–9, 153, 195, 210–12, 227

shipping 10–11, 16, 24–6, 50, 54–7, 60–7, 70, 72, 134, 142, 149–50, 156–7, 159, 164, 194, 228, 232, 235–6; American 16, 44, 52–54, 60–67, 71, 116; Mediterranean 16, 52, 59, 61, 63–5; neutral 52, 60, 67; Scandinavian 94, 117, 119–22, 150, 164
Simpson, James 56
SKF 15, 17–18, 173–7, 180–96, 211, 217, 233
Skjolderbrand, Per Eric 56
slave trade 99
slavery 55, 61, 96, 98
slaves 61, 103–4
small states 13, 15, 17, 19, 24, 47, 50, 52–3, 142–3, 146–7, 151, 198, 232, 234
Soviet 14, 18, 196, 213–14, 228–30
Soviet Union 18, 196, 213, 215–18, 220–3, 229–30
Spain 13, 20, 25, 32, 41, 53, 55, 59, 68, 84–5, 122, 147–9, 150–3, 211, 224
St Petersburg 75–6, 79, 88, 90–1, 93–4
State Department (United States) 60, 154, 159, 164–5, 227
statutory list *see* blacklist
Sweden 3–9, 13, 15–17, 21, 23, 25, 30, 41, 44–5, 54, 56, 59–60, 74, 116–19, 121, 123, 127, 129–31, 133–7, 147–8, 150–3, 156, 173–5, 177–8, 180–3, 187, 189, 191–2, 194–207, 211, 213–18, 220–2, 224–5, 227, 229, 233–4
Swedish Riksbank 178–9, 193–5
Switzerland 6, 13, 20, 144, 147–54, 211, 213–18, 220, 222, 224–5, 227, 229

tariffs 23, 88, 116–32, 135–7, 191
taxation 16, 21, 44, 95–6, 99
Taylor, George 32
Tena Junguito, Antonio 11
Thirteen Colonies 52, 62–3

Tito, Josip Broz 234
tobacco 43, 76–7, 101–3, 121–2, 126, 130–1
tonnage 4–5, 7, 34, 39–42, 117, 163–6, 170
trade policy 16–17, 116, 119, 122, 124, 127, 133–6, 155, 221
transportation 77, 118, 178, 233
Trieste 56, 66, 68
Triple Entente 177, 188–90
Tripoli 55–8, 60–1, 68, 71
Tunis 55–6, 64, 66, 68, 70
Turkey 59, 142, 147

UK 3–8, 22–6, 33, 38–40, 49–51, 123, 136–7, 150, 154, 156, 159, 166, 171, 195, 219, 225–6
United Kingdom 4–5, 182, 194, 214, 226
United States of America 4–6, 50, 151, 154
US Foreign Economic Administration 186–8
USA 2–7, 18, 71, 121, 221, 224, 234
USSR 148, 230, 234

Venice 56, 59, 64

Wagner, Conrad Frederick 56
War of 1812 32, 39, 49–51
War Trade Board (WTB) 166–8, 170–1
War Trade Department (WTD) 159, 167
Warsaw Pact 214–15
weak states 2, 16, 23, 30, 47, 49–50, 93, 234
wheat 43–4, 46, 62–4, 79, 156
Wilson, Woodrow 153
World War I 3–5, 9, 11, 13, 15–18, 20, 22–3, 37, 116, 118–34, 136, 145, 171, 173–7, 181–2, 186–90, 194, 196–8, 203–7, 209, 232–4
World War II 2, 4–5, 8, 13, 17, 23, 37, 151, 153–4, 191, 196–8, 209, 211–12, 216, 218, 232